Abstracts of Wills
Montgomery County, Maryland
1776-1825

Willow Bend Books
Westminster, Maryland

Willow Bend Books

65 East Main Street
Westminster, Maryland 21157-5026
1-800-876-6103

WB0359

Source books, early maps, CDs -- Worldwide

For our listing of thousands of titles offered
by hundreds of publishers, see our website
at
www.WillowBendBooks.com

Visit our retail store

Copyright ©1977 Mary Gordon Malloy,
Jane C. Sween and Janet D. Manuel

Fourth Printing, 2001 Willow Bend Books

All rights reserved. No part of this book may be reproduced or transmitted in any form or by any means, electronic or mechanical, including photocopying, recording or by any information storage and retrieval system without written permission from the author, except for the inclusion of brief quotations in a review.

International Standard Book Number: 1-58549-139-X

Printed in the United States of America

INTRODUCTION

For some reason the period of thirty or forty years after the Revolutionary War is extremely difficult for researchers in Maryland genealogy to bridge. Whether it was because so many families were leaving for western territories, or the fact that new county government officials were not always careful to record documents, or whatever the reason, still this can be a specially difficult period in which to do research. Whenever a new volume of source records for this period appears, genealogists can be grateful.

Created in 1776 from Frederick County, Montgomery County is surrounded by Frederick, Howard and Prince Georges Counties, the District of Columbia and the Virginia counties of Loudon and Fairfax. Despite its location on the threshhold of Western Maryland, very few of Montgomery County's records have been published. Marriage licenses for 1796 to 1850 have been published and the censuses for 1790, 1800 and 1810 have been published and indexed. This volume of will abstracts, the first of a projected two parts, will be welcome to genealogists.

Covering the years 1776 thru 1825, the 695 wills in this volume cover 155 pages with a name index of more than five thousand persons. The compilers have abstracted the wills from original documents and, where these have not been available, have used the copies of wills in the record books. Each abstract gives the name of the testator, the book and page number where the will can be found, the dates the will was signed and filed, and the names of all legatees. Where land has been bequeathed, a summary of its disposition has been included. Finally, the names of executors and witnesses have been given.

The compilers have long been familiar with Montgomery County history and genealogy. Mary Gordon Malloy and Jane C. Sween have been active with the Montgomery County Historical Society and several years ago prepared the Selective Guide to the Historic Records of Montgomery County, Maryland. Currently, Mrs. Sween is Librarian for the Society. Janet D. Manuel, the third compiler, has copied the 1850 Census for Montgomery County and has, also, copied many tombstone inscriptions in the county. She is currently Curator of Graphics for the Society.

                                            ROBERT W. BARNES

                                            Chairman Genealogy Committee,
                                            Baltimore County Historical Society

                                            Author of Maryland Marriages 1634-
                                            1777 and Marriages and Deaths from
                                            the Maryland Gazette 1727-1839

11 March 1977
9219 Snyder Lane
Perry Hall, Maryland 21128

PREFACE

These wills were abstracted from the original wills or, where the original was not available, from the recorded copy, and have been proofread for accuracy. The following explanations are called to your attention.

Although Montgomery County was created from Frederick County in September 1776, the first will was not probated until 11 June 1777.

The first date given in the abstract is the date the will was written; the second is the date it was probated.

The first liber and folio is that of the original record; the second liber and page numbers refer to the book at the Montgomery County Court House in which xeroxed copies of the original are bound. Where only one liber appears, it indicates that the original will does not exist as far as the compilers could determine.

Libers I and J are interchangeable and are recorded in one book.

All spellings are as they appear in the will.

Oral wills are designated by (nunc.) after the testator's name.

All questionable readings of the original wills were checked against the recorded copy and any illegible items are indicated by ----.

Copies of the entire will may be obtained for a fee from the Office of the Register of Wills for Montgomery County, 50 Courthouse Square, Rockville, Maryland 20850, or the Hall of Records Commission, 350 Rowe Blvd., Annapolis, Maryland 21401.

ADAMS, STEPHEN   L F f 181   13 Nov 1807
                                            L 2 p 137   18 Dec 1807

Lucy McDonald, "a young woman that was raised in my family"
Wife: Hennaritta
Children: Ann Adams, James Adams, John Adams, Benedict L. Adams, Stephen Adams
Ex: Wife, Hennaritta
Wit: Thomas Cramphin, Isaac Riley, Warren Magruder

ALDRIDGE, JOHN   L D f 145   21 Jun 1789
                                            L 1 p 431   11 Jun 1799

Wife: Dolly Aldridge - "Add. to Moore's Rest" where testator now lives: at her
      decease to son Joshua
Daus: Mary Beddo, Eleanor Dunn, Sarah Dunn, Nancy Beall, Elizabeth Aldridge,
      Rebecca Aldridge, Ann Aldridge
Sons: John Aldridge, Joshua Aldridge, James Aldridge, Isaac Aldridge
"Aldridge's Discovery" to be sold
Ex: Wife, Dolly
Wit: Charles Soper, Zachariah Downs, James Soper

ALLEN, ARCHIBALD   L B f 108   27 Sep 1782
                                            L 1 p 125   24 Jan 1783

Sell plantation "Greenbrier"
Wife: (not named)
Dau: Elizabeth Allen at age 16
Brother: Thomas
Wit: Robert Whitaker, James Orme, Thomas Allen

ALLISON, BENJAMIN   L C f 219   4 Aug 1795
                                            L 1 p 329   5 Sep 1795

Father: Charles Allison - pt. of "Allison's Park", "P--ks Lot"
Children of William Spates: Charles Spates, Samuel Spates, Casandry Spates
                           (minors)
Benjamin Sansberry, son of Thomas Sansberry
Sister: Priscilla Spates
Brother: Jonathan Allison
Exs: William Spates, Jonathan Allison
Wit: William Willson, Martin Fisher, Zephaniah Offutt

ALLISON, ELISHA, farmer   L D f 16   28 Jun 1796
                                            L 1 p 399   30 Mar 1798

Wife: Ann - at her decease half estate to be returned to testator's father's
       family
Ex: Wife, Ann
Wit: John Mitchel, James McLaughlin, John Deur

1

ALLISON, JOHN   L C f 123   12 Aug 1793
                                                          L 1 p 279   10 Dec 1793

Wife: Elizabeth
Children: Joshua Allison, John Allison, Hezekiah Allison, William Allison,
          Thomas Allison, Zachariah Allison, Ruth Allison now Prather, Ann
          Allison now Fields, Presus (dau) Allison, Polly Allison, Daniel
          Allison, Eleanor Allison now Usher
Grandson: Loyd Allison, son of dau. Eleanor Allison
Grandson: John Prather, son of dau. Ruth
Exs: Sons, Joshua Allison and William Allison
Wit: Michael Letton, John Ball, William Richards

ALLISON, SILVESTER (nunc.)   L C f 118   10 Oct 1793
                                                          L 1 p 270   16 Oct 1793

Sister: Nelly
James Watters
James Colier and William Colier
Henry Allison
Mary Hickman
Wit: Mrs. Fielder Hardy, Mrs. Hiland Watter

ALLNUTT, JAMES   L B f 231   17 May 1786
                                                          L 1 p 207   8 Aug 1786

Wife: Jane Allnutt - pt. of "Thomases Discovery" including dwelling house
Daus: Ann Coats, wife of Charles Coats; Sarah Price, wife of William Price,
      dec'd; Mary Peck, wife of Richard Peck; Susanna Allnutt; Rebecker
      Allnutt - land at wife's decease
Son: Jesse Allnutt
Son: William Allnutt - 100 a. pt. of "Thomases Discovery"
Sons: Lawrence and James Allnutt - remainder of "Thomases Discovery"
Sons: John Allnutt, Joseph Allnutt, Talbert Allnutt, Daniel Allnutt - pt. of
      "Mersars Land" lying on Buck Marsh, Fred. Co., Va., unless warrent for
      land at Kaintucke on w. waters of Va. approved; then "Mersars Land" to
      go to five daus.
Ex: Wife, Jane
Wit: Samuel Dyson, Maddox Dyson, Elijah Veirs

ALLNUTT, LAWRENCE   L O f 171   13 Nov 1824
                                                          L 3 p 296   10 Jun 1825

Wife: Eleanor Allnutt
Sons: Benoni and Lawrence Allnutt - 171 a. pt. of "Thomas' Discovery" where
      testator now lives; 88 a. pt. of "Thomas' Discovery"
Daus: Mary Harper, wife of Thomas Harper; Ann Dawson, wife of James Dawson;
      Elizabeth Dawson, wife of William Dawson, dec'd; Susannah Dawson, wife
      of Thomas Dawson; Verlinda Darby, wife of George Darby

Hrs. of dec'd son, James Allnutt
Hrs. of dec'd dau, Eleanor Soaper
Ex: Son, Benoni
Wit: John B. Dyson, William Vinson, Basil Darby

ANDERSON, JOHN   L I f 196   13 Feb 1815
                                            L 2 p 426   22 May 1815

Wife: Mary Anderson
Sons: Robert (minor), Richard
Children: (not named)
Ex: Wife, Mary Anderson
Wit: Robert Wallace, Richard Anderson, Richard Anderson, Jr.

ANDERSON, RICHARD, planter   L A f 24   21 Dec 1777
                                            L 1 p 21   4 Feb 1778

Wife: Priscilla
Sons: John, Edward, Richard, Jeams
Daus: Ann, Catherine (minors)
Ex: Son, Edward
Wit: William West of John, Basil West, Osborn West

ANDREWS, CHARLES   L I f 452   14 Dec 1780
                                            L 2 p 511   1 Oct 1816

Wife: Elizabeth Andrews - 50 a. "Andrew's Folly"; "Richland" (formerly
                "Sapling Ridge") where testator now lives
Son: Charles Kilbourn Andrews - 50 a. "Andrew's Folly" where he now lives at
                wife's decease
3 youngest sons: Richard, Edward, Jonathan
Children: William, Elizabeth, Charles, Rachel, Richard, Edward, Comfort, Ruth,
            Jonathan
Grandson: Elijah Medly
Exs: Sons, Charles and Richard Andrews
Wit: Thomas Hinton, Nathan Burditt, William Medley

ANDREWS, EDWARD   L I f 214   28 Sep 1815
                                            L 2 p 464   5 Dec 1815

Wife: Ann Andrews
2 sons: William Andrews, Phillip Andrews
Amsey Peters
Exs: Sons, William Andrews, Phillip Andrews
Wit: William Willson of John, Philip Edelen, Benjamin Cecill

ARNOLD, JOHN of Frederick Co., Md. L C f 154   27 Apr 1782
                                    L 1 p 315   12 Feb 1795

Wife: Lucy Arnold - dwelling plantation
Sons: Peter Arnold, David Arnold
Susana Randall and Elizabeth Randall
Epharim Arnold
Ann Gassaway
Ex: Wife, Lucy; son, Peter
Wit: Alex. Todd, Basill Todd

ATWOOD, JAMES   L D f 298   5 Dec 1799
                                    L 1 p 443 16 Jan 1800

Wife: Mary Atwood
Daus: Mary Elliot, Elizabeth Green, Ann Medley, Cela, Ellioner
Sons: James Atwood, John L. Atwood, Willy, George Perry, Charles
Unborn child
Ex: Wife, Mary; son, John L. Atwood
Wit: Joseph Jarboe, Henry Belwood, Josiah Beeding

AWBREY, WILLIAM (indexed Aubrey)   L E f 115 17 Jan 1804
                                    L 2 p 23 17 Mar 1804

John R. Campbell - entire estate
Ex: John R. Campbell
Wit: Solomon Holland, John Fleming

AUSTIN, JOHN, Sr.   L N f 456 21 Feb 1818
                                    L 3 p 231 12 Nov 1823

Wife: (not named)
Son: Amos Austin - pt. of "Conclusion"
Son: John Austin
Grandsons: Barrach Austin, son of Hezekiah Austin; John Austin, son of
           Zachariah Austin
Exs: James Austin, Amos Austin
Wit: Benjamin White of Nathan, Brooks Jones, Benjamin Greentree

AYTON, HENRY   L E f 10   6 Jan 1803
                                    L 1 p 532 15 Feb 1803

Wife: Eleanor Ayton
Children: Samuel Ayton, Beal Ayton, Deborah Prather, Jane Ayton - land in
          Hampshire Co., Va. on Capon; land in Pa. on the Monongahalea
          called "Sugar Tree Bottom"
Grandson: Richard Ayton - pt. of "Charles and Benjamin"
Granddaus: Eleanor Ayton, Eleanor Prather
Exs: Wife, Eleanor; son, Beal
Wit: James Brooke, Samuel Thomas, Jr., Jonathan Duley

BARBER, JOHN, Sr.   L G f 405   7 Sep 1811
                                            L 2 p 297   28 Jan 1812

Granddau: Delilah Mobley - all real estate
Grandchildren: Samuel Barber, John Barber, Reazen Barber, Ann Barber
Ex: John Mobley
Wit: William Willson of John, James Hawkins, Charles Miles

BARBER, LUCEY (nunc.)   L F f 210   Mar 1808
                                            L 2 p 172   14 Jun 1808

Son: John Barber
Dau: Nancy Barber
Husband deceased
Wit: Richard Young and Elisha Walker

BARNES, ELIZABETH, widow   L B f 214   28 Sep 1785
                                            L 1 p 183   19 Nov 1785

Children: Elizabeth Aldridge, Richard Weaver Barnes, Thomas Barnes
  Nancy Hocker
Grandchildren: Jacob, son of Richard Weaver Barnes; Nancy, dau of Richard
               Weaver Barnes; Ann Johns; Elizabeth, dau of Richard Weaver
               Barnes
Ex: Richard Weaver Barnes
Wit: Ezekiel Waters, Nathan Waters

BARNES, WEAVOUR   L B f 20   12 Jan 1781
                                            L 1 p 90   27 Feb 1785

Wife: Elizabeth - dwelling plantation "Snowden's Add. to his Manner"
Son: Thomas Barnes - 150 a. "Inspection"
Son: Joseph Barnes
Son: Richard Weavour Barnes - pt. of "Second Add. to Snowden" and "Snowden's
                               Addition"
Dau: Dorcas Hocker
Grandsons: Richard Weavour Johns; Weavour Barnes, son of Joseph; Weavour
           Hocker, son of Philip Hocker
Granddau: Ann Johns
Exs: Joseph Barnes and Richard Weavour Barnes
Wit: Edward Burgess, John Farrall, Archibald Mason

BATES, HENRIETTA MARIA of Hanover Co., Va. L H f 310   4 Jan 1813
                     Quaker   L 2 p 349   27 Jan 1813

Brother: William Henry Pleasants - testator's interest in "Brook Meadow" in
                         Mont. Co. which testator holds in common
                         with Tarlton Woodson Pleasants, purchased
                         by them from Thomas Moore
Children of dec'd husband Banjamin Bates: Lucy Bates, Micajah Bates, Martha
                         Bates, Tace Bates, William Bates

5

Elizabeth Bowles, Widow of Richard C. Bowles
Margaret Willing Pleasants
Rebecca Russel
Thomas Hatton
Nieces: Elizabeth Ann Pleasants, Hannah Pleasants
Nephews: Basil Pleasants, Thomas Snowden Pleasants, Joseph Jordan Plesants
Sister: Deborah Stabler
Nieces and nephews, children of dec'd sister Mary Stabler: William Stabler,
        Elizabeth Stabler, Anna Stabler, Robertson Stabler, Thomas Snowden
        Stabler
Ex: Brother, William Henry Pleasants
Wit: N.M. Vaughan, Lemuel Crew, Fleming Bates

BAXTER, GABRIEL   L A f 229   8 Nov 1779
                                                                              18 Dec 1779

Wife: Elizabeth Baxter - all property that was "hers when I married her for
                    the use of her children she had before I married her."
Dau: Mary Baxter
Wit: Clement C. Walter, James Fyffe

BEALL, ARCHIBALD   L B f 438   10 Sep 1785
                                                                                12 Apr 1791

Wife: Jane, dau of James Edmonston
Dau: Celina Beall, wife of Samuel Beall - pt. of "Labyrinth", pt. of "Resurvey
                                            of James' Gift"
Son: James Edmonston Beall - dwelling plantation called "Owens Rest", pt. of
                    "Batchelor's Forrest" which was bequeathed to
                    testator by his brother Alexander Beall
Daus: Rachel Beall, Nancy Beall
Exs: Wife Jane Beall and son James Edmonston Beall
Wit: Richard Berry, Nicholas Berry, H. Dunn

BEALL, EDWARD, Sr.   L D f   4   7 Dec 1797
                                                                       L 1 f 383   3 Jan 1798

Wife: (not named)
Sons: Eli, Eden
Exs: Wife and son Elijah
Wit: John Bowie, Samuel Charles Beall, Nathan Talbert

BEALL, ELIZABETH   L G f 354   20 Dec 1809
                                                              L 2 p 270   7 Mar 1811

Mother: Sabrina Beall
Sisters: Mary Magruder, **wife** of John Burgess Magruder; Rachel Beall,
         Henrietta Beall

Nieces: Eliza Holland (under age 16), Sarah Holland, Mary Ann Holland, daus.
of Nathan Holland, Jr.; Nancy Ford, dau. of James Ford; Sarah Beall,
dau. of James Edmonston Beall
Nephews: Elias Holland, son of Nathan Holland, Jr.; Jeremiah Beall, son of
Daniel Beall, Jr.; Caleb Beall, son of James Beall
Ex: Nathan Holland, Jr.
Wit: Daniel Beall, Sr., Cephas Lazenby, John L. Beall

BEALL, ELIZABETH, widow   L M f 278   30 Jan 1810
                            L 3 p 111   24 Oct 1820

Daus: Selah, Polly, Elizabeth, Dorathy
Sons: James, Alexander, Archibald, Zebedee, Basil
Grandsons: James Brooke Beall; Emmery Montgomery Beall; Elemleck Beall, son
of Basil; Alpheus Beall, son of Basil
Granddau: Anna Beall, dau. of Basil
Exs: Son James and dau. Selah
Wit: Thomas P. Willson, Gazway Perry, Daniel Leach

BEALL, GEORGE   L A f 262   15 Mar 1780
                            L 1 p 69   24 Mar 1780

Son: George Beall
Son: Thomas Beall - houses and lots in Georgetown, tract "Conjuror's Dis-
appointment", pt. of "Dunbarton"
Dau: Elizabeth Evans
Wit: Richard Cheney, W. Smith, Abraham Boyd

BEALL, GEORGE of Washington Co. State of   L F f 346   11 Jun 1802
              Columbia (Washington, D.C.)   L 2 p 197   20 Oct 1807

Wife: Elizabeth Beall
Eldest son: George Beall
Grandchildren: Patrick S. Beall and Ann Beall, children of George Beall; John
Beall and Anna Beall, children of Levin C. Beall; Thomas Beall,
son of Erasmus Beall
Sons: Levin C. Beall, Hezekiah Beall
Son: Thomas Brook Beall - land on Seneca Creek
Rev. Stephen B. Balch
Lewis W.P. Balch, George Balch, Anna Balch, Harriet Balch
Capt. John Rose
Children: Hezekiah Beall, Capt. Thomas B. Beall, Elizabeth Balch, Anna Rose -
dwelling house and lots in Georgetown, "Thomas Beall's of George
Addition to Georgetown"
Exs: Sons Hezekiah Beall and Capt. Thomas B. Beall - to inherit graveyard lot
Wit: Matthew Steel, Samuel Duvall, Jonathan Bloyce

```
BEALL, JAMES, son of James                      L E  f 112        3 Sep 1801
                                                L 2  p  16       15 Feb 1804
```

Wife: Elizabeth
Son: Alexander Edmonston Beall - 200 a. "Black George"
Dau: Dothary Brook Carten - estate of testator's brother Alexander Beall
Son: Archibald Allen Beall
Son: Basel Musgrave Beall - pt. of "Prevention", pt. of "Philadelphia"
Dau: Cela Beall - pt. of "Greenland"
Dau: Elizabeth Brook Beall - pt. of "Greenland"
Son: Zebedee Beall - pt. of "Greenland", pt. of "Philadelphia"
Son: Jemme Beall - "Resurvey on Meadow Hall" where testator now lives
Dau: Polly Orme - "Fairwell"
Wit: Robert Wallace, Charles Wallace, John Wallace of Wm.
Codicil dated 12 Dec 1803
Grandchildren: James Brook Beall, Selea Beall children of dau. Elizabeth
Wit: Robert Orme, Sr., Priscilla Orme, Anne Edmonston


```
BEALL, JAMES, son of Ninian, planter            L A  f 282       14 Apr 1778
                                                L 1  p  70       22 May 1780
```

Wife: Ann
Brother: Robert
Children of brother Benjamin: Lloyd, Ninian, Cephus and Nancy Beall (minors)
Children of brother John: Sebert and Ruth Beall (minors)
Ex: Ann Beall
Wit: Thomas Read, Zadock Magruder, Rebecca Tannehill


```
BEALL, JAMES, son of Robert, planter            L B  f 139       25 Jan 1781
                                                L 1  p 136       14 Aug 1783
```

Wife: Margaret - "Enster" and "Resurvey on Batchelor's Purchase"
Sons: Jeremiah, Zephaniah - "Resurvey on Enster Rectified and Divided"
Son: Daniel
Daus: Catrine Loveless, Margery Loveless, Mary Suter
When land sold reserve family burying ground
Exs: Sons Jeremiah and Zephaniah, wife Margaret
Wit: Andrew Heugh, Elias Harding, John Farrall


```
BEALL, JANE                                     L C  f 180       18 Jun 1788
                                                L 1  p 319       17 Jan 1795
```

Sons: Zachariah Beall, Samuel Beall - "James' Gift"
Grandson: Alexander Robert Beall - "James' Gift" jointly with two sons above
Granddaus: Mary White, dau. of Zachariah White; Jane Beall, dau. of Zachariah
           Beall; Jane Beall, dau. of Samuel Beall
Mary White, wife of Zachariah White
Margery Beall, wife of Alexander Beall
Dau: Jemima Beall
Exs: Sons Zachariah Beall and Samuel Beall
Wit: Archibald Beall, Samuel Thomas 3rd, George F. Warfield

BEALL, JANE   L D f 437   14 Feb 1801
                                                 L 1 p 465   21 Mar 1801

Daus: Rachel Owing, Nancy Admonston
Son: James E. Beall
Granddaus: Anna Beall (under age 16), dau. of Samuel and Celina Beall, "in
            full for her deceased mother Celina Beall's part cf testator's
            estate; Ruth Beall, dau. of James E. Beall; Nancy Owens and Tavy
            Owens, daus. of Edward Owen (both under 16)
Trustee: Son-in-law, Edward Owen
Wit: Jeremiah Berry of Richard, Washington Owen, Walter C. Williams

BEALL, JEREMIAH   L D f 537   20 Oct 1801
                                                 L 1 p 480   19 Jan 1802

Wife: Sabrina Beall
Sons: James Beall, Daniel Beall
Daus: Mary Beall, Elizabeth Beall, Rachel Beall, Hanna Beall, Sabra Ford,
      Margaret Beall, Martha Holland
Exs: Wife Sabrina and son James
Wit: J. F. Beall, William P. Williams, Walter C. Williams

BEALL, JOHN   L K f 221   16 Aug 1816
                                                 L 2 p 516   1 Apr 1817

Wife: Margaret Beall
Sons: Hezekiah Beall, Elisha Beall, Basil Beall, Nehemiah Beall
Grandson: Reuben Lishure
Dau: Elizabeth
Ex: William Willson of John
Wit: Valentine Rine, Daniel Browning, Jeremiah Browning

BEALL, JOSEPH, Sr.   L D f 447   11 May 1801
                                                 L 1 p 476   12 Jun 1801

Wife: (not named)
Daus: Rachel Swearingen, Martha Swearingen
Sons: Horatio Beall, Josiah Beall - pt. of "Lay Hill" on Northwest Branch
Sons: Jeremiah Beall, Nathaniel Beall, Joseph Beall
Grandchildren: Elemeleck Beall, Anna Beall and Alpheus Beall children of dau.
               Eleanor Beall; Eleanor Swearingen dau. of Obed and Rachel
               Swearingen; Elizabeth Swearingen, dau. of Samuel and Martha
               Swearingen
Ex: Son-in-law Obed Swearingen
Wit: J.F. Beall, John Hobbs, James Bonifant, Aaron Henry

BEALL, NINIAN   L B f 413   14 Jan 1790
                                                                  2 Mar 1790

Dau: Ruth Gassaway

9

Dau: Susanna Catlett
Grandchildren: children of Ruth Gassaway when they come of age; children of
Susanna Catlett when of age; children of dec'd dau. Mary Watkins
when of age
Grandson: Gassaway Watkins, Thomas Watkins
Sons-in-law: Zachariah Offutt, Hardage Lane and Benjamin Edwards - land ajoining "land already claimed by them by virtue of their marriages and which was before the property of Andrew Beall, dec'd."
Daus: Eleanor Offutt, Rachel Lane, Margaret Edwards
Grandchildren: children of dec'd. son Charles Beall
Ex: Son-in-law Mr. Hardage Lane
Wit: William Smith, Daniel Query, Henry Query

BEALL, RICHARD, son of Samuel	L A f 39	12 Sep 1775
	L 1 p 35	19 Aug 1778

Wife: Sarah
Brother: Samuel - guardian to children if wife remarries
Children: (not named)
Ex: Wife Sarah
Wit: Samuel Cecil, John Cecil, Joseph Franeway, James Cecil

BEALL, ROBERT	L B f 370	4 May 1788
	L 1 p 232	4 Jul 1788

Wife: (not named) - dwelling plantation
Children: Basil, Kinzey, Benjamin, Zadock, Middleton and Axy Beall, Verlinda Dent, Sarah Adams
Grandson: Rezin Beall Offutt (under 21), son of Lucy Offutt
John Dent to continue to dwell on testator's land
Ex: Wife and John Dent
Wit: John Fleming, Richard Elliott, John Hawkins

BEALL, SABRINA	L N f 110	10 Feb 1813
	L 3 p 172	12 Feb 1822

Dau: Elizabeth Beall, dec'd. - terms of her will dated 20 Dec 1809 to be fully carried out
Ex: Nathan Holland, Jr.
Wit: John L. Beall, George Cashell, Rachel Owen

BEALL, SAMUEL	L O f 157	10 Oct 1824
	L 3 p 266	17 Feb 1825

Heirs of dau. Jane Prather
Grandchildren: Samuel Beall, James A. Beall and Eveline Beall, children of Lloyd
Ann Wilmington, wife of John Wilmington
Son: Enoch Beall - "James' Gift" and resurvey of it
Son: Elijah Beall - pt. of "Batchelor Forrest" and resurvey of it

Sons: Elisha and Samuel D. Beall
Dau: Mary Beall
Sell pt. of "Batchelor's Forrest", "Owen's Rest", and house and lot
    purchased of Lloyd Beall
Exs: Friend, Eden Beall; son Elijah Beall
Wit: Richard D. Butt, Thomas L.F. Higgins, Levin Easton

BEALL, SAMUEL, Sr.   L B   f 10   5 Sep 1780
                                      L 1   p 80   12 Dec 1780

Wife: Jane
Daus: Mary White, Elezebeth Crafford, Rachel Crafford, Margaret Crafford,
      Jemima Beall, Margery Beall
Sons: Zachariah, Samuel, Archibald Edmonston and Joseph Belt Beall
Exs: Wife Jane, Zachariah Beall
Wit: James Beall of Jas., John Busey, Lucy Michel

BEANES, JOSIAH   L N   f 295   9 Feb 1822
                                      L 3   p 194   14 Dec 1822

Children: (not named)
Granddau: Priscilla Kisner "who now resides with me" - pt. of Harding's
                    Choice" where testator lives
Josiah Beanes of Christopher
Granddau: Tabitha Gittings, wife of Joseph Gittings - remainder of land
Ex: Granddau. Priscilla Kisner
Wit: Thomas Gittings, Henson Clark, Erasmus Perry, Jr.

BEAR, JOHN   L K   f 226   20 May 1817
                                      L 2   p 519   3 Jun 1817

Wife: (not named)
Sons: Jacob Bear, John Bear, George Bear
Michael Bear
Daus: Elizabeth, Margaret, Catherine
Granddau: Mary, dau. of Elizabeth
Ex: Son George Bear
Wit: George Herring, Adam Boyer, James Day

BEATTY, CHARLES of Frederick Co.   L E   f 124   23 Dec 1776
                                      L 2   p 43   21 Nov 1804

Wife: Martha - lots #83 and #84 in Frederick Town, Frederick Co. (south of
            Market House Ground) with improvements
Children: John Meddagh Beatty, Charles Affordly Beatty, Thomas Johnson Beatty,
      Mary Franckfeld Beatty, Randle Hulse Cradock Beatty (some are
      under age 21)
Wife's brother and sisters: John Meddagh, Mary Rickey, Susannah Johnson
Testator's brothers and sisters: Thomas Beatty, James Beatty, Susanna Maynard,
                    Sarah Maynard

Ex: Wife Martha
Wit: Frederick Henop, Philip Bier, Peter Hoffman (witnesses appeared in Balt.
    Co. and original will is filed and recorded there)

BEATTY, VOLINDA   L F f   3   21 Nov 1806
                                         L 2 p 107   2 Mar 1807

Brother: Dr. Ozias Offutt - "Brother's Industry" deeded testator by Elizabeth
                            Clements, Jacob Clements and Joseph Clements
Father: James Offutt, dec'd.
Brother: Zadock Offutt, dec'd.
Mother: Rebecca Offutt
Ex: Brother Ozias Offutt
Wit: James Wade, Kinsey Gittings, Alexander Allen

BECKWITH, KEZIA   L E f   4   6 May 1802
                                         L 1 p 519   13 Oct 1802

Son: John Beckwith
Daus: Ann Williams, wife of Thomas Swearingen Williams; Barbary Nicholas,
    wife of Simon Nicholas
Ex: Son John
Wit: Elemeleck Swearingen, Thomas H. Wilcoxon

BECRAFT, BENJAMIN   L E f 331   7 Oct 1797
                                         L 2 p 78   10 Apr 1806

Ann Purnell, dau of Charlotte and Richard Dixon late of Md.
Jonathan Becraft who lived with testator at one time
Children of brother Peter Becraft "by Mary his present wife"
Children of sister Leonora, wife of James Higgins
Wit: Doct. Peter Becraft, James Higgins (appeared at probate)

BEDDO, ABSOLEM   L F f   1   23 Dec 1806
                                         L 2 p 104   2 Mar 1807

Wife: Mary - 1/3 land including testator's dwelling house
Son: James - "Snowden's Mill" purchased from Peter Kemp
Dau: Martha Beddo - rent from land in Prince George's Co.
Daus: Sarah Beddo, Dorcas Beddo, Eleanor Beddo, Nancy, Harriott
Granddau: Margaret Maclish
Grandsons: William, Absolem, Robert Maclishes
Exs: Son James and testator's wife
Wit: Benjamin Duvall, Eden Edmonston, John R. Bussard
Codicil: Wit. same as above
Dau: Deborah living in Kentucky

BELT, CARLTON, Sr.   L D f 570   8 Mar 1802
                                                L 1 p 500   16 Jun 1802

Wife: Ann Belt - plantation where testator lives
Children: Esther Belt, Lloyd Belt, Anna Campbell Belt, Elizabeth Belt, Henny
           Campbell Belt (minors)
Refers to wife's "own born children"
Son: Carlton Belt - pt of "The Whole Included" on Sugarland Road
Brother: John Belt
Dau: Molly Magruder, wife of Joseph Magruder
Father-in-law: Aeneas Campbell
Sons: Aeneas Belt, Alfred Belt, Tilghman Belt - land in Allegany Co., Md.
                                                  called "Dispute"
Grandsons: Carlton Magruder and Lloyd Magruder, sons of dau. Molly and
            Joseph Magruder
8 of children by present wife
Ex: Wife Ann
Wit: Thomas Veatch, Sr., John Beard, Sr., Christian Hempstone, Hugh S. Dunn

BELT, HIGGINSON   L B f 361   15 Jul 1786
                                                                 15 Nov 1788

Wife: Sarah
Son: John Belt - land
Sons: Carlton Belt, Higginson Belt
Dau: Beckey Peddicoart
Grandsons, sons of Greenbury Belt: Westley and Higginson Belt (under age 21)
Ex: Son John
Wit: H. Griffith, Joshua Griffith, Elizabeth Griffith

BELT, JOHN   L H f 321   26 Aug 1811
                                                L 2 p 264   4 Jan 1814

Sons: Evan Belt, William Belt
Dau-in-law: Margaret Belt, widow of son Greenbury Belt
Granddau: Rebecca Belt
Grandson: Rufus Belt
Dau: Mary Gatril - lot of 1 1/2 a. of "Three Brothers"
Sons: Otho Belt, John Smith Belt - equal division 281 1/2 a. dwelling plant.
Daus: Ann Belt, Dolly Belt
Exs: Sons Otho Belt and William Belt
Wit: Mesheck Browning, Nacy Waters, John Turnbull, G. Howard
Codicil dated 25 Oct 1812
Wit: Mesheck Browning, Joshua W. Dorsey, Robert Plummer

BELT, LEONARD   L C f 117   14 Sep 1793
                                                L 1 p 266   20 Sep 1793

Nephew: John Belt, son of brother Higginson Belt - pt. of "Dann" where test-
                                                    ator lives
Lucy Beckwith, relict of William Beckwith - pts. of "Paradise Enlarged" and
                                                "Magruder's Hazard"

13

Sister: Sarah Peddicoart
Niece: Althea, dau. of Sarah Peddicoart, wife of William Selman
Rebecca Peddicoart, wife of Jasper Peddicoart
Elizabeth Beckwith, wife of Samuel Beckwith
Brother: Joseph Belt
Henry Watson, Sr.
Mary Belt, dau. of John Belt
John Watson, son of Henry
Ex: John Belt, son of Higginson
Wit: William Glaze, Edward Harding, Kinsey Gittings of Benjamin

BENSON, ANN	L F f 187	27 Dec 1796
	L 2 p 141	8 Feb 1808

Nicholas Pagno and Mary, his wife, adms. of William Benson - agreement
　assigned by testator to Daniel Candler
Daus: Sarah Hanks, wife of William Hanks; Margaret Clarke, wife of Neill
　　　Clarke; Sarah Selby, wife of Thomas Selby; Rosanna Candler, wife of
　　　Daniel Candler; Alice Holland, wife of Benjamin Holland
Grandson: William Benson, son of Fleetwood Benson
Granddau: Sarah Benson, dau. of William Benson
Ex: Thomas Selby
Wit: Brice Selby, Zachariah Selby, Richard Groome

BENSON, ANNE HENRIETTA	L N f 463	16 Nov 1804
	L 3 p 237	6 Oct 1823

Daus: Ann Henritta Gladman, Prissilla Ford, Margaret Smith Benson
Son: Archibald Brook Orme
Granddaus: Oliva Cattrol Orme; Elizabeth Ann Orme (under age 16), both daus.
　　　of testator's son Nathan Orme
Ex: Basil Musgrove Beall
Wit: Thomas Swearingen, James Beall (son of James the 3rd), Cela Beall, Basil
　　　M. Beall

BENTON, JOSEPH	L F f 5	20 Jul 1803
	L 2 p 112	6 Mar 1807

Wife: Rachel Benton
2 sons by last wife: Nathaniel Offutt Benton and Leaven Benton (minors)
11 children by 1st wife: Joseph Benton, William Benton, Mordacai Benton,
　　　　　　　　　　　　Erasmus Benton, Benjamin Benton, Nathan Benton,
　　　　　　　　　　　　Hezekiah Benton, Marian Sedwick, Elizabeth Ford,
　　　　　　　　　　　　Thomas Benton (dec'd. leaving children), Ann
　　　　　　　　　　　　Sedwick (dec'd. leaving children)
Dwelling plantation located on Captain John Run
Exs: Wife and son Joseph Benton
Wit: James Wallace, Samuel B. Magruder, Walter Magruder
Codicil dated 21 Jul 1803
Sons: Nathaniel O. and Levin - pt. "Doull's Park" and "Trouble Enough"
Wit: James Wallace, William Wallace, Charles Wallace

BENTON, JOSEPH   L I   f 432   3 Apr 1815
                                     L 2   p 472   6 May 1815

Wife: Ann Benton
Son: Theodore - his widow, Henrietta Benton and children to live with wife Ann
Son: Thomas Benton
Children: Eleanor Bennett, Benjamin Benton, Casandra Bennett, Thomas Benton,
           Ann Wallace
Hrs. of Theodore Benton: Sarah Ann Benton, Samuel S. Benton
Legacy to be received from dec'd father after death of step-mother to be sold.
Ex: Son Thomas Benton
Wit: Nichalas Rhoades, William Suter, William Murphy

BERRY, JOHN   L B   f 237   31 Oct 1785
                                     L 1   p 216   17 Mar 1786

Wife: Eleanor Berry - "Drumelderey", "Beary's Meadow" and pt. of "Snowden's
         Manor Enlarged"
Son: Benjamin (under age 21) - above land at mother's decease or remarriage
Daus: Cassandria Berry, Eleanor Bowie Berry, Mary Clagett Berry, and Ocatia
         Berry (under age 16)
Sons: John Wilks Berry, Elisha Clagett Berry (under age 21)
Exs: Wife Eleanor and son Benjamin
Wit: Allen Bowie, Richard Estep, Clement Williams

BERRY, MILDRED   L D   f 307   26 Dec 1799
                                     L 1   p 456   3 Dec 1799
                                                        (as recorded)
Dau: Mary Douglass
Ex: Dau Mary Douglass
Wit: Joseph Hall, Zachariah Maccubbin

BERRY, NICHOLAS   L B   f 402   8 Feb 1780
                                                        31 Mar 1788

Sell "Charles and Benjamin", it being the land where testator now lives,
    which fell to him by the death of his father Rev. Mr. Jeremiah Berry
Wife: Eleanor Berry - remainder of land
Brothers: Jeremiah and William Berry - land at death of wife
Ex: Wife Eleanor
Wit: Samuel White, Samuel Brooke, Jeffrey Magruder

BERRY, RICHARD   L L   f 110   26 Aug 1818
                                     L 3   p 33   30 Nov 1819

Daus: Mary Moody, Ruth Griffith, Elizabeth W. Beall, Eleanor Gittings,
         Amelia Gassaway, Ann Thomas
Dau: Deborah D. Berry - "Pig Park" and pt. of "Charles and Benjamin"
Son: Elisha D. Berry - pt. of "Charles and Benjamin" and "Shepherd's Hard
                        Fortune"

15

Son: Richard Berry in Kentucky
Grandchildren: Michael R. Berry, Sarah G. Berry, Sarah B. Offutt
Ex: Son Elisha D. Berry
Wit: Richard K. Watts, Wilson Birdsall, John Birdsall

BIGGS, SAMUEL of Frederick Co., Innholder   L B f 82   26 Dec 1768
                                                                      L 1 p 117   15 Jul 1782

Wife: Hennerita - dwelling plantation and 1/2 of land
Father: John Biggs, dec'd.
Brother: John Biggs, who owned "St. Georges" in Charles Co.
Dau: Jane Posey, baptised Jane Biggs, eldest child of Jemima Posey - 1/2 land
Exs: Wife and dau. Jane
Wit: Andrew Heugh, Mordecai Madding, Thomas Nicholls

BIRDWHISTELL, THOMAS   L E f 11   9 Nov 1802
                                                                   L 1 p 536   21 Feb 1803

Wife: Susanna Birdwhistell
Dau: Ann Pelley - 50 a. land to include a field called Shop field
Dau: Eleanor
Sons: Thomas, James, William
Exs: Son Thomas; son-in-law Benjamin Pelley
Wit: Osburn Trail, Basil Mullican, John Higdon

BIRNSIDE, JOSEPH (indexed Burnside)   L I f 444   24 Feb 1816
                                                      L 2 p 495   12 Mar 1816

Wife: Ann
2 youngest children: Margaret and James (under age) - dwelling plantation
Sons: Aquilla and Henry
Son: John Nelson - two unimproved lots in Clarksburg and lot purchased from
              Evan Belt on north side of testator's dwelling plantation
Exs: Wife Ann Birnside and sons Aquilla and Henry Birnside
Wit: John Winemiller, Evan Belt, Henry Fister, Jr., Samuel Soaper

BOGELY, ANN   L I f 186   15 Feb 1815
                                                               L 2 p 408   2 Mar 1815

Daus: Cassandra Welsh and Sarah Bogely
Exs: William Huddleston, Basil Greenfield
Wit: Charles Evans, Jonathan Huddleston

BOHRER, PETER   L D f 129   7 Jun 1798
                                                      L 1 p 406   30 Jun 1798

Wife: Mary
Children: John, Mary, Peter, Jacob, George, Benjamin, Elizabeth, Abraham,
            and Barbary Bohrer. Last three named children are blind.

Ex: Wife Mary
Wit: C. Worthington, William Cary, William Ratrie

BOLING, GEORGE (indexed Bowling)   L G f 397   17 Nov 1811
                                    L 2 p 286   10 Dec 1811

Mother: Elizabeth Myers
Sister: Pelly Ellis
Son: William Bowling
Children of sister Pelly Ellis
Children of brother Joseph Boling
Wife: Margaret
Exs: Dennis Lackland, William Burns, Sr.
Wit: John Harwood, Thomas Green, Isaac Cawood

BONIFANT, WILLIAM   L E f 108   11 Dec 1801
                                    L 2 p   9   18 Nov 1803

Brothers: John Bonifant, Samuel Bonifant, James Bonifant, Benjamin Bonifant
Ex: Brother John Bonifant
Wit: J.F. Beall, John Hobbs

BOONE, ARNOLD, Quaker   L B f 76   7 Nov 1779
                                    L 1 p 111   21 May 1782

Brothers: Samuel and Isiah Boone
Wife: Mary - "I Will Not, Yet I Will", pt. of "Boon's Good Luck", "Rockey
       Spring", 2 lots in "Addition to Georgetown"
Ex: Wife Mary
Wit: William Willett, James Fleming, Ninian Willett

BOONE, ISAIAH   L H f 318   20 Jan 1809
                                    L 2 p 359   17 Nov 1813

Son: Arnold Boone - land where grist and saw mills stand of about 50 a.
Daus: Elizabeth Hughes, wife of Benjamin Hughes; Mary Hopkins, wife of
      Philip Hopkins; Hester Brooke, wife of James Brooke; Susannah Janney,
      wife of George Janney; Anne Boone
Son: Mordecai Boone - remainder of plantation
Ex: Son Mordecai Boone
Wit: William Morgan, John Thomas, Mordecai Morgan
Codicil dated 11th mo. 15th dy. 1812
Anne Boone has become Anne Elgin
Wit: James Anderson, James Johnson, William Morgan

BOSWELL, LEONARD   L N f 461   30 May 1823
                                    L 3 p 235   27 Jan 1824

Wife: Rena Anna Boswell - land

17

Youngest son: Otho (minor)
Eldest son: William
Second son: Clement
Dau: Christiann Harding, wife of John S. Harding
Ex: Wife Rena Anna Boswell
Wit: Isaac Williams, William Clagett, Edward Harper

BOWIE, ALLEN   L E f 104   19 May 1803
                                          L 1 p 546   15 Aug 1803

Wife: Ruth Bowie - plantation where testator dwells and others he owns
Sons: John Bowie, Washington Bowie, Thomas Bowie
Dau: Elizabeth Davis, wife of Thomas Davis - land on Seneca called "John's
              Delight" and pt. of "2nd Res. on Wolf's Cow" 267 a.
Son Washington's wife and children
Ex: Son John Bowie
Wit: Thomas Cramphin, Daniel Beall, William Duley

BOWMAN, JACOB   L M f 397   18 Jan 1815
                                          L 3 p 131   9 Mar 1821

Son: Richard P. Bowman - 175 a. on s. side of rd. from mouth of Monocacy to
             Green's Bridge
Son: Frederick Bowman - 85 a. on n. side of rd. above with storehouse and lot
Dau: Amelia Alnut, wife of Aden Alnut - 50 a. land
Dau: Elizabeth Case, wife of James Case - 50 a. land
Granddau: Matilda Bowman, dau. of son George - 50 a. land
Grandson: Jacob Merrick, son of dau. Verlinde Merrick and Michael Merrick -
             10 a. to include lot and house occupied by Michael
             Merrick
Sons: George Bowman, Shadrach Bowman
Daus: Rachel Leach, wife of John Leach; Verlinde Merrick
Granddau: Rachel Merrick, dau of Verlinde
Other children of Verlinde Merrick
Exs: Sons Richard and Frederick
Wit: Henry Griffith, Edward House, John Allnutt, Ephraim Gaither of William
Codicil dated 10 Apr 1819
Land given to granddau. Matilda to go to son George for his lifetime
Wit: Ephraim Gaither, Samuel Darby, Jesse Allnutt

BOYER, PETER   L E f 139   4 Apr 1805
                                          L 2 p 71   7 Oct 1805

Wife: Mary Boyer
Children: (not named)
Exs: Wife Mary Boyer and eldest son Adam Boyer
Wit: Abednego Baker, Johnnes -------, James Day

```
BRADSTREET, LYONEL, Fen Court, Fenchurch St.,      L B  f 211      29 Jan 1785
                   London, Capt. of merchant      L 1  p 177      24 Jan 1786
                   ship Potomack
```

Friends: John Gooch and Michael Danby of Fencourt, Brokers - trustees and
                   guardians of 2 sons below
Son: Lyonel Bradstreet (under age 21) - land in Georgetown purchased from
                   Thomas Beall
Son: William Bradstreet (under age 14) - 1/4 share of ship "Potomack"
Exs: John Gooch and Michael Danby
Wit: James Fell, Jane Atter, Jane Grimes
Note: Above will probated in England; examined in Mont. Co. 4 Mar 1786.
      Lyonel Bradstreet died in London.

```
BRAGG, WILLIAM                                    L B  f  67      27 Dec 1781
                                                  L 1  p  99      10 Jan 1782
```

Wife: Mary Bragg
Son: William Bragg
Ex: Wife Mary
Wit: Basil Magruder, Edward Alphin, Ann Alphin

```
BRISCOE, ROBERT                                   L D  f 127      29 May 1788
                                                  L 1  p 404      28 May 1798
```

Wife: Sarah - 200 a. dwelling plantation
Wife's grandsons: James Caise, Elexander Caise, Robert Caise, sons of
                   Margaret Caise, dau. of Sarah Briscoe - land in
                   Harrison Co., Va. on the Ohio River
Ex: Wife Sarah
Wit: Richard Conner, Battus Folks, William Fulks

```
BRISCOE, SARAH                                    L D  f 300      13 Jul 1798
                                                  L 1  p 445       6 Nov 1799
```

Dau: Margaret Ricketts, wife of Anthony Ricketts
Granddaus: Mary Ann Case and Nancy Ricketts (under age 16)
Children: Thomas, Alexander, John and James Wilson; Sarah Boyd, wife of
          William Boyd
Grandson: Samuel Mount
Ex: Son-in-law Anthony Ricketts
Wit: John Chambers, John Belt
Codicil dated 1 Jan 1799
Son-in-law Anthony Ricketts to have crops where dec'd husband Robert Briscoe
    lived in 1798
Wit: John Tumbell, Benjamin Ricketts, Marry Harison

```
BROOKE, BASIL                                     L C  f 145      20 Feb 1794
                                                  L 1  p 292      26 Feb 1794
```

Wife: Elizabeth Brooke - dwelling house where testator now lives

Dau: Deborah Pleasants, wife of James
Sons: James Brooke, Gerard Brooke, Basil Brooke
Richard Thomas, Samuel Brooke, James Brooke, William Hammond Dorsey, George
   Ellicott, Gerard Brooke to be trustees of property of children of Basil
   Brooke
Exs: Sons James Brooke and Gerard Brooke
Wit: Evan Thomas, Richard Hopkins of Gerrard, Gerrard Hopkins of Richard

BROOKE, GERARD   L N f 88   3 May 1819
                                            L 3 p 154   15 Dec 1821

Son: Richard Brooke
Dau: Elizabeth P. Stabler, wife of Thomas P. Stabler - 288 a. "Spring
             Garden" where they now live
Exs: Son Richard Brooke and son-in-law Thomas P. Stabler
Wit: Robert E. Dorsey, Maria A. Dorsey, James M. Dorsey

BROOKE, HENRY   L H f 25   12 Jun 1811
                                            L 2 p 327   11 Aug 1813

Burial according to the rites of the Roman Catholic Church "of which I pro-
   fess myself a member"
Wife: Eleanor
Daus: Elizabeth Susannah, Eleanor
Son: Nicholas Basil
Ex: Wife Eleanor
Wit: John Wailes, H.H. Young, Charles H.W. Wharton

BROOKE, JAMES of Frederick Co.   L B f 160   13 Feb 1770
                                            L 1 p 143   5 May 1784

Granddaus: Deborah Brooke and Elizabeth Brooke, daus. of son James Brooke, Jr.
             dec'd. - 1/6 of testator's lands. Their father had already
             purchased "Brooke's Addition, "The Forke" and "Brooke Black
             Meadow" on the Hawlings River
Sons: Roger Brooke, Richard Brooke, Basil Brooke, Thomas Brooke - each 1/6
         of land, to include where they now live
Dau: Elizabeth Pleasants - 1/6 of land including where Edward Penn, Michael
         Murphy, James Parradice and Jeremiah ------ live
Cousin: Richard Thomas
Sell pt. of "Addition to Brooke Discovery" and 2nd addition located on the
   Monocacy and Piney Creek
Exs: Sons Roger, Richard and Basil
Wit: John Thomas, Paul Hoye, Samuel Thomas, 3rd

BROOKE, RICHARD   L B f 348   10 Apr 1786
                                            L 1 p 231   11 Jun 1788

Sister-in-law: Rose Lynn
Brother: Roger Brooke

Dau: Ann Brooke (under age 21)
Ex: Brother Roger Brooke
Wit: Richard Thomas, William Robertson, Samuel Thomas, George F. Warfield

BROOKE, THOMAS   L B f 405   14 Feb 1789
                                                             20 Jun 1789

Children of brother Roger Brooke: Samuel, Mary, Deborah, Peggy, Sarah, Hannah,
                                   Roger, and Dorothy Brooke - 2,000 a. being
                                   land left testator by his dec'd. father
Children of brother Basil Brooke: James, Deborah, Gerrard and Basil Brooke -
                                   remainder of land left by dec'd. father
Deborah Pleasants, dau. of Thomas Pleasants - 260 a. "Penn Brooke" and
                                                    "Mount Radnor"
Mary, Sarah, Henrietta and Margaret Pleasants, daus. of Thomas Pleasants
Deborah Chandler, wife of George Chandler
Elizabeth Brooke, sister of Deborah Chandler
Brother: Roger Brooke
Richard Thomas, Jr.
Ex: Brother Roger Brooke
Wit: Nathan Holland, Nathan Holland, Jr., Ignatius Waters, Thomas Knott

BROOKES, HENRY   L F f   8   9 Feb 1807
                                        L 2 p 116   17 Apr 1807

Wife: Martha
Dau: Margaret Gaither - pt. of "Deer Park" and pt. of land purchased from
            Jeremiah Crabb of 219 a.
Grandchildren: Martha and Eviline (both under age 21), daus. of dau. Margaret
Children: James Bowie Brookes, Letitia Brookes, Arabella Brookes, Walter
          Brookes, Eleanor Magruder, Martha Wallace
Grandsons: Edwin Wallace (under age 21), Henry Brookes Magruder
Ex: Son James Bowie Brookes
Wit: John Henderson, Benjamin Ricketts, Ephraim Gaither of Wm.

BROOME, THOMAS   L O f 162   22 Sep 1824
                                        L 3 p 281   12 Nov 1824

Wife: Mary Broome - property to be sold at her decease
Sons: John M., Benjamin M., Alexander and Thomas Broome
Two children of son Benjamin (not named)
Three children of son James (not named)
Daus: Mary H.D., Sarah M. and Isabell Ann Broome
Ex: Son Alexander Broome
Wit: John Candler, William Clagett, Richard Poole

BROWN, JOSEPH   L M f 397   18 Jul 1820
                                        L 3 p 130   3 Mar 1821

Wife: Mary Brown
Son: Jeremiah Brown
Wit: Camden Riley, Sarah Yates

BROWN, WILLIAM   L B f 130   6 Apr 1762
                                                  L 1 p 127   4 Nov 1782

Friend: Brooke Beall - "Addition to Mill Seat"
Ex: Brooke Beall
Wit: Zadock Magruder, Samuel Beall, Jr., Thomas Beall

BROWNING, EDWARD, Sr. of Frederick Co.   L B f 208   9 Mar 1776
                                                  L 1 p 173   9 Apr 1788

Wife: (not named)
Eldest son: William
Sons: Edward, Jonathan, Benjamin, Nathan, Jeremiah
Wit: Joseph Hall, Nehemiah Holland, James Butler, Samuel Baker

BROWNING, EDWARD, Sr., planter   L D f 440   4 Dec 1800
                                                  L 1 p 468   1 Jan 1801

Wife: Rebecca Browning
Dau: Lucretia Mitchel, wife of Walter Mitchel - "Snowden's Manor Enlarged"
              where testator now lives and "Browning's Folly"
Daus: Keziah Casey and Delilah Brashear
Son: Edward Browning - land on Bennet's Creek
Grandsons: Edward Browning, Josias Browning and Thomas, son of Sarah and
              James Case
Ann Mitchel
Elizabeth Tucker
Jeremiah Browning
Ex: Walter Mitchel
Wit: James Wilson Perry, Benj. Waters, Archibald Mason, Charleton Smith

BROWNING, JONATHAN   L E f 137   21 Apr 1801
                                                  L 2 p 68   13 Apr 1805

Wife: Elizabeth Browning
Sons: Nathan Browning, Jesse Browning, Masheck Browning, Samuel Browning
Daus: Elizabeth Purdom, Priscilla Purdom
Exs: Nathan, Jesse and Masheck Browning
Wit: Greenberry Howard, Bazil Soper, Samuel Soper

BROWNING, VERLINDA   L J f 21   23 Feb 1814
                                                  L 2 p 371   1 Apr 1814

Children: Elias, Nathan, Rachel and Priscilla Browning
Grandsons: John Baker Browning and Nathan Crummel (under age)
Son: Samuel
Ex: Son Samuel Browning
Wit: Ashford Laton, Jonathan Browning, James Day

BRYN, MARY   L B f 205   19 Feb 1785
                                              L 1 p 152   2 Feb 1786

Daus: Virlinda Bryn, Mary Bryn and Elizabeth, wife of Baxley Davis
Ex: Son Mathaias Bryn
Wit: Charles Sanders, Aneas Campbell, Bedder Phillips, Hendery Allison
Note: Bryn also spelled Burn when referring to daus. Virlinda and Mary

BUCKSTON, WILLIAM   L N f 296   22 Nov 1822
                                              L 3 p 196   27 Dec 1822

Wife: Ellenor Buckston
Nine children (not named)
Ex: Wife Ellenor Buckston
Wit: William J. Bright, Matthew Connelly, Isaac Williams

BURGESS, EDWARD   L O f 149   27 Jan 1824
                                              L 3 p 247   11 May 1824

Sisters: Elizabeth Burgess, Jane Burgess, Ann Burgess
Massa Davis of Frederick Co.
Nephews: Edward Burgess, son of brother John Burgess; Thomas Burgess, son
         of brother Ephraim Burgess
Ex: Basil Burgess of Ann Arundel Co.
Wit: Horace Willson, Nathan M. Clagett, James Day

BURGESS, ELIZABETH   L O f 163   25 Aug 1824
                                              L 3 p 279   12 Nov 1824

Sisters: Jane Burgess, Nancy Burgess, Margrett Clagett
Mary D. McGill
James Hook
Niece: Sarah Burgess
Brother: Edward Baring
Wit: Jonathan Fry, Elisha Etchison, James Day

BURGESS, JANE   L P f 314   6 Jul 1825
                                              L 3 p 415   8 Aug 1825

Sisters: Ann Burgess, Margaret Clagett
Sarah Burgess
Jane Clagett
Ex: Ninian Clagett
Wit: Elisha Etchison, Jonathan Fry, James Day

BUTLER, ELIZABETH   L A f 263   15 Jun 1779
                                              L 1 p 68   29 Mar 1780

Daus: Elizabeth Flemmon, Margaret Butler and Ann

23

Sons: (not named)
Exs: Three daughters
Wit: James Beall of Jas., Elizabeth Beall, Thomas Edmonston Beall

BUTLER, HENRY of Baltimore City   L D f 133   9 Jul 1798
                                              L 1 p 414   21 Sep 1798

Brother: Walter living in Kilkenney Co., Ireland
Nephew: James, eldest son of brother Walter
Pastor of Catholic congregation where he dies
Poor of county where he dies
Ex: Friend, Charles O'Brian
Wit: J. DuBois, E.B. Medley, B.H. Clements, Jr.

BUTT, RIGNAL   L N f 116   7 Nov 1821
                                              L 3 p 164   5 Mar 1822

Sons: Aaron Butt, Basil Butt, Proverb Butt
Daus: Elizabeth Butt, Jane Butt, Ann Lanham, Ruth Burress, Virlinda Burress
Elizabeth Prather, dau. of Aaron Prather - testator's share of Aaron Prather's
                                      estate
Ex: Son Proverb Butt
Wit: John Rabbit, Daniel Beall, Sr., John L. Beall

BUTT, SAMUEL, planter   L B f 210   28 Aug 1783
                                              L 1 p 176   6 Sep 1786

Wife: Elizabeth Butt
Sons: Hazel, Swearingen, Richard, Samuel, John, Aron, Rignal and Basil Butt
Daus: Keziah Butt now Harding, Ann Butt now Green, Lidia Butt now Hawker,
      Elizabeth Butt now Ray, Ruth Butt now Harding, Mary
Exs: Wife Elizabeth and son Hazel
Wit: Samuel Glaze, William Richards

BUXTON, SARAH   L I f 210   Oct 1815
                                              L 2 p 455   14 Nov 1815

Daus: "Ann or Brittania", Sarah
Sons: William, James
Dau: Eleanor, wife of John Buxton - 2 a. at upper end of land where testator
          lives to include that pt. of the 5 a. granted testator by hrs.
          of William Buxton that extends to the garden of John Buxton of
          Thomas
Dau: Rachel - remainder of 5 a. to include present dwelling house which is
          pt. of "Fertile Meadows"
Wit: Richard J. Orme, Richard Green, Asa Holland

BYRNE, MARTHA   3 Oct 1821
                                      L 3   p 150   Not probated

Sons: John Byrne, Augustine Byrne, Patrick Byrne
Grandchildren: John Alexander Whitaker (under age 21) and his brothers and
               sisters "by his mother"
Ex: Son Patrick Byrne
Wit: John Aldridge, Clement Wheeler, Thomas Wheeler

CAHELL, WILLIAM   L B   f 101   11 Nov 1782
                                      L 1   p 121   26 Nov 1782

Wife: Jane Cahell
Grandsons: William and Astere Cahell, sons of William Cahell, Jr., dec'd -
                     "Hole" and pt. of "Leakings Lot"
Grandchildren: Joseph and Mary Cahell, children of William Cahell, Jr., dec'd.
Mary Swany's child, Elizabath Swany (under age 16)
Son: Dennis
Ex: Joseph White
Wit: Zadock Dickerson, William Clark, George Ham

CAMPBELL, AENEAS   L H   f 13   7 Oct 1809
                                      L 2   p 311   14 Feb 1812

Wife: Henrietta Campbell
Sons: Aeneas Campbell and James Campbell
Daus: Hester Beall, wife of Levin Beall; Lydia
Two great-grandchildren: Thomas Noland Davis; Catherine Noland, dau. of
                     Thomas Noland, dec'd.
Trustee: Friend, Solomon Davis
Ex: Wife Henrietta Campbell
Wit: Richard Lyles, John Harwood, Henry O'Neale
Codicil dated 14 Feb 1812
Wit: Elizabeth Simmons, Richard Davis, Aeneas Belt

CAMPBELL, GEORGE, Gentleman   L E   f 117   28 Jul 1801
                                      L 2   p 31   19 Jun 1804

Wife: Sarah Campbell
Wife's 3 sons: Lisbon W. Collier, James Campbell, George Campbell
Exs: Wife Sarah Campbell and Lisbon W. Collier
Wit: John Culp, John Lucus

CAMPBELL, JOHN (indexed James)   L L   f 104   10 Apr 1818
                                      L 3   p 26   18 Jun 1819

Wife: Mary Campbell
Ex: Wife Mary Campbell
Wit: Solomon Holland, Upton Beall, Brice Selby

Attached to above will was a "List of payments by John Campbell of Rockville"
Dated 13 Apr 1818
$2,000 for house and lot in Rockville; clothing, boarding and schooling of 4
   children for 3 yrs. and 5 mos.
Wit: Brice Selby

CAMPBELL, JOHN R.   L J   f   38   3 Aug 1814
    L 2   p 400   14 Mar 1815

"George Riley is to ce (see) to my property and after the deth (death) of
myself and my wife, Mary Campbell, when my just debts are pade (paid) then
the ballons (balance) of my Estate to goe to Sarey Riley, Daughter of George
Riley"
At probate Isaac Riley and Wm. Sands state the above will is in the handwriting of John Campbell.

CANBY, WHITSON, Quaker   L N   f 469   9 Apr 1821
    L 3   p 244   13 Mar 1824

Wife: Mary Canby
Children: Joseph Canby, Thomas Canby, Martha Canby, Charles Canby, Amos Canby
Exs: Sons Joseph and Thomas Canby
Wit: Ger. Brooke, Edward Stabler, Jr., Eliza S. Canby

CANDLER, DANIEL   L G   f 152   8 Apr 1808
    L 2   p 243   18 Jun 1810

Wife: Rosetta Candler
Sons: William Candler, John Candler
Dau: Mary Gatton
Ex: Son John Candler
Wit: William Darne, Jr., Daniel Query, John Doud

CARROLL, DANIEL   L C   f 268   9 Apr 1796
    L 1   p 354   21 May 1796

Brother: John Carroll
Friends: Notley Young and Robert Brent, trustees
A letter to his brother John Carroll is a part of this will. In it he names
   grandchildren William Carroll and George Carroll and indicates there are
   others
Ex: John Carroll, Notley Young, Robert Brent
Wit: Ann Brent, Charles Minor, John Steuart, William Brent
Codicil dated 4 May 1796
Son: Daniel Carroll, dec'd.
Catholic Chapel on testator's land

CARROLL, ELIZABETH "of Pollymony", Mont. Co.   L M f 395   23 Jan 1821
                                               L 3 p 127   29 Jan 1821
Nephew: Daniel Brent
Robert Young Brent
Children of William Brent
Jane Brent
Mary and Anna Maria Pearson
Anna Maria Livingston
Catherine Digges
Mrs. Elizabeth Carroll
William Carroll and George A. Carroll - legacy in trust with Rev. Wm. Matthews
Ex: Daniel Brent
Wit: Frederick May, Catherine W. Brent, George Naylor, Robert Brent
Will probated in Washington, D.C.

CARROLL, ELLEANOR   L C f 224   25 Jan 1796
                                               L 1 p 344   15 Feb 1796

Daus: Nancy Carroll, Elizabeth Carroll
Exs: Sons Daniel and John Carroll and dau. Elizabeth Carroll
Wit: Robert Plunkett, Notley Young

CARTWRIGHT, THOMAS   L A f 151   10 Sep 1778
                                               L 1 p 50   11 Feb 1779

Burial according to rites of Church of England
Wife: Barbara Cartwright
Son: John Sliegh Cartwright
Ex: Wife Barbara
Wit: Aeneas Campbell, John Taylor, Elisha Hickman, Thomas Chilton

CARTWRIGHT, WILLIAM of St. Mary's Co., Md.   L C f 316   26 Mar 1794
                                               L 1 p 365   6 Mar 1797

Brother: Henry Greenfield Cartwright
Sister: Julia Cartwright
Aunt: Elizabeth Courts
Ex: Nathaniel Ewing of St. Mary's Co.
Wit: Stephen B. Balch, Charles W. Beatty, Richard Forrest

CASEY, JOHN of Georgetown   L C f 220   25 Oct 1794
                                               L 1 p 331   30 Oct 1794

Children: Pamela Casey, John Casey, Thomas Casey
Exs: Henry Rozier and Notley Young
Wit: Robert Molyneaux, William Casey, James Cook

CASEY, PHILIP, planter   L B f 224   20 Mar 1787
                                                L 1 p 197   12 Jun 1787

Daus: Rebecca S. Casey, Anna Stacy Casey, Elizabeth Casey, Mary Casey
Exs: Lawrence Oneill and sister Alice Casey
Wit: Michael Letton, Benjamin Allison

CASEY, REBECCA   L E f 135   7 May 1805
                                                L 2 p 65   11 Jun 1805

Brother: Joseph D. West
Aunt: Ailce Casey, dec'd.
Lawrence O. Holt
Ex: Brother Joseph D. West
Wit: Edward Willett, Lawrence Offott, John Ball

CASH, ANN   L D f 445   25 Jun 1795
                                                L 1 p 473   20 Jun 1801

Sons: William Cash, Rezin Cash, Jonathan Cash, Isaiah Cash
Ex: Son Jonathan Cash
Wit: Archibald Nicholls, John Dailey, Joshua Pearre

CASH, DAWSON (signed Dorson)   L C f 204   9 Jun 1795
                                                L 1 p 328   28 Jul 1795

Friend: Richard Cash
Brother: John Cash
Wit: John Cecill, Archibald Cecill, William Cecill

CASH, JOHN   L C f 141   15 Dec 1793
                                                L 1 p 286   18 Mar 1794

Wife: Ann Cash - land where testator lives
Sons: John, William, Rezin, Jonathan, and Isaiah Cash - "Dawson's Mill Land"
Daus: Henrietta Cash, Mary Plummer, Dorcas Plummer
Son: Richard Cash
Other children (not named)
Exs: Wife Ann and son William
Wit: Joseph Jones, James Wilson, Joseph Jones, Jr.

CAWOOD, MARY   L B f 412   30 Dec 1789
                                                                   2 Mar 1790

Brother: Stephen Cawood
Ex: Brother Stephen Cawood
Wit: John Veirs, Josias Heighton

CAWOOD, STEPHEN   L D f 545   16 Jan 1802
                                          L 1 p 492   10 Mar 1802

Wife: Priscilla
Son-in-law: Josiah Heighton and his wife (not named)
Other children: (not named)
Grandchildren: William, Milly, Stephen, and Thomas who are children of
               Josiah Heighton
Ex: Son Erasmus
Wit: Robert D. Dawson, Samuel Carrington, Lenox Martin

CECIL, SABRIT, Planter (indexed Talbert) L G f 147   12 Apr 1805
                                          L 2 f 238   4 Jun 1810

Wife: Mary Cecil
Children: Samuel and Mary (until death or marriage) - "Kilmamock" and
          "Charles and William"
Children: John and Mary (until death or marriage) - "Beall's Contest"
Sons: James, William, Thomas
Daus: Ann, Jemima, Eleanor Barret
Granddau: Rebecca Hall
Exs: Sons Samuel Cecil and John Cecil
Wit: Benjamin Gittings, Robert B. Beall, Josiah Bean, Richard James

CECILL, WILLIAM, Sr.   L F f 183   10 May 1807
                                          L 2 p 138   13 Oct 1807

Dau: Mary Ball - pt. of "Widow's Purchas" and "Chance" formerly belonging to
          Phillip Cecill and William Ball
Daus: Elizabeth Toole, Susannah Kirk
Sons: Archibald, William, Thomas, George, Phillip and John Cecill
Son: Benjamin - pt. of "Widow's Purchase" and "Chance" formerly belonging to
          Phillip Cecill and William Ball
Wit: Samuel Soaper, Richard Andrews, Henry Cooley

CHAMBERS, ANN   L F f 184   13 Oct 1807
                                          L 2 p 139   5 Nov 1807

Ex: Friend, Simpson Trammell
Wit: William Darne, Jr., John H. Galwith, Benjamin Sparrow, Alexander Adams

CHAMBERS, ANNE   L E f   7   5 Sep 1795
                                          L 1 p 524   6 Jan 1803

Son: William Chambers - land in Va. where he now lives, bequeathed to test-
                ator by her father Robert Booth
Sarah Fields Hamilton
Dau: Nancy Chambers
Ex: Dau. Nancy
Wit: Archibald Orme, Upton Beall, Josiah Leatch

CHAMBERS, WILLIAM   L A f 332   1 May 1780
                                                    L 1 p 73   30 Aug 1780

Daus: Violet Grant, Ann, Sarah, Kesiah, Eleanor
Son: William Chambers
2nd son: John Chambers - "Chamberlains Desire", Boydstones (Boylston's)
           Discovery", "I Was Not Thinking On It"
Ex: John Chambers
Wit: Brooke Beall, William Thompson, Tobias Butler, Jacob Tice, William
     Roberts

CHENEY, HENRY   L C f 220   9 Aug 1793
                                                    L 1 p 333   2 Feb 1795

Wife: Susanna - pt. "Resurvey on Miller's Beginning", pt. "Bachelor's
                     Forrest Enlarged"
Ex: Wife Susanna
Wit: John Aldridge, Basil Burton, Byrno Brunen

CHENEY, RICHARD   L B f 243   Dec 1785
                                                    L 1 p 222   20 May 1786

Brothers: Samuel Cheney, Hezekiah Cheney
Sister: Fannutta Cheney
Exs: Brothers Samuel and Hezekiah
Wit: William Dunn, Sr., Hugh Nixon, Jonathan Nixon, Jr.

CHESHIRE, JOHN   L C f   4   19 Dec 1789
                                                    L 1 p 242   18 Jul 1792

Only son: Birch Cheshire
Jane, wife of Birch
Granddau: Jane Cheshire, dau. of Birch
Dau: Sarah Allison
Ex: Son Birch Cheshire
Wit: William Glaze, James Moore, James Henry Moore

CHESLEY, ALEXANDER   L D f 392   10 Feb 1800
                                                    L 1 p 457   9 Apr 1800

Wife: Ann Chesley - land
Ex: Wife Ann
Wit: Jane Clagett, H. Morsell, Henry Townsend

CHILDS, MARY   L L f 103   22 Apr 1819
                                                    L 3 p 24   20 May 1819

Sons: Edmond P., Joseph, Cephas, William, Henry, and Enos Childs
Daus: Elizabeth, Eleanor, Mary

Ex: Dau. Elizabeth Childs
Wit: Burgess Willett, Edward W. Gatton

CHILDS, WILLIAM   L L   f 87   13 Jan 1818
                                               L 3   p   1   31 Aug 1818

Wife: Mary Childs
Daus: Elizabeth, Eleanor, Mary - all land while unmarried
Sons: Joseph, Cephas, Enos, William, Henry, Edmond P.
Ex: Wife Mary Childs
Wit: David Clagett, Edward W. Gatton

CHINA, SHADRICK (indexed Chaney)   L M   f 280   7 Oct 1820
                                               L 3   p 114   14 Nov 1820

Daus: Elizabeth China, Catharine Riney
Wit: Elisha Medley, William Willson, Brock Case

CHISWELL, STEPHEN NEWTON   L E   f 134   18 Jun 1804
                                               L 2   p 63   17 May 1805

Son: Joseph Newton Chiswell - "Chiswell's Lodge" on Dry Seneca
John Augustus Chiswell (under age 25)
Dau: Frances Elizabeth Vinson, wife of William Vinson - 10 a. "Chiswell's
                Lodge" and "Resurvey on Hanover"
Daus: Ann, Peggy Presberry
Children: Joseph Newton Chiswell; Ann, wife of Jesse Allnutt; Sarah, wife of
          Robert D. Dawson; Frances E., wife of William Vinson; Peggy P.,
          wife of Nathan White; Rebeckah P., wife of Benjamin White
Exs: Joseph N. Chiswell, Thomas Fletchall
Wit: Lawrance Allnutt, James Allnutt, Basil Darby

CLAGETT, ANN   L I   f 188   19 Apr 1810
                                               L 2   p 410   12 Mar 1815

Son: Thomas Clagett - 100 a. land adjoining where testator now lives
Dau: Ann Offutt, wife of Alexander Offutt
Granddau: Ann Clagett (under age 16)
Sons: Zachariah, Joseph, Henry, David
Children of son Samuel
Children of son Josiah
Ex: Son Joseph Clagett
Wit: Levin Beall, Samuel West, Jesse Leach

CLAGETT, ANNA   L G   f 399   7 Aug 1811
                                               L 2   p 291   20 Dec 1811

Desires to be "interred in the burying ground at the old place and by the
   side of my husband"

Children: Thomas and Mary Anna Clagett - 166 a. where testator now resides deeded to her by William Leach 2 Apr 1803
Son: Samuel Clagett - 51 3/4 a. "Laws Purchase" on Muddy Branch deeded to her 20 Nov 1809
Children: Ann Clagett, Elizabeth Fisher, William Clagett, Samuel Clagett, Thomas Clagett and Mary Anna Clagett
Exs: Henry Jones of Edward and son William Clagett
Wit: Charles H.W. Wharton, Charles Offutt, James Lackland
Codicil dated 28 Oct 1811
Within three months after testator's decease personal property to be sold and Gerard Brooke, Henry Warren and James Lackland, trustees, to buy negro, John Ayres and free him and pay him interest on remainder of money. After his decease, money to go to four youngest children: William Clagett, Samuel Clagett, Thomas Clagett and Mary Anna Clagett
Wit: A. Taney, C.H.W. Wharton

CLAGETT, HENRY   L A f 22   13 Jul 1777
                                         L 1 p 19   2 Feb 1778

Wife: Ann - "Clagett's Folly" and land where testator now lives
Son: Samuel - "Magruder's Chance"
Sons: Joseph and Zachariah - land where widow Jervis and Joseph Compton live
Sons: Thomas, Henry, David (all minors) - land at wife's decease
Sons: Hezekiah and Josiah - "Quince Orchard" and land where William Pack lives
Daus: Ann and Sarah
Exs: Wife Ann and son Samuel
Wit: John Fleming, Zachariah Offutt, Peter Becraft

CLAGETT, JOHN   L J f 189   25 Nov 1812
                                         L 2 p 413   20 Mar 1815

Wife: Mary Clagett - 250 a. dwelling plantation
Daus: Mary Offord Glaze, Rebeckah Magruder Clagett, Anne Magruder Clagett
Sons: King Magruder Clagett, William Magruder Clagett, Samuel Magruder Clagett, John Clagett
Son: Nathan Magruder Clagett (youngest) - dwelling plantation at dec. of wife
Sons: William and Samuel - "Pleasant Plains of Damascus"
Son: John - 30 a. "Dan"
Exs: Wife and son Nathan
Wit: Jeremiah Watkins, Edward Warfield, Larkin Baker

CLAGETT, JOHN, Sr.   L B f 428   17 May 1788
                                                            17 Nov 1790

Son: Horatio Clagett
Dau: Ann Clagett
Son: Walter - pt. of "Clagetts Purchase", pt. of "Pritchetts Purchase", pt. of "Laybrinth"
Ex: Son Walter Clagett
Wit: Aaron Lanham, Henry Janes, King English

CLAGETT, MARY   L M f 284   24 Dec 1817
                                                     L 3 p 121   27 Dec 1820

Daus: Mary Glaze, Rebeckah Clagett, Ann
Sons: Ninian, William, Samuel, John and Nathan Clagett
Exs: Sons John and Nathan
Wit: James Day, Joshua Purdum, Jeremiah Watkins

CLAGETT, THOMAS   L A f 30   5 Jan 1778
                                                     L 1 p 26   14 Apr 1778

Wife: Ann
Son: John - pt. of "Dan", pt. of "Greenland" in Prince George's Co.
Son: Nathan - pt. of "Dan" where testator now lives
Son: Ninian
Dau: Elizabeth Wilcoxen
Ex: Son Nathan
Wit: Baruch Odel, Rezin Offutt, John Herring

CLARK, ANN   L I f 25   3 May 1814
                                                     L 2 p 378   6 May 1814

Sons: Henson Clark, Judson Clark, Johnson Clark, Henry Clark, John Beeden,
      Levin Clark, Lawson Clark, Baley E. Clark
Daus: Henrietta Peerce, Ann Wilson
Granddau: Caroline Wilson
Ex: Son Judson Clark
Wit: Thomas Gittings, William Clark, Josiah Beanes, Sr.

CLARK, BALEY E.   L I f 440   5 Jan 1816
                                                     L 2 p 486   13 Feb 1816

Wife: Eliza Clark - claim to estate of Gabriel P. Van Horn, dec'd.
Sons: Baley Liverot Clark and Mason Earls Clark
Brother: Henry Clark
Dau: Moriah - claim to estate of Gabriel P. Van Horn, dec'd.
Trustees: Henson Clark and Thomas Gittings
Exs: Wife Eliza Clark and Henson Clark
Wit: Spencer Mitchell, Richard Nixon, Samuel A. Jackson

CLARK, HENRY, Sr.   L F f 12   18 Dec 1806
                                                     L 2 p 124   9 Jun 1807

Wife: Ann
Son: Henry Clark - plantation where he now lives on n. side of rd. from
                    Bladenburgh to Montgomery Court House, pt. of "Charles
                    and William", "Fenwick"
Son: Lawson Clark - plantation where he now lives which testator purchased
                    from Richard James

Son: Hanson Clark - plantation where testator now lives, pt. of Charles
                and William", "Fenwick"
Daus: Ann Wilson, Henrietta Peerce
Sons: Judson and Johnson Clark - pts. of Charles and William" and "Hills
                and Dales"
Sons: Levin and Baley E. Clark
Trustees: Henry Clark, Lawson Clark, Hanson Clark
Wit: Thomas Simpson, Henry C. Peerce, Obed Swearingen

CLARK, JOHN   L E f   9   31 Dec 1802
                                             L 1 p 530   9 Feb 1803

Wife: Ane Clark - place where testator now lives
Son: John Clark (minor) - land in Ky. on Green River and in Randolph Co., Va.
Son: Nelson Clark (minor)
Dau: Sarah Willson - house and lot in Clarksburg where she now lives
Daus: Jane Clark (minor), Ann Clark (minor), Maryann Read
Ex: William Willson
Wit: John Willson, John Buxton, Jr., Rezin Cash

CLARKSON, NOTLEY   L E f 113   2 Oct 1801
                                             L 2 p 20   20 Feb 1804

Wife: Vilettee Clarkson
Children: Elexus Clarkson; Ignatius Clarkson; William Clarkson; Ann
            Beckwith, wife of George Beckwith
Exs: Wife Vilettee Clarkson and son Elexus Clarkson
Wit: Elemeleck Swearingen, John Soper, Jonathan N. Becraft

CLEMENTS, BENNET HANSON   L E f 125   5 Oct 1804
                                             L 2 p 47   24 Dec 1804

Wife: Charity Clements
Daus: Ann Clements, Martha Clements, Mary Bowie
Wife's daus: Sary Smith, Mary Hoggins
Grandsons: Basil and Thomas Medley, sons of dau. Mildred Medley
Sons: Basil Clements, William Clements, Wilford Clements, Gustavus Clements
Exs: Sons William and Wilford Clements
Wit: Matthias Byrn, Sr., Matthias Byrn, Jr.

CLEMENTS, FRANCIS   L C f 120   Aug 1793
                                             L 1 p 273   14 Nov 1793

Wife: Elizabeth - pt. of "Brother's Industry"
Sons: Joseph Clements and Jacob Clements - pt. of "Brother's Industry"
Daus: Catherine Clements and Rebecca Sanders Clements
Exs: Wife Elizabeth, son Jacob, brother-in-law Edward Sanders
Wit: Charles A. Beatty, David Parker, Henry O'Reiley

COLLINS, WILLIAM   L B f 453   19 May 1792
                                                                 24 May 1792
Patrick Dougherty of Georgetown, laborer
Wit: John Hickey, John Atkinson

COLLYAR, SARAH, widow of William   L D f 441   2 Oct 1800
                                                L 1 p 469   16 Apr 1801
Daus: Elizabeth Greenfield, Sarah Camel, Ann Culp, Eleanor Adams
Granddaus: Sarah and Harriott Greenfield, daus. of Elizabeth Greenfield
Grandsons: Lilbourn W. Collyar, James Camel, George Camel, sons of Sarah
           Camel
Ex: Elizabeth Greenfield
Wit: Peter Becraft, William Glaze
Note: Camel should be Campbell

COLLYAR, WILLIAM, Sr.   L C f 136   4 Jan 1792
                                                L 1 p 281   15 Jan 1794
Wife: Sarah Collyar
Son: William Collyar, Jr. - pt. of Stubb Hill" (lease of 99 yrs)
Son: James Collyar - pt. of "Dann". pt. of "Elders Delight", "Collyar's
     Resurvey Corrected"
Son: John Collyar - pt."Stubb Hill" after 99 yrs.,"Sine of the Meadows"
Daus: Keziah Wilson, wife of Zadoc Wilson; Ann Collyar; Eleanor Collyar;
      Elizabeth Greenfield; Sarah Campbell
Exs: Wife Sarah and son James Collyar
Wit: Frederick Wetzel, Philip Yost, King English

CONSTABLE, ROBERT   L A f 211   16 Aug 1779
                                                L 1 p 59   4 Sep 1779
Wife: Susanna Constable
Son: John Constable - "Mexico"
Son: Stephen Constable - "Precious Springs"
Son: Thomas Constable - "Thomas's Choice"
Son: Samuel Constable - "Howard's Chance"
Sarah Kenny and her brother David Kenny
Nathan Burditt "who married one of my daughters"
Daus: Ruth, Ann, Eleanor, Rachel
Ex: Son Thomas
Wit: Thomas Hinton, Josiah Leach, Rebecca Hinton

COOK, ELIZABETH   L F f 190   18 Jan 1808
                                                L 2 p 145   19 Mar 1808
Children: John Cook, Zadoc Cook, Rezen Cook
Granddau: Mary Cook, dau. of James Cook, dec'd.
Ex: Son Zadoc Cook

Wit: John Adamson, Garrett Crown
Codicil dated 18 Jan 1808
Son: Zadoc - extra inheritance for "trouble and expense" testator has been
     to him
Wit: John Adamson, Garrett Crown

COOKE, JAMES   L E f 103   10 May 1803
                                          L 1 p 545   10 Aug 1803

Mother: Elizabeth Cooke
Ex: Zadoc Cooke
Wit: Robert Ricketts, Alexander Willson, John Beaden

COOKE, JOHN   L A f 32   14 Mar 1778
                                          L 1 p 29   31 Jul 1778

Wife: (not named)
Eldest brother: Basil (under age 21) - "Cook's Range" where testator now
                lives, "Cook's Choice", pt. of "Needwood", pt. of
                "Dublin", pt. of "Fellowship", pt. of "Lucky Range",
                pt. of "Resurvey on Small Purchase", "Charles and
                John's Choice"
Youngest brother: Nathan (under age 21) - "Crabb's Purchase", "Anns Garden",
                pt. of "Needwood", pt. of "Resurvey on Mill Trail", pt.
                of "Resurvey on Small Purchase", pt. "Charles and
                John's Choice"
Eldest sister: Sarah Cooke (minor) - "Rum Punch", pt. of "Cooke's Range", pt.
                of "Resurvey on Lakin's Lott", pt. of "Resurvey on
                "Dublin"
Sister: Ruth (minor) - pt. of "Lakin's Lott"
Youngest sister: Rachel (minor) - pt. of "Cooke's Range" where William
                Ricketts lives, pt. of "Raddle Snake Denn", pt. of
                "Needwood"
Ex: Friend, Nathan Holland
Wit: John Bruce, Nathaniel Pigman, Richard Wootton
Codicil dated 2 May 1778
Charges Nathan Holland to distribut father's estate and appoints him guardian
 to sisters and brothers
Wit: John Kennedy

COSTIGAN, DENNIS   L E f 106   17 May 1803
                                          L 2 p   4   10 Oct 1803

Dau: Mary Costigan
Son: Michael
Ex: Mary and Michael Costigan
Wit: Richard Selby, Nathan Cooke, Benjamin Gaither

COUPLAND, HUGH of Lower District of   L A   f 36   26 Aug 1776
            Frederick Co.   L 1   p 32   4 Jun 1778

Friend: Jane, wife of Archibald Beall
Ex: Jane, wife of Archibald Beall
Wit: H. Dunn, William Lanham

CRAFFORD, NATHANIEL   L B   f 138   21 Jan 1783
                                                L 1   p 134   11 Oct 1783

Wife: Rachel Crafford - pt. of "Prevention"
Son: Robert - "Prevention" at wife's decease
Son: Alexander Crafford
Daus: Elizabeth Crawford (sic), Rachel Crafford
Exs: Sons Alexander Crafford and Robert
Wit: William Richards, William Magrath, Sarah Richards

CRAWFORD, JOHN SUTTON   L J   f 21   18 Mar 1814
                                                  L 2   p 370   28 Mar 1814

Wife: Elizabeth Crawford
Daus: Betsey Sutton Crawford, Patty Allen Crawford, Lethe Crawford
Tyson Beall (minor), an orphan boy raised by testator
Grandchildren: Louisa, James, Emmaline, Basil Mockbee
Ex: Wife and son Nathaniel
Wit: James Anderson, J. Elgan

CROW, EDWARD, Sr.   L B   f 418   21 Mar 1783
                                                                          8 Jun 1790

Wife: (not named)
Son: Edward - 150 a. pt. of Able's Levils" and "Resurvey on Shady Grove"
Son: Samuel - 100 a. "Able's Levils"
Sons: Joshua, Basil (under age 21), James
Daus: Martha, Priscilla, Lucy, Nancey
Granddau: Cloe Owen (under age 16)
Ex: Wife and sons Edward and Samuel
Wit: H. Griffith, Samuel Griffith, Jacob Crumblick

CROWN, JERRARD   L L   f 84   20 Jun 1818
                                                           L 3   p 86   22 Jul 1818

Wife: Dorothy Crown
Granddaus: Mary and Kitty Eleanor, children of dau. Elizabeth Duley
Daus: Elizabeth Duley, Sophia, Susan, Mary
Sons: Elisha, Joseph, Jerrard, Samuel, Thomas
Ex: Robert P. Magruder
Wit: Thomas Read, Phillip Connelly, Sarah Read

37

CULP, GEORGE, Sr.   L G f 394   22 Jan 1803
                                        L 2 p 283   6 Nov 1811

Daus: Elizabeth Culp and Katherine Culp - each 1/2 dwelling plantation
Son: John Culp - land purchased from Thomas Aldridge and Edward Crow near
                 the head of the Seneca in Mont. Co.
Son: George Culp
Land on Seneca where John now lives, purchased from Gideon Davis and George
   Ellicott, to be sold and divided between Elizabeth, Katherine, John and the
   children of George Culp, they to have their father's 1/4 share.
Ex: Son John Culp
Wit: Robert Wallace, Thomas P. Willson, Charles Willson
Codicil dated 12 Feb 1803
Grandchildren: James McCormick, George McCormick, Edward McCormick, and
               Christina McCormick
Wit: Upton Beall, Thomas P. Willson, Charles Willson, Lewis Beall

CUSHMAN, JOHN H.   L J f 451   23 Jun 1816
                                        L 2 p 507   2 Jul 1816

To be interred in some burying ground of the Roman Catholic Church
Sons: George Washington Cushman, John Franklin Cushman
Ex: Henry Waring
Wit: Richard J. Orme, Nicholas Lowe Dawson, James Walker

DARBY, ANN of Ann Arundel Co.   L L f 78   10 Jun 1809
                                        L 3 p 76   5 Mar 1818

Sons: Sammuel Darby, John Darby, Aden Darby, Zadock Darby
Dau: Ann Blowers
Granddaus: Rada, Drusillar and Ann Darby, daus. of Samuel Darby
Grandsons: James Ray, William Alford Ray, George Washington Ray, Asa Ray
Granddau: Martha Ann Ray
Ex: Son John Darby
Wit: Richard Green, Zaddock Windsor
Final account of Anne Darby 28 Nov 1822 lists other children: Asa Darby,
   Basil Darby, Caleb Darby, Elizabeth Allnutt, Rezin Darby

DARBY, GEORGE   L B f 227   27 Feb 1788
                                        L 1 p 204   5 May 1788

Wife: Anna - dwelling plantation
Son: Rezin - dwelling plantation at wife's decease
Sons: Basil and John Darby - "Amsterdam"
Son: Caleb - "Dry Spring"
Sons: Samuel Darby and Aden Darby - "Ray's Adventure"
Son: Zadock Darby - "Hutchcraft Range"
Children now living with testator as they come of age (not named)
Ex: Wife Anna and sons Basil and John
Wit: Richard Thomas, Richard Thomas, Jr., Nicholas Boswell

DARBY, JOHN   L L f 101   24 Oct 1818
                                                 L 3 p 22   20 May 1819

Wife: Ruth Darby - plantation where testator now lives
Nephews: John Washing(ton) Darby and Charles Alexander Darby
Niece: Rebeckah R. Bailey
Nephew: Nicholas R. Darby - plantation at wife's decease
Ex: Brother Aden Darby
Wit: Samuel Darby, William Gartrell, Rezin Bowman

DAVIS, ANN   L B f 190   15 Dec 1778
                                                 L 1 p 157   22 Mar 1785

Son: Isiah Davis - "Widdow's Lot" where testator lives
Daus: Ann Davis, Susanah Davis and Lucretia Sanders
Grandsons: Azariah Weaver Sanders and Rhodum Weaver Sanders
Ex: Son Isiah Davis
Wit: Thomas Veatch, Thomas Dowdon, John Nobs

DAVIS, LODOWICK, planter   L A f 28   13 Feb 1778
                                                 L 1 p 24   28 Mar 1778

Wife: Eleanor - land
Son: Rezin
Other children: (not named)
Ex: Wife Eleanor
Wit: Charles A. Warfield, Charles Greenbury Griffith, Hezekiah Griffith

DAVIS, WILLIAM, Sr., of Frederick Co.   L A f 222   22 Jul 1775
                                                 L 1 p 62   11 Nov 1779

Children: William Davis; Mary Dowden, wife of Thomas Dowden; Eleanor Harding,
          wife of Charles Harding; Lucy Swearingham, wife of Van Swearingham.
          All of Frederick Co.
Son: Leonard Davis - remainder of estate, especially my right to the estate
                     of Mary Welch, dec'd., of Prince George's Co., Md.
Ex: Son Leonard Davis
Wit: Robert Ferguson, James Campbell

DAVIS, ZACHARIAH   L D f 135   20 Feb 1799
                                                 L 1 p 417   18 Apr 1799

Mother: Susan Davis
Archibald Pitts and Thomas Crauford
Brother: Luke Davis
Ex: John Templeman, Esq.
Wit: James S. Morsell, Thomas Quaid, Truman Crown

39

DAVISS, ISAIAH   L C   f 114   22 Aug 1792
                                                        L 1   p 261   20 Jul 1793

Nephew: Azariah Weaver Sanders - "Widow's Lott"
Ex: Sister Lucretia Sanders
Wit: John Williams, Henry Russell, Henry McGlocklin, Matthias Byrn

DAWSON, ELIZABETH   L F   f 507   12 May 1809
                                                        L 2   p 214   4 Aug 1809

Sister: Eleanor Allnutt
Lawrence Allnutt
Elizabeth Dawson, dau. of Robert D. Dawson
Elizabeth Johns, dau. of Richard W. Johns
Elizabeth Dawson, wife of William Dawson
Elizabeth Allnutt, dau. of James Allnutt
Father, dec'd.
Brother: Robert D. Dawson
Wit: Basil Darby, William Vinson, John B. Dyson

DAWSON, THOMAS   L D   f 434   6 Jan 1794
                                                        L 1   p 461   2 Oct 1800

Wife: Elisabeth Dawson
Son: Robert Doyne Dawson - 110 a. "Mother's Delight", 50 a. "Addition to
                Mother's Delight", 16 a. "Fair Prospect"
Daus: Mary, Elenor, Virlinder, Rebecah, Elizabeth, Sarah, Jane
Sarah Blackmore and Rebecah Blackmore, daus. of Sarah and William Blackmore
Mary and Elizabeth, children of dau. Jane
Sons: Nicholas Dawson, Benoni Dawson
Exs: Robert Doyne Dawson and wife Elizabeth
Wit: Isaac Waters, Edward Digges, John Jenes

DEAKINS, WILLIAM, Jr. of Georgetown, merchant   L D   f   1   2 Mar 1798
                                                L 1   p 379   12 Mar 1798

Wife: Jane Deakins - 3 lots in Georgetown where they now dwell, lot and
                dwelling where James Clark now lives, approx. 150 a.
                tracts "Seneca Landing" and "Fortune" nr. mouth of
                Seneca Creek in Mont. Co.
Brothers: Francis Deakins, Leonard Marbury Deakins, and Paul Hoy
Ex: Brother Francis Deakins
Wit: Benjamin Stoddart, C. Worthington, John Weems, John T. Mason

DENNIS, WILLIAM   L F   f 179   24 Jul 1805
                                                        L 2   p 132   28 Sep 1807

Niece of present wife: Elizabeth Clark - plantation where testator now lives,
                                "Chelmsford"
Wife: Easter Dennis

Ex: Friend, John Poole, Jr.
Wit: Joseph Poole, Jr., Benjamin Poole, Charles Willson

DICKERSON, HANNAH   L M f 285   12 Jul 1816
                                                     L 3 p 123   29 Dec 1820

Son: Surratt Dickerson, lately of Ky., dec'd.
Elizabeth Dickerson of Ky.
Rueben Collins
Ex: Elizabeth Dickerson of Ky.
Wit: Jonathan Duley, Charles B. Hutton

DIGGES, CATHERINE   L F f   4   8 Apr 1805
                                                     L 2 p 109   4 Mar 1807

Husband: William Digges
Grandnieces: Catherine Kirwan, dau. of testator's dec'd. niece Mary Kirwan;
             Eleanor Sewall, dau. of nephew Robert Sewall; Maria Sewall, dau.
             of nephew Nicholas Sewall; Sally Blake; Catherine Chamberlaine,
             formerly Catherine Blake
Grandnephews: Robert Sewall and William Sewall, sons of nephew Robert Sewall;
              Nicholas Sewall, son of nephew Nicholas Sewall
Brother: Robert Darnall, dec'd.
Nephews: Robert Sewall and Nicholas Sewall
Ex: Nephew Robert Sewall
Wit: Philip B. Key
Codicil dated 23 Dec 1805
Wit: Joseph Belt, David Parker, Richard Ball

DOUGLASS, SAMUEL   L E f 107   9 Oct 1803
                                                     L 2 f   5   8 Nov 1803

Wife: Susanah Douglass - plantation where testator lives
Sons: Hugh Douglass, John Douglass
Dau: Mary Douglass
Step-dau: Cassandra Swan
Children: John, Elizabeth, Charles, Ann, Samuel, Rebecca, Jane, Levey,
          Josias, Mary, Hugh
Exs: Wife Susanah Douglass, son John Douglass
Wit: Thomas Benson, Henry Fowler, John Harding

DOWDEN, ZACHARIAH   L N f 86   11 Nov 1820
                                                     L 3 p 152   8 Dec 1821

Sell estate
Wife: Sarah Dowden
Dau: Lucy Mullican, wife of John Mullican
Ex: Friend, Solomon Holland
Wit: Gassaway Perry, John Heeter, Henson Pritchett

DOWNS, MARY   L H f 315   11 Oct 1804
                                                     L 2 p 355   7 Oct 1813

Dau: Lucy Hallsal
Son-in-law: Leonard Hurdle
Grandchildren: Mary Duritty, Ann Griffin, Rebecca Ridgeway, Lucretia Parsons,
               Thomas Hurdle, Elizabeth Hurdle, Sarah Hurdle, Anna Hurdle,
               Zachariah Hallsal, Mary Hallsal, Stacy Hallsal
Children: Mary Holly, Zachariah Downs, Henry Downs, Lucy Hallsall
Ex: Son Zachariah Downs
Wit: William Culver, John Needham

DOWNS, MARY   L N f 300   8 Oct 1822
                                                     L 3 p 201   28 Jan 1823

Father: (not named, but living)
Eldest Sister: Ann M. Downs
Brothers: Richard M. Downs, William Downs
Sisters: Elizabeth Wheeler, Leanah Jones
Eldest nephew: Alfred Wheeler
Exs: Brothers Richard and William
Wit: Burgess Culver, Joshua Brown

DOYLE, ALEXANDER of Georgetown, D.C.,   L C f 149   7 Mar 1787
                 storekeeper   L 1 p 301   20 Nov 1794

Land in Stafford Co., Va. may be sold
Wife: Elizabeth
Daus: Mary Doyle, Anne Doyle
Dau: Margaret Doyle - lot and house in which testator lives in Georgetown
Dau: Gracy Doyle - lot with storehouse and granery
Sons: James Doyle, Alexander Doyle, Joseph Doyle, John Doyle
Exs: Notley Young of Prince George's Co. and Marsham Waring of Mont. Co.
Wit: Henry King, Thomas Connelly, Samuel Wesley

DRANE, THOMAS   L N f 308   28 Jan 1823
                                                     L 3 p 213   4 Feb 1823

Step-grandson: Thomas Burch of City of Washington
Brothers and sisters of Thomas Burch (not named)
Ex: Friend, William Trail
Wit: John Poole, Sr., Samuel S. Hayes, Sarah Vermillion

DUVALL, AQUILLA   L B f 141   29 Sep 1783
                                                     L 1 p 138   3 Nov 1783

Brother: Lewis Duvall
Dau: Rachel Musgrove
Sons: Levin, Zadock, Frederick
Son: Aquilla - 100 a. land where testator now lives

5 youngest children: Eleanor, Elizabeth, William, Claudia, Aquilla
Ex: Brother Lewis Duvall
Wit: Henry Griffith, Jr., Ann Purdis, Ann Russell

DUVALL, ANN   L O f 461   Oct 1818
                                        L 3 p 366   9 Aug 1825

Dau: Elizabeth Owen
Son: Lewis W. Duvall
Ex: Son Lewis W. Duvall
Wit: Ephraim Etchison, Samuel Welsh Sr.

DUVALL, MAREEN   L F f 180   2 Apr 1805
                                        L 2 p 134   5 Nov 1807

Dau: Sarah Duvall - 1/2 dwelling plantation "Hermitage"
Son: Benjamin Duvall - 1/2 dwelling plantation "Hermitage"
Son: William Duvall
Ex: Son Benjamin Duvall
Wit: Peter Becraft, James Lee, Edward Harding

DYER, ELEANOR   L N f 311   25 Feb 1822
                                        L 3 p 215   3 Mar 1823

Daus: Elizabeth H. Chilton, wife of Joshua Chilton; Mary Carr, wife of
      William Carr of Loudoun Co., Va.; Ann Dyer, Catherine Dyer
Son: Henry Dyer, dec'd.
Ex: Thomas T. Wheeler
Wit: Daniel Trundle, Clement Wheeler, Patrick Byrn

DYER, HENRY   L N f 92   21 Dec 1821
                                        L 3 p 158   7 Jan 1822

Sister: Ann Dyer
Mother: Eleanor Dyer
Ex: Thomas T. Wheeler
Wit: Clement Wheeler, Gustavis Clements, John H. Hughes

DYSON, LYDIA   L G f   2   4 Jan 1810
                                        L 2 p 227   29 Jan 1810

Daus: Mary Neal, wife of Barton Neal; Darcus Viers, wife of Nathan Veirs;
      Nancy Brashears, wife of Edward Brashears; Mily Higdon, wife of
      Ignatius Higdon
Sons: John B. Dyson, Jeremiah Dyson
Children of dec'd dau. Sarah Bird
Children of dec'd son Samuel Dyson
Ex: Son John B. Dyson
Wit: William Dawson, James Allnutt, Lawrance Allnutt

EDELIN, PHILIP   L N f 441   27 Jul 1823
                                                    L 3 p 228   20 Aug 1823

Sell all but house and 10 a. of plantation
Mary Mathews, Priscilla Mathews, Betsy Mathews - dwelling house and 10 a.
James Mathews
Eight children of Thomas Knott
Four children of Philip Knott
Brother: Leonard Edelin - house and 1 a. lot on Ten Mile Creek
Ex: Friend, Nacy Griffith of Clarksburgh, Md.
Wit: Mesheck Browning, Daniel Bennett, Lamack Saffell

EDMONSON, MARY   "late of Mont. Co. and at   L J f 210   3 Oct 1815
                  present on a visit to my   L 2 p 456   4 Nov 1815
                  children in Alexandria"

Dau: Dorothy Waters
Sons: Eden Edmonson and Robert Edmonson
Ex: Son Robert Edmonson
Wit: Thomas Jacobs, R.G. Lanphies, George Jacobs
Note: Will probated in Alexandria Co., District of Columbia

EDMONSON, WILLIAM   L C f 113   6 May 1793
                                                    L 1 p 260   18 Jun 1793

Wife: Elizabeth Edmonson
Children: Ann Edmonson, Thomas Edmonson, Sarah Edmonson, William Edmonson,
          John Edmonson, Elizabeth Edmonson
Ex: Wife Elizabeth
Wit: Hezekiah Magruder, Philip Jackson, Samuel Nicholls, Ninian Magruder

EDMONSTON, ARCHIBALD   L A f 44   28 Dec 1764
                                                    L 1 p 41   9 Jan 1779

Wife: Dorrithy
Daus: Jean and Elizabeth
Grandson: Archibald Brooke Beall - "Addition to Deer Park" and land purchased
                                    of Nicholas Jackson
Daus: Mary, Priscilla, Dorrithy, Ann Henrietta, Margaret Smith - "Sisters
                                Goodwill", "Debate", "Locust Thicket"
Friends: James, Richard and Basil Brooke
Son: Roger
Son: Thomas - land where testator now lives
Ex: Wife Dorrithy
Wit: Nasey Brashear, Mary Simpson, Musgrove Simpson

EDMONSTON, THOMAS, Sr.   L E f 129   30 Jan 1805
                                                    L 2 p 55   9 Mar 1805

Son: Edward Edmonston - pt. of "Greenland" where he now lives, "Tom's Lot"

Sons: Alexander Edmonston, dec'd.; Thomas Edmonston, Robert Edmonston
Son: Eden Edmonston - pt. "Deer Park Enlarged", "Edmonston Range"
Daus: Elizabeth Schoolfield, Dolly Edmonston - pt. "Bear Garden"
Grandchildren: Franklin Edmonston and Olivia Edmonston (minors)
Grandsons: Decious Edmonston and Brook Edmonston (minors)
Sell 211 3/4 a. "Edmonston Enclosure"
Wife: Mary - testator's home plantation of "Bear Garden" and "Deer Park
       Enlarged"
Ex: Wife Mary
Wit: Josiah Jones, James W. Perry, Tyson Beall

ELDER, JOHANNAH	L D f 393	17 Mar 1800
	L 1 p 460	10 May 1800

Grandson: Hugh Glover
Ex: Hugh Glover
Wit: William Glaze, Susannah Lee

ELLIS, JOHN, planter	L E f 136	1 Jul 1805
	L 2 p 67	13 Aug 1805

Daus: Ruth, Elizabeth, Sarah Palmmer, Mary Lewis
Sons: John, Philip, Joseph - 95 a. testator's plantation
Ex: Sons John and Philip Ellis
Wit: Zadock Summers, Jonathan Browning, ------- -------

ESTEP, BETSEY	L M f 132	25 Dec 1818
	L 3 p 95	22 Mar 1820

Daus: Sarah Estep, Eleanor
Son: Rezin Estep
Ex: Dau. Sarah Estep
Wit: William Culver, Elizabeth Hayes

ESTEP, ELIZABETH	L J f 20	1 Jan 1814
	L 2 p 441	9 Jul 1815

Grandsons: Richard Estep, Richard Holmes, Edward Tillard, Rezin Tillard
Granddaus: Elizabeth Tillard, Ann Lyles Estep, Martha Eleanor Tillard,
           Eleanor Maria Estep
Sister: Ann Leach, dec'd.
Daus: Sarah Tillard, Eleanor Holmes
Son: Rezin - retain possession of Sarah Tillard's part until decease of her
     husband
Wit: Benjamin Duvall, Washington Duvall
Codicil dated 1815 - not probated

ESTEP, RICHARD   L B f 245   28 Mar 1785
                                                  L 1 p 226   26 Mar 1787

Wife: Elizabeth
Son: Alexander Estep - dwelling plantation which is pt. of "John and Jane's
            Choice"
Son: Rezin Estep - pt. of"John and Jane's Choice"
Daus: Mary Williams, Eleanor (minor), Sarah (minor)
Ex: Wife Elizabeth and son Rezin
Wit: Edward Tillard, Benjamin Allein, Charles Drury

ESTEP, SARAH   L N f   2   31 Jul 1820
                                                  L 3 p 147   14 Mar 1821

Brother: Resin Estep
Sister: Eleanor Howison
Ex: Brother Resin Estep
Wit: Ruth Wheeler, John Bowie

EVANS, WILLIAM   L B f 188   9 Feb 1785
                                                  L 1 p 159   4 Mar 1785

Dau-in-law: Elizabeth Essex who is "helpless"
Peggy, sister of Elizabeth Essex
William Evans Ferguson (under age 21), nephew of Elizabeth Essex
Children of Nathaniel Ferguson
Friend and neighbor: Thomas Fletchall
John Ferguson, son of Nathaniel
Ex: Thomas Fletchall
Wit: John Peter, John Heugh

FARR, ISAAC   L L f 100   11 Jul 1815
                                                  L 3 p 19   18 May 1819

Sons: Cyrus Farr, Edward Farr, James Farr
Daus: Mary Newcomb, Hannah Farr, Jane Farr
3 granddaus: Hannah Farr, Agsnath Farr, Elizabeth Farr, whom testator has
             raised
Ex: Son James Farr
Wit: David Newlin, John H. Riggs, William Layman

FARRALL, JAMES of Frederick Co.   L A f 12   5 Oct 1776
                                                  L 1 p   5   7 Jun 1777

Sons: Henry, John
Daus: Ann, Mary Verlinda, Mary, Kezia, Rebekah and Mary Rosemond Farrall
Married sons and daus: (not named)
Ex: "All my unmarried children as named above"
Wit: Thomas Belt, Jeremiah Beall

FEE, WILLIAM   L B f 440   20 Dec 1790
                                                            14 Jan 1791

George Washington Haymond (under age 21), son of Margaret Haymond - "William
                                Meadows otherwise Netherlands", pt. "Rockey Point"
Eli Fee Haymond (minor) , son of Margaret Haymond - "Adamson's Choice"
Elizabeth Haymond, second dau. of Margaret Haymond
Brothers: Thomas Fee, George Fee
Sisters: Mary Cox, Rebecca Jones, Elizabeth Ancrim
Margaret Haymond
Land "Pippin" to be sold
King English, Richard Wootton, Esq., John Gainer Hamilton, Atty., Michael
   Lytton to be guardians of above children
Exs: King English and Margaret Haymond, George Washington Haymond when of age
Wit: Walter Lanham, Lawrence Owen Holt, Joseph Fish

FERGUSON, CATHARINE of Frederick Co.   L A f 197   16 Mar 1779
                                       L 1 p 58   30 Aug 1779

Granddaus: Katherine Lovelace, Catherine Lanham, Ann Skinner Ferguson
Ex: Son John
Wit: John Lacklen, Elias Harding, John Wilcoxen

FERGUSON, REZIN   L F f 203   30 Jun 1808
                                       L 2 p 161   14 Sep 1808

Wife: Elizabeth Ferguson
Children: Elizabeth, Nancy, Caroline and Addison Ferguson (minors)
Exs: Frederick Whetzel, Philip Yost
Wit: Zadok Lanham, Aquila Lanham, Robert L. Beall

FISH, ROBERT, Sr.   L D f 580   26 May 1802
                                       L 1 p 503   19 Jul 1802

Wife: Priscilla Fish
Daus: Elizabeth Fish, Henrietta, Ann, Eleanor, Mary, Harriot
Sons: Robert, George, Francis, James, Richard, Levin, and William Fish
Ex: Wife Priscilla
Wit: James Anderson, Benjamin Gaither, Robert P. Magruder

FISHER, MARTIN   L I f 40   15 Nov 1814
                                       L 2 p 403   21 Feb 1815

Half acre where graveyard is never to be sold
Children: Eleanor, Matilda, Elizabeth, William, Selah, Artaxerxes, Thomas,
           Aquilla
Ex: Son Artaxerxes
Wit: Archibald Mullikin, Zadock Mullikin, Edward W. Gatton

FISHER, MARTIN   L N f 83   6 Sep 1821
                                        L 3 p 148   15 Nov 1821

Land to be sold
Dau: Ann Fisher
Sons: Thomas, Nelson, John, George, William, Martin
Exs: Sons William and Martin
Wit: William Brewer, John Douglass, Richard Spates

FISHER, MARY   L B f 401   1 May 1787
                                                           9 Jun 1789

Sons: Stephen and Arthur Tall
Dau: Jane Moffett
Granddaus: Ann and Mary Moffett; Ruth Tall, dau. of son Stephen; Anne Shears
Ex: states no letters of administration to be taken out
Wit: James Beall, Elizabeth Beall

FLEMING, JAMES   L C f   1   14 Apr 1792
                                        L 1 p 235   12 Jun 1792

Wife: Elizabeth Fleming
Daus: Mary, Catherine
Son: John
Other children: (not named - minors)
Land on Bennet's Creek to be sold
Ex: Wife Elizabeth and son John
Wit: Joseph Magruder, Ninian Willett, James Anderson

FLEMING, JOHN   L C f 315   Jan 1795
                                        L 1 p 349   16 Jan 1797

Wife: Ann - "Hensley", "Fleming's Addition","Bedfordshire Carrier"
David Lowe and Margaret Lowe - "Hensley"
Elizabeth Fleming, widow of late son James - "Fleming's Addition to Hensley"
Hrs. of son James Fleming: John, Robert, Burgess, Cephas, Mary and Catherine
                            Fleming
Catherine Magruder
Ann Willet, wife of Ninian Willet
Son: John Fleming
Balance of estate to be divided into 5 parts: David and Margaret Lowe;
    Catherine Magruder; John Fleming; Ann Willet, wife of Ninian; hrs. of
    James Fleming
Ex: Wife Ann and David Lowe
Wit: James Anderson, Ozias Offutt

FLEMING, JOHN   L I f 37   10 Dec 1814
                                        L 2 p 397   29 Dec 1814

Brother: Robert W. Fleming - houses and lots in Rockville

48

Burgess Willett
Father, dec'd.
Brothers, dec'd.
Sister: Mary Summers
Ex: Brother Robert W. Fleming
Wit: Thomas Linstid, John Braddock, John A. Smith

FLEMING, ROBERT W.   L J f 38   4 Jan 1815
                                            L 2 f 399   7 Jan 1815

Sister: Mary Summers
Father, dec'd.
Burgess Willett - estate of testator's brother John Fleming
Ex: Burgess Willett
Wit: John Wootton, Robert Wallace, Brice Letton

FLETCHALL, BETTY   L B f 198   17 Mar 1785
                                            L 1 p 168   27 Oct 1785

Daus: Ann Fletchall, Cynthia Fletchall
Wit: Samuel Trammell, William Chaney

FLETCHALL, JOHN   L A f   7   20 Apr 1777
                                            L 1 p   9   14 Jun 1777

Wife: Betty Fletchall
Sons: Thomas, John
Daus: Jean, wife of William Hickman; Elizabeth, wife of William Hickman
Dau: Ann - "Flints Grove"
Dau: Cinthy (under age 16)
Patrick Locker, overseer of plantation
Ex: Son Thomas with wife as guardian until he reaches legal age
Wit: Margrate Campbell, Thomas Beeding, Aneas Campbell

FLETCHALL, THOMAS   L L f 123   10 Aug 1819
                                            L 3 p 60   15 Sep 1819

Wife: Sarah Newton Fletchall - "Mount Nebo" 487 a.; 7 1/4 a. "Simpson's
            Avenue"; 2 8/10 a. "An Hours Work"; 152 3/8 a. "Flints
            Grove"; 190 a. "Friends Advice" and "Resurvey on the
            Beginning"; 123 1/2 a. "Woolfs Cow"; 1,200 a. land in
            Harrison Co., Va.; 15 a. pt. of "Forrest" adjoining land
            of Colmore Williams and Ann Scearcy
Son: James Fletchall - 76 a. plantation where he now lives purchased from
            William Brewer, Thomas Hickman et al; 87 a. lease from
            Cumminger heirs; 400 a. plantation where George Fletchall
            now lives which is pt. of "Forrest"; 700 a. pt. of lands
            in Harrison Co., Va.
Dau: Sarah Chiswell, wife of William Chiswell - land devised to wife at her
            decease, except only 500 a. of land in Harrison Co., Va.;

none of "Forrest", only pt. of "Mount Nebo"; also to
have 100 a. of lease from Cumminger heirs
Son: George W. Fletchall - remainder of testator's plantation, which is
"Mount Nebo" and pt. of "Forrest", at wife's
decease
Grandson: Thomas Fletchall Chiswell (under age 21), son of William Chiswell,
and his brothers and sisters
Thomas Fletchall Linthicum (under age 21) and his brothers and sisters
Sarah Ann McElfresh and her sisters
Daniel, Ann and John Fletchall, children of John Fletchall, dec'd. - 1/2 of
lot in Georgetown
Executor to convey land sold to Benjamin White and Ann Scearcy
Ex: Son George Fletchall, William Chiswell
Wit: Colmore Williams, Ezekiah Linthicum, John M. Williams

FOWLER, ELISHA, Jr.   L C f 181   5 Feb 1794
                                        L 1 p 321   10 Jan 1795

Wife: Ann Fowler - lot # 265 in "Hawkin's and Beatty's Addition to George-
                    town, lot #113 in "Threlkeld's Addition to Georgetown",
                    "Second Addition to Culver's Chance"
Sister: Rebecca Doherty
Joseph Clarke, son of Robert
Francis Xaverius Simms, son of Joseph Milburn Simms
Ex: Wife Ann
Wit: George Fenwick, Abner Cloud, Joseph Brooke

FRAZIER, JOSHUA of City of Annapolis   L D f 303   17 Aug 1791
                                        L 1 p 448   23 Mar 1799

Nephew: Richard Frazier (under age 25) - house and lot in Annapolis where
                    testator lives; rents from other houses and lots
Sister: Elizabeth Tastell
Niece: Mary Middleton
Nephew: James Frazier
Ex: Richard Frazier
Wit: Archibald Chisholm, John Long, John Rigby

FREEMAN, SAMUEL   L E f   1   29 Aug 1801
                                        L 1 p 510   31 Aug 1802

Wife: Ann Freeman - pt. of "Cow Pasture" where testator lives
"To my brother and sister children Aaron Freman and Sarah Stalling" - land
                    where testator lives at wife's decease
Wit: Henry Leeke 3rd, Edward Jones, Greenberry Griffith, Jr.

FRENCH, GEORGE   L D f 131   12 Dec 1798
                                        L 1 p 410   28 Dec 1798

Wife: (not named)

Children: (not named - minors)
Sister-in-law: Margaret Scott
Ex: Wife
Wit: Isabella Scott, Elizabeth Scott, Elijah Walker

FRYER, JOHN, planter   L A f 46   28 Dec 1777
                                              L 1 p 43   27 Jan 1778

Son: Walter Fryer - plantation where testator now lives
Son: Richard Fryer
Other children: (not named)
Exs: Son-in-law David Trail, Jr., son Richard
Wit: Ninian Mockbee, William Benson, Elizabeth Grossman

FYFFE, JAMES   L B f 445   17 Oct 1791
                                                                22 Nov 1791

Wife: Sarah
Sons: Abijah, Joseph, James, Jonathan, John
Daus: Sarah, Elizabeth
Ex: Son John
Wit: Richard Shekell, Lewis Howser, Benjamin Ward

GAITHER, DANIEL   L L f 91   12 Sep 1818
                                              L 3 p   6   7 Oct 1818

Wife: Henrietta Gaither - pt. "Timber Neck" with grist and saw mills; pt.
                          "Mill Race", pt. "Hobson's Choice"
Son: Samuel Riggs Gaither - above land at wife's decease
Sons: William Beal Gaither, Henry Gaither, George R. Gaither, Elisha Gaither
Daus: Paulina Ould, wife of Robert Ould; Ann Willcoxen, wife of Horatio
      Willcoxen
Children of brother William Gaither, dec'd - 40 a. of "The Meadow" and
                                             "Ritch Level"
Ephraim Gaither - pt. "Hobson's Choice"
Ex: Wife Henrietta Gaither
Wit" Ephraim Gaither, H. C. Gaither, Jesse Wilcoxen

GAITHER, EDWARD, son of Benjamin   L A f 1   26 Mar 1777
                                              L 1 p 1   11 Jun 1777

Wife: Elloner Gaither
Son: Benjamin Gaither - "Gaither's Purchase", "What's Left"
Son: Basil Gaither - "Mitchell's Garden", "Mitchell's Range"
Son: Eli Gaither - dwelling plantation purchased from Isaac Snider
Sons: Greenberry Gaither, Nicholas Gaither, Burgess Gaither, Jonsey Gaither,
      and Brice Gaither - first and second resurvey on "Mitchell's Range",
                          "Gaither's Range", "Good Luck", land purchased
                          from Zachariah Lynthicum

Daus: Eloner Prather, Sarah Gaither, Cassandra Gaither, Lyla Gaither
Exs: Wife Eloner, sons Benjamin and Basil
Wit: John Ray, Jr., Benjamin Ray, John Suter, Samuel Hardesty

GAITHER, GERRARD   L I f 442   9 Jan 1816
                  L 2 p 489   15 Feb 1816

Wife: Agnes Gaither
Son: Beal Gaither
Brother: Frederick Gaither
House and lot in Unity not fully paid for, land adjoining where son Beal now resides
Exs: Son Beal Gaither and brother Frederick Gaither
Wit: Thomas Davis, Henry Griffith, Nathan Musgrove

GAITHER, HENRY, planter   L B f 143   24 Aug 1780
                  L 1 p 140   21 Aug 1783

Son: William - "Presley" in Ann Arundel Co.
Son: Henry Chew Gaither - "Gaither's Forrest, 4 a. "Snoden Purchase", "Diamond"
Son: Beale Gaither - "Gaither's Forrest", "Barren Ridge", pt. of land in Hampshire Co., Va.
Son: Ephraim Gaither - "Addition", "Good Friday", "What's Left"
Son: Gerrard Gaither - "Green Spring", "Hold Fast of What You Have Got", "Resurvey on Hammond's Strife"and "Grove" in Frederick Co., Md., "Simpson's Chance"
Son: Benjamin Gaither - pt. of Moab in Frederick Co., pt. of "Presley"
Son: Daniel Gaither - "Timber Neck", "Rich Level", "The Meadows", "Providence", "Lakin's Desire"
Son: Frederick Gaither - "Benjamin's Lott", "Frederick's Grove", "Gaither's Forrest", "Addition", "Fox Hall"
Dau: Ann Ayton - remainder of land in Hampshire Co., Va. devised to son Beale
Daus: Elizabeth, Deborah, Mary and Amelia Gaither - land in Hampshire Co., Va.
Sell pt. of "Resurvey on Hammond's Strife" and "Black Acre"
Exs: Wife Martha and sons William and Henry
Wit: H. Griffith, Weaver Barnes, H. Griffith, Jr., Henry Leeke

GAITHER, HENRY, Col. "of Carenot"   L G f 389   **Not dated**
                  L 2 p 276   **27 Aug 1811**

Sister: Amelia Holland - property in and adjoining village of Unity
Henry Chew Gaither, William Henry Gaither, Henry Gaither of Daniel, Henry Gaither of Frederick, Henry Chew Dorsey - property in City of Washington and Georgetown, property in Annapolis, lots in Brewins Burrough in Mississippi Territory, land warrant for "Yazzo" in Allegany Co., Md., land in Northwestern Territory
Thomas John Davis
Henry Prather of Walter
Beal Gaither of Gerard
Will originally probated in District of Columbia, 26 Aug 1811

52

GAITHER, JOHNSEY   L D f 13   12 Dec 1797
                                          L 1 p 396   1 Jan 1798

Sell land in Roan Co., N.C. and 150 a. adjoining Benjamin Gaither's land
Wife: Mary Gaither who is pregnant
Daus: Harriot, Matilda
Son: James
Exs: Wife Mary, brother Greenbury Gaither, friend Charles Gassaway (they
         also to be guardians of minor children)
Wit: Archibald Orme, James Lackland, John Orme

GAITHER, MARTHA   L D f   8   2 Feb 1795
                                          L 1 p 390   7 Nov 1797

Daus: Amelia Holland, Deborah Gaither
Son: Frederick Gaither
Ex: Son Beale Gaither
Wit: Thomas Davis, Nathan Musgrove, Ephraim Gaither of Wm.

GARRETT, EDWARD   L B f 186   5 Feb 1785
                                          L 1 p 160   10 Mar 1785

Elizabeth Garrett Gittings (minor)
Sisters: Elizabeth Philpot, Casander Philpot
Children of dec'd brother Middleton Garrett
Brothers: John Garrett, Barton Garrett
Niece: Susannah Garrett
Nephews: Lemelick Garrett, John Garrett, Aron Garrett, children of Middleton
            Garrett
Sell pt. of "Hermitage" and "Resurvey of Hermitage" where testator lives
Ex: Brothers Barton and John Garrett
Wit: Allen Bowie, Elias Harding, Erasmus Berry

GARTRELL, AARON   L D f 542   21 Feb 1801
                                          L 1 p 488   1 Mar 1802

Son: William Gartrell - land on Seneca where he now lives purchased from
            John Perry
Son: Ignatius Gartrell - land purchased from William Simpson where Caleb
            now lives
Son: Benjamin Gartrell - pt. of "What's Left", "Addition to Brooke Grove",
            "Burgesses Look Out" and "Not Worth Naming" where
            he now lives
Son: Caleb Gartrell - pt. of "Benjamin's Lott" where testator lives
Son: Samuel Gartrell - pt. of "Resurvey on Little Worth" and "Beggars
            Purchase"
Daus: Amelia Holland, Sarah Darby, Rebecca Griffith, Elizabeth Belt, and
         Jane Gaither
Grandson: Aaron Gartrell, son of William
Niece: Mary Gartrell, dau. of brother Stephen Gartrell
Ex: Son Benjamin Gartrell
Wit: Philemon Plummer, Nathan Musgrove, Philemon Plummer, Jr.

GARTRELL, IGNATIUS   L E f 129   20 Feb 1805
                                            L 2 p 53   7 Mar 1805

Brother-in-law: Frederick Gaither
Nephew: Ignatius Griffith, son of Greenberry Griffith
Ex: Brother-in-law Frederick Gaither
Wit: Thomas Davis, Ephraim Gaither, Nathan Musgrove

GARTRELL, SARAH   L H f 324   29 Oct 1813
                                            L 2 p 367   5 Feb 1814

8 grandchildren: Charles A., Rachel, Davage, Phillemon, Sarah, Ann, Basil
                 and John Griffith
Ex: Basil Griffith
Wit: Philip Holland, Samuel Gartrell, William Plummer

GA(R)TRELL, SARAH   L B f 135   10 Feb 1777
                                            L 1 p 132   14 Oct 1783

Daus: Rachel, Sarah
Granddau: Ruth Gatrell
Grandson: Stephen Penn (under age 21)
Ex: Brother Thomas Gatrell
Wit: H. Griffith, Luke Davis

GARVIS, JARRETT   L E f 114   2 Mar 1804
                                            L 2 p 21   15 Mar 1804

Sons: Zadock, Washington, Hillery
Daus: Alley, Polly
Exs: Friends, John Aldridge and William Darnes
Wit: Joseph Forrest, Robert D. Allnutt, Joseph Astlin, Thomas Brome

GASSAWAY, CHARLES   L J f 453   18 Nov 1816
                                            L 2 p 512   11 Dec 1816

Wife: Ruth Gassaway - 400 a. of dwelling plantation including house
Dau: Polly Catlett
3 children of Polly Catlett: Deborah Edwards, Eliza Dorsey, Evelina Dorsey
Dau: Elizabeth Darne - pt. "Mt. Pleasant", "Resurvey on Mitchell's Range",
                       "The Promise Fulfilled", "The Addition to the Promise
                       Fulfilled", " Morton's Island" in the Potomac River
Dau: Rachel Owings - pt. "Mt. Pleasant" 282 a., 141 a. "**Hartly Hall**",
                     "Pleasant Hills" where testator resides, "Morton's
                     Island"
Son: Thomas Gassaway - pt. "Pleasant Hills" where testator lives, "Overplus",
                       "Thomas' Discovery Fortified", "Morton's Island", a
                       parcel of land purchased from Thomas Plater with mills
Son: Charles - pt. "Pleasant Hills" where testator lives, "Resurvey on Mitch-
               ell's Range", "Promise Fulfilled" and remainder of "Morton's
               Island"

Exs: Son-in-law William Darne, son Charles Gassaway
Wit: Leonard Boswell, John Candler, John Doud

GATTON, ANN   L H f 37   17 Oct 1811
                                           L 2 p 344   10 Feb 1813

Son: Samuel Franklin
Dau: Kitty, dec'd.
Dau: Matilda
"All my children": (not named)
Wit: Richard Wootton, John Wootton

GATTON, BENJAMIN   L A f 180   31 Jan 1779
                                           L 1 p 56   4 Aug 1779

Buried in form of Church of England
Wife: Elizabeth - dwelling plantation
Son: Samuel Gatton (under age 19)
Dau: Vhelander Gatton
Ex: Wife Elizabeth
Wit: Elenour Lewis, Aneas Campbell, John Lewis

GATTON, JAMES   L A f 50   19 Jan 1777
                                           L 1 p 47   9 Jun 1778

Wife: Mary - all land
Son: Azeriah - plantation where testator now lives at wife's decease
Children: Elisha, Elizabeth, Rebeccah
Ex: Wife Mary
Wit: Charles Barkley, Benjamin Gatton, Sarah Barkley

GATTON, JAMES   L F f 185   7 Sep 1807
                                           L 2 p 140   12 Nov 1807

Sons: John Gatton, Thomas Gatton, James Gatton
Dau: Susannah Reid
Dau-in-law: Mary Ann Gatton
Ex: Son James Gatton
Wit: Hezekiah Veatch, Thomas Veatch, Richard Veatch

GATTON, SAMUEL FRANKLIN   L L f 82   25 Oct 1817
                                           L 3 p 82   11 Jun 1818

Edward W. Gatton
Hrs. of Aquilla Gatton: Ann, Sarah, William and Zachariah Gatton
Solomon Holland
Ex: Solomon Holland
Wit: Dr. James Anderson, Robert Anderson

55

```
GENTLE, STEPHEN                              L C  f 205        5 Jan 1795
                                             L 1  p 236        5 Aug 1795
```

Wife: Sarah
Granddau: Ann Collier, dau. of dau. Jane
Grandson: Fielder Gentle, son of William Gentle
Grandson: Samuel Gentle, son of Samuel Gentle
Ex: Wife Sarah
Wit: Philbird Greenwell, Hyram Seers

```
GITTINGS, BENJAMIN                           L B  f  52       20 May 1781
                                             L 1  p  96       14 Aug 1781
```

Wife: Ann Gittings
Sons: Kinsey, Ason, James - pt. of "Dan" and "Club's Delight"
Daus: Amelia, Virlinda, Elizabeth, and Sarah Gittings
Wife Ann and brother Jeremiah to be guardians of children
Wit: Allen Bowie, Jr., James Higgins, Edward Harding

```
GITTINGS, ELIZABETH                          L N  f 310       23 Jan 1823
                                             L 3  p 214       25 Feb 1823
```

Step-father: Thomas Drane
Ex: Step-father Thomas Drane
Wit: John Poole, Sr., William Trail, John Parklington

```
GODMAN, EDWARD                               L M  f 133       15 May 1812
                                             L 3  p  96       23 May 1820
```

Wife: Sarah Godman - 52 a. "Edmonston's Range" where testator lives
Children: Julia, Rachel, Samuel, Elijah (minors)
Ex: Wife Sarah Godman
Wit: Josiah Jones, Jr., Patrick Orme, -.-. Edmonston

```
GOLDSBURRY, JONATHAN, planter                L C  f 312       29 Aug 1796
                                             L 1  p 363        5 Oct 1796
```

Dau: Mary Drury
Sons: John Goldsburry, Jonathan Goldsburry, Ignatius Goldsburry
Ex: Ignatius Drury
Wit: Ch. Decandry, John Douglass, Raphael Jarboe

```
GOTT, ELEANOR                                L O  f 374       25 Jul 1822
                                             L 3  p 310       25 Feb 1825
```

Dau: Sebell Gott
Elizabeth Parkerson
"All my children"
Sary Ann Fisher

Dau-in-law: Sary Gott
Samuel Harris
Wit: Stephen White of N

GOTT, RICHARD   L E f 115   20 Feb 1804
                                            L 2 p 24   24 May 1804

Wife: Eleanor
Son: Richard Gott - land where testator lives
Son: John Gott
Dau-in-law: Sarah Gott, wife of Richard Gott
Daus: Sebell, Mary Spencer, Elizabeth Allnutt, Eleanor Allnutt
Grandchildren: Elizabeth Harris, Thomas Harris, Nancy Harris
Ex: Son Richard Gott
Wit: Nathan S. White, John Hoyle, Charles Howard

GRAHAM, JUDITH SWAN   L J f 191   2 Dec 1814
                                            L 2 p 418   11 Apr 1818

5 grandchildren: John Marzhel Taylor, Charles William Taylor, Rawleigh
                  Colston Taylor, Howard Tapscott Taylor, Allen Griffin
                  Taylor (all minors), children of dau. Frances Bell
Daus: Sarah Fauntlery Howard, Ann Tapscott, Frances Bell
Granddau: Alcindia Graham Howard
Land in Kentucky
Ex: Son-in-law Henry Howard of John
Wit: Henry Griffith, David Newlin, H.C. Gaither

GREEN, FRANCIS   L L f 93   28 Mar 1814
                                            L 3 p 11   17 Oct 1818

Father: Benedict Green
Sister: Jane Green
Nieces and Nephews: Letitia, Juliet, Benedict Hanson, Basil and George
                     Clemons, children of sister Chloe, dec'd, wife of
                     Basil Clemons
Ex: Sister Jane Green
Wit: Joshua Chilton, John D. --emmons, William S. Chilton

GREEN, HUGH   L D f 544   21 Jan 1802
                                            L 1 p 491   3 Mar 1802

Wife: Rachel
Sons: William Green and Richard Green
Wit: James Trail, Jr., John Buxton, William Tracy

GREEN, RICHARD   L L f 88   23 May 1815
                                            L 3 p   3   17 Sep 1818

Son: Allen Green - 257 1/4 a. "Peasant Farms" which is testator's dwelling

57

                    plantation, on condition he make it his permanent
                    residence within 1 year
Daus: Elizabeth Griffith, Mary Israel, Anna Dorsey, Amelia Dorsey, Ruth Darby
Ex: Son Allen Green, who lives in Cincinnati, Ohio. If he is unable to serve
    then ex. to be friend and neighbor Thomas Davis
Wit: James Holland, John W. Leeke, Remus Riggs

GREEN, THOMAS   L N f 457   28 Sep 1820
                                                                  30 Oct 1823

Wife: Margaret Green - house and land where testator now lives
Son: Thomas W. Green - "Elizabeth" which was purchased from Solomon **Davis**
Son: William
Daus: Elizabeth Clark, Margaret Douglass, Jemima Green, Susannah Green,
    Kitty Green
Ex: Son Thomas W. Green
Wit: Robert Maginniss, Overton Williams, Dennis Lackland

GRIFFITH, HENRY   L C f 152   14 Jan 1794
                                            L 1 p 308   10 Oct 1794

Son: Henry Griffith - "two plantations where his two sons live" near the
       Hawlings River
Son: Samuel Griffith - plantation where he now lives, "That's All", "Inman's
       Plains"
Son: Joshua Griffith - testator's dwelling plantation
Grandchildren: William Ridgely, Juliett, Pheby and John Griffith, children
       of dec'd. son John (all minors)
Grandchildren: Children of Amon Riggs and his wife Ruth - "Griffith's Park"
       in Allegany Co., Md.
Grandchildren: Children of Samuel Welsh and his late wife Rachel -
       "Sherewood Forrest"
Grandchildren: Children of Nicholas Hall and his wife Ann
Grandson: Lyde Griffith (under age 21)
Sell "Mill Land" and mill, pt. "Tusculum", "New Design Place"
Lands in Ann Arundel and Frederick Cos., Md.
Son: Philemon Griffith
Dau: Sarah Todd, dec'd
John Burgess for his wife's part
Joale Waters for his wife's part
Exs: Sons Philemon and Joshua
Wit: Benjamin Griffith, Charles G. Griffith, John H. Griffith

HARBIN, ELIAS   L D f 445   25 Apr 1801
                                            L 1 p 475   4 Jun 1801

Wife: Dorcas Harbin
Children: John Hatton Bevly Harbin, James Harbin, Jeremiah Harbin, John
      Harbin, William Harbin, unborn child (all minors)
Exs: Wife Dorcas and Benjamin Cross
Wit: Robert D. Dawson, Samuel McFarland, Joseph Jarboe

HARBIN, JAMES   L A f 42   3 Jan 1778
                                       L 1 p 38   12 May 1778

Wife: Eleanor
Sons: Joshua, Gerrard, Elias, William - land
Daus: Mary, Dorcas, Ann Ellis
Exs: Wife Eleanor and son Joshua
Wit: James Fyffe, Director Smallwood

HARDESTY, MARY   L N f 336   29 Sep 1818
                                       L 3 p 223   15 May 1823

Sister: Elizabeth Hinton
Relatives: John and Samuel Tannehill, sons of Leonard Tannehill
Relative: Elizabeth Ward, dau. of Joseph Crosby
Ex: John Poole, Sr.
Wit: William Wilcoxen, Leonard Hays, Abraham Hays

HARDING, CHARLES   L B f 448   12 Feb 1790
                                                        14 Feb 1792

Wife: Eleanor Harding
Daus: Millisent and Joeaster
Sons: William, Clement, John, Elias, Vachel, Benjamin, Lewis, Rezin, Charles
Ex: Wife Eleanor
Wit: Thomas Cramphin, Edward Harding, Erasmus Perry

HARDING, ELIAS   L D f 295   10 Nov 1799
                                       L 1 p 439   10 Mar 1800

Wife: Elizabeth Harding
Sons: Edward Harding, Josiah Harding
Son: John Harding - 150 a. "Forest" where testator lives
Son: Nathan - remainder of "Forest" where John now lives
Grandson: Thomas Noble Harwood Harding (under age 18), son of John Harding
Grandchildren: Elias Harding; Philip Harding; Mary Drane, wife of Thomas O.
               Drane; Elizabeth Williams, wife of Benjamin Williams - all
               children of dec'd son Walter Harding
Grandchildren: Mary, Sarah, Elizabeth and Walter Harding, children of dec'd
               son Basil Harding
Daus: Elizabeth Perry, wife of Erasmus Perry; Deborah Wheeler, wife of John
      Hanson Wheeler
Exs: Sons Edward and John
Wit: Alexander Whitaker, Walter Williams, Hugh Dunne

HARDING, WALTER   L B f 88   6 May 1782
                                       L 1 p 119   16 Aug 1782

Wife: Mary
Children: Anna, Elias, Polly, Elizabeth, Philip

Ex: Wife Mary
Wit: John Beard, Simon Reeder, Zachariah Knott

HARRISON, JOSIAS   L E f 107   20 Apr 1803
                                         L 2 p   7   16 Nov 1803

Wife: Elizabeth Harrison
Sons: Henry Harrison, unmarried and living at home; Joshua Harrison;
      Greenbury Harrison; Nathan Harrison, dec'd.
Daus: Elizabeth Harrison, unmarried and living at home; Sarah Hawkins,
      Amy Hawkins
Grandchildren: Peggy, Linny, Ann, Rebecca and Sarah Hawkins Harrison,
               children of son Nathan, dec'd.
Ex: James Day
Wit: John Simpson, Thomas Winsor, Zachariah Thompson

HARRISS, BARTON   L C f 138   28 Jan 1794
                                         L 1 p 285   11 Feb 1794

Friends: Jonathan Granger and Cloe Stephens
Ex: Jonathan Granger
Wit: Richard Wootton, Jesse Mills, Elias Mills

HARRISS, BARTON   L O f 367   22 Mar 1822
                                         L 3 p 298   30 Aug 1825

Wife: Elizabeth Harriss - to live on farm
Son: Maddison Franklin Harriss - house and lot in Rockville
Sons: John Harriss and Barton Harriss - pt. "Hamond's Addition"
Dau: Elizabeth Harriss (minor) - 2 a. "Hamond's Addition"
Dau: Mary Ann Harriss - house and lot in Rockville jointly with brother
                       Madison Franklin, 1 a. "Hamond's Addition"
Exs: Wife Elizabeth and Robert Wallace
Wit: Robert Wallace, Brice Selby, Thomas P. Willson

HARRISS, ELIZABETH   L D f 443   8 Jun 1797
                                         L 1 p 472   1 Jun 1801

Sisters: Mary, Sarah
Brother: Jesse Harriss
Wit: James Denning, Hezekiah Veatch, Jacob Stier

HARRISS, JOSEPH   L C f 320   27 Aug 1796
                                         L 1 p 372   19 May 1797

Grandson: Joseph Harriss, son of John Harriss - 150 a. pt. of "Mt. Zion"
                    including pt. lot #1 where son John formerly lived
Dau: Priscilla - remainder of lot #1 89 a.

Son: Joseph Harriss - 150 a. "Mt. Zion" including pt. lot #2 including
   his dwelling plantation
Dau: Elizabeth - remainder of lot #2
Son: Nathan Harriss - 153 a. "Mt. Zion" including lot #4
Dau: Mary Harriss - 100 a. "Mt. Zion" taken out of lot #5 including
   plantation where John Sargeant formerly lived
Son: Jesse Harriss - remainder of lot #5 of 210 3/4 a. to include remainder
   of dwelling plantation and saw and grist mill and all
   of lot #3 of 23 a.
Dau: Sarah Harriss - pt. of proceeds of mill
Son: Barton Harriss - pt. "Mt. Zion" including 65 a. pt. of lot #7 includ-
   ing his dwelling plantation and 25 a. of lot #6
Dau: Elenor - pt. "Mt. Zion" including 65 a. pt. of lot #7 and 25 a. of
   lot #6
Wit: Hezekiah Veatch, William Norris of George, Jacob Stier

HARRISS, MARY   L F f   9   4 Mar 1807
                                        L 2 p 119   22 Apr 1807

Sister: Sarah Harriss - dwelling plantation and 100 a. "Mt. Zion"
Children of brother Nathan Harriss, dec'd.; children of brother Barton Harriss,
   dec'd.; children of brother Joseph Harriss; children of sister Priscilla
   Hilton, "former wife of James Hilton" - proceeds from sale of 34 1/4 a.
   "Basil's Lot" and "Mt. Zion"
Dwelling plantation to be sold at decease of sister Sarah
Ex: Joseph Harriss
Wit: Samuel Clements, Leonard Wathen, Joshua Pearre
Codicil dated 3 Apr 1807
Brother-in-law James Hilton to be ex. instead of brother Joseph Harriss
Wit: Samuel Clements, Leonard Wathen, Joshua Pearre

HARRISS, SARAH   L N f 313   1 Mar 1823
                                        L 3 p 217   12 Mar 1823

Elizabeth Harper
Wit: John H. Beall, Thomas N. Davis

HARWOOD, JOHN   L N f 301   1820
                                        L 3 p 204   21 Jan 1823

Wife: Mary Harwood
Sons: Gassaway W. Harwood and John H. Harwood - 200 a. "Harwood's Delight"
   where testator now lives
Sons: Henry Harwood, Levin Harwood
Daus: Elizabeth Jones, Margaret Lyles, Rebecca Breathert, Maryann Harwood
Exs: Wife Mary and son Gassaway W. Harwood
Wit: Colmore Williams, Aeneas Belt, John H. Hughes

HAWKER, WILLIAM, Sr.   L D f 396   28 May 1793
                                           L 1 p 458   15 Jul 1800

Wife: Susanna Hawker - 77 1/2 a. purchased from Benjamin Veatch and Richard
                Bennett Hall
Daus: Deanna, Elizabeth
Son: William
Grandson: Hezekiah Swan
Children: (not named)
Ex: Son William
Wit: Robert Peter, Elisha O. Williams, John Suter, Jr.

HAWKINS, DOROTHY   L I f 34   4 Jul 1814
                                           L 2 p 392   20 Sep 1814

Son: James Hawkins
Grandchildren: John Hawkins, Elizabeth wife of John H. Clagett, Nathaniel
                Hawkins, James Hawkins, children of son John Hawkins, dec'd.
Granddaus: Ara Clagett, Elizabeth Clagett, Susanna Clagett
Grandchildren: Juliet, Eleanor, Elizabeth, daus. of son Peter Hawkins
Dau: Susanna Clagett
Exs: Joseph Clagett, James Hawkins, Peter Hawkins
Wit: Thomas Scott, Jr., Kinsey Beall

HAYES, JEREMIAH   L B f 142   15 Sep 1783
                                           L 1 p 123   18 Oct 1783

Sell "Jeremiah Park", Hopson's Choyes"
Sons: Richard, Thomas, William, Jeremiah, Levin Hayes and George Hayes if he
         shall return
Daus: Sarah Stoakes, Elizabeth Clagett, Margaret Hoskinson, Mary Rollins
         wife of John Rollins, Priscilla Hayes wife of George Hayes
Exs: Sons Thomas Hayes and Richard Hayes
Wit: Simon Reeder, Charles Hayes, William Hilton

HAYS, CHARLES, planter   L B f 229   8 Jan 1787
                                           L 1 p 205   3 Feb 1787

Wife: Elizabeth Hays
Sons: Thomas Hays, Charles Hays
Daus: Eleanor, Patty, Anne Rawlings, Lily Rawlings Hays
Ex: Wife Elizabeth
Wit: Alexander Hall, George Howard

HAYS, GEORGE B.   L N f 460   26 Sep 1823
                                           L 3 p 233   16 Dec 1823

Wife: Elizabeth Hays
Son: William H. Hays

Children and grandchildren: (not named)
Ex: Wife Elizabeth and son William H. Hays
Wit: William Darne, William S. Hays, Gabriel Wathen, John Plummer

HAYS, LEONARD   L N f 283   9 Sep 1822
                                           L 3 p 180   1 Oct 1822

Wife: Eleanor Hays - land in Barnesville
Son: Leonard Hays - land in Barnesville, house where Mrs. Shearman now
                resides, land devised wife at her decease, 220 a.
                land purchased from Thomas Drane
Son: William S. Hays - 225 a. "Hobson's Choice", other land, house and
                lot where testator lives at wife's decease
Son: Abraham S. Hays - land in Barnesville, land purchased from Lewis
                and Joseph Knott
Dau: Sarah Candler - 20 a. land where Asa Nicholson resides, lots in
                Barnesville
Son: Samuel S. Hays - land on which he now resides purchased from Alex-
                ander Reed and Samuel Hebburn, land purchased from
                Thomas Drane, house and lot in Barnesville purchased
                from Samuel Hilton
Dau: Eleanor Howard - 20 a. land purchased from Edward Knott, house where
                Arthur Leeman now lives
Dau: Abigail Trail, wife of William Trail - 120 a. land, lots in Barnesville
Sons: Abraham S., Leonard, and William S. Hays - lot and houses on which
                storehouse, blacksmith's shop and barn stand for 3 yrs.,
                then to be sold
Exs: Sons Abraham and Samuel S. Hays
Wit: William Darne, Richard Beall, Gabriel Wathen
Codicil dated 12 Sep 1822
Dau: Sarah - money instead of 20 a. land
Wit: William Darne, Gabriel Wathen, Henry Wathen

HAYS, WILLIAM   L B f 435   13 Apr 1790
                                                            9 Feb 1791

Son: George B. Hays - "Resurvey on the Addition and Troublesome" 129 a.,
                50 a. "Cool Spring Manner"
Sons: William and Notley - 120 a. "Resurvey on Jeremiah's Park" originally
                deeded as "Friendship"
Daus: Mary Norriss, Eleanor Hemstone
Granddaus: Patty and Priscilla Hays
Ex: Son George B. Hays and William Norriss
Wit: William Jarrett, Joseph Harriss, Jr., George Lashley

HENDERSON, RICHARD of "Spring Hill"   L E f   1   17 Jun 1800
                                           L 1 p 511   4 Sep 1802

Wife: Sarah - "Spring Hill"
Son-in-law: James Maccubbin Lingan

63

Dau: Ariana, wife of Patrick Sim. He has children by a former marriage
Daus: Sarah; Janet, wife of James Maccubbin Lingan; Ann, wife of McCarty Fitzhugh
Son: John
Exs: Son-in-law James Maccubbin Lingan and son John
Wit: Francis Gantt, T.T. Gantt, Samuel Hambleton, Alies Nicholson
Codicil dated 3 Apr 1801
Codicil dated 25 Nov 1801
Grandson: William Simm sent to school 16 Apr 1799 and not doing well
Codicil dated 16 Dec 1801
Codicil dated 2 Jun 1802
Codicil dated 9 Jul 1802
Dau: Ariana has left husband and returned to parents

HEUGH, ANDREW   L B f 391   22 Dec 1788
                                         10 Feb 1789

Wife: Sarah - 1/2 land during life, to include dwelling
Children: Martha, Elizabeth, Sarah, Ann, Margaret, Jane, John, Mary, Andrew
          (under age 21), Harriet (minor), Christina (minor)
Daus: Martha and Margaret - have already received their share of estate
Son: John - 1/2 land and "Clean Gleanings"
Son Andrew and all unmarried daus. - wife's 1/2 at her decease
House or houses in Town of Folkirk in Scotland to be sold
Brother: Charles, dec'd.
Father: dec'd. (not named)
Wit: Nathan Clagett, Frederick Wetzel, Robert Tilley

HICKMAN, ELIZABETH   L E f 329   3 Jan 1806
                      L 2 p 75   31 Jan 1806

Children: Sarah, Hanson, John, Richard, William, Thomas, Mary, Ann F. Cross, Betty
Son-in-law: Benjamin Cross - to care for dau. Sarah and son Hanson until
                             they are of age
Exs: Brother Thomas Fletchall and son Thomas Hickman
Wit: Joseph Hall, Eleoner Collins

HICKMAN, JOSHUA   L L f 80   16 Jan 1818
                      L 3 p 79   17 Mar 1818

Wife: Mary Hickman - 100 a. plantation called "Accord" where testator lives
Daus: Margaret White Strider, Mary Waters Hickman - plantation at wife's
                                                    decease
Son: Joshua Hickman
Grandson: John Strider
Ex: Wife Mary
Wit: John Aldridge, Clement Wheeler, Thomas T. Wheeler

HICKMAN, MARY   L B f 167   23 Oct 1783
                                                                    4 Oct 1784

Sons: Samuel Doughlass, Levy Doughlass if he is still alive
Ex: Son Samuel Doughlass
Wit: Aeneas Campbell, Benjamin Lovelass, El-onis Loveless, Lucy Loveless

HICKMAN, WILLIAM   L F f 201   4 May 1808
                                               L 2 p 159   15 Jul 1808

Wife: Nancy Hickman
Sons: Thomas and Gary - tracts purchased from Long William Hickman and
              Elizabeth Hickman
Son: John
Youngest son: Greenberry (under age 21) - dwelling plantation called
              "Bassheba" and "Saturday Morning"
Daus: Jane Luckett, Mary, Litha, Nancy, Kitty, Sitha
Dau: Elizabeth McIntosh - 200 a. purchased from Nathan Ellis
Granddau: Mary Ann Luckett - her portion of her father's estate
Ex: Son Thomas
Wit: John Poole, Jr., Benjamin Poole, Walter Williams

HIGGINS, ELIZABETH, Mrs. (nunc.)   L N f 440   2 Sep 1823
                                               L 3 p 227   28 Oct 1823

Sons: Martin and Montgomery
Granddau: Lucretia Ann
Dau: Matilda
Wit: Eleanor Garrett, Eliza Higgins, John Wootton

HIGGINS, JAMES   L I f 437   30 Feb 1808
                                               L 2 p 480   18 Jan 1816

Wife: (not named) - to live on in testator's home
Son: Benjamin Higgins - "The Fork" and "Additions to the Fork" where he now
              lives 200 a.
Son: James Becraft Higgins - 367 a. "The Addition" where he and testator now
              live
Son: John Higgins - 202 a. "The Last Coat"and pt. of "Joseph's Park" where
              he now lives, which was obtained from Benjamin Becraft
Daus: Sarah Prather, Ann Prather, Rebekah Soper, Susanah Swearingen,
      Luranah Becraft, Elizabeth Allison, Elinor Garrett
Granddau: Susanna Swearingen
Ex: Son James B. Higgins
Wit: John Fleming, Benjamin Ray, Zadock Lanhan

HIGGINS, JOHN   L F f 209   20 Sep 1808
                                               L 2 p 170   10 Nov 1808

Wife: Jamima Higgins

65

Dau: Rachel Tucker
Son: William Higgins
Exs: Wife Jamima Higgins and Richard Tucker
Wit: Dennis Lackland, Robert D. Dawson, Margaret Moreland

HILLEARY, HENRY					L C f 2		19 Apr 1792
						L 1 p 239		13 Jul 1792

Wife: Elizabeth - Lot #102 in Hamburgh on the Potomack River
Sister: Sarah West
Nephew: Thomas West, son of Joseph and Sarah West
Nephew: Thomas Hilleary, son of John
Niece: Sarah Hilleary, dau. of John
Henry West, son of Benjamin and Verlinda West
Niece: Sarah Wheeler, dau. of Samuel Hanson and Nancy Wheeler
Brother: Tilghman Hilleary
Niece: Elizabeth Hilleary, dau. of Rignal Hilleary - "Pickaix" in Fred. Co.
Ex: Wife Elizabeth
Wit: Samuel Hocker, William Smith
Codicil
Sister: Nancy Wheeler
Wit: Basil Magruder, William Smith

HILTON, WILLIAM					L N f 113		21 Sep 1821
						L 3 p 169		 6 Feb 1822

Sell plantation where testator now lives
Wife: Elizabeth Hilton
Easther Hilton
Daus: Elizabeth, Ann, Delila and Darcus Hilton
Sons: Archibald and Otho Hilton
Exs: Wife Elizabeth and son Archibald
Wit: Joseph A. Murphy, Richard Beall, Leonard Hays

HINTON, THOMAS, Sr.				L C f 1		 2 Jan 1792
						L 1 p 237		12 Jun 1792

Wife: Rebeckah Hinton
Sons: Thomas, James, Pillip, Michal Hinton
Daus: Mary Ward, Ann Andrews, Rachel Ball
Grandson: James Hinton, son of Thomas
Will written by Jonathan Willson
Wit: Daniel Bennett

HOBBS, SAMUEL, Sr.				L E f 339		 7 Aug 1806
						L 2 p 96		 1 Dec 1806

Sons: Samuel Hobbs, William Hobbs, Jesse Hobbs
Grandson: Rezin Hobbs (minor)

Daus: Marcy Hobbs, Priscilla Hobbs, Martha Hobbs, Polly Hobbs, Nancy
      Browning, Tessy Houser, Salla Beltt
Exs: Son Samuel Hobbs and son-in-law Samuel Browning
Wit: Joseph Benton, Jr., James Hawkins, Jesse Hyatt

HOGGINS, JOHN   L E f 131   19 Sep 1802
                                           L 2 p 58   29 Mar 1805

Daus: Ellender Hoggins, Kitty Hoggins
Sons: John Hoggins, William Hoggins, Benjamin Hoggins
Wife: Tamer Hoggins
Ex: Wife Tamer Hoggins
Wit: Martin Fisher, Thomas Fletchall, John Douglass

HOGGINS, RICHARD   L I f 203   20 May 1811
                                           L 2 p 444   27 Jul 1815

Wife: Ann Hoggins - 200 a. "Discovery" and "Addition"
Daus: Milliann, Elizabeth Rhiney (widow), Ann Austin, Deborah Austin,
      Bellinder Ann Plummer
Granddau.'s children: Stephen Lloyd Jones and Elizabeth E. Jones
Son and 2 daus. of Deborah Austin, daus. of Elizabeth Rhiney
Daus. of Bellinder Ann Plummer
Son: Richard Hoggins
Teacle Hoggins
Friends: Mescheck Browning, Leonard Wathen, Thomas Knott
Exs: Wife Ann Hoggins and dau. Milliann Hoggins
Wit: M. Browning, Leonard Wathen, Thomas Knott
Codicil dated 8 Jun 1812
Granddau: Ann Jones
Wit: Mescheck Browning, Phillip Knott, Leonard Wathen

HOGGINS, PETER   L D f 132   Not dated
                                           L 1 p 412   3 Oct 1798

Wife: Catharine - land
Son: William Hoggins
Other children: (not named)
Granddau: Mary Eleoner Hoggins
Ex: Son William
Wit: Charles Hungerford, Caleb Darby, Matthew Reid, Jonathan Tucker

HOGGINS, WILLIAM   L E f 11   Not dated
                                           L 1 p 535   16 Feb 1803

Brother's sons: John and William
William Wilcoxon, son of Jesse
Exs: Richard Beall, William Hempston
Wit: Newton Chiswell, Jesse Wilcoxon, Benjamin White

HOLLAND, BENJAMIN, Sr.　　　　　　　　　L G f 153　　　2 Dec 1806
　　　　　　　　　　　　　　　　　　　　L 2 p 245　　21 Jun 1810

Grandson: Zadok Holland - 100 a. "Quince Orchard"
Ex: Grandson Zadok Holland
Wit: Benjamin Gaither, Benjamin Williams, William Mullican

HOLLAND, JOHN　　　　　　　　　　　　　L I f 443　　　9 Feb 1812
　　　　　　　　　　　　　　　　　　　　L 2 p 491　　23 Feb 1816

Dau: Mary Holland - legacy in trust with John H. Riggs and James Brown
Sons: James Holland, Samuel Holland
Children of dec'd. son Stephen Holland
Children of dec'd. son John Holland
Children of dec'd dau. Sarah Taylor
Ex: Son James Holland
Wit: John H. Riggs, Basil Griffith, Richard Johnson, James Brown
Codicil dated 27 Feb 1812
Dau: Mary Holland - testator's dwelling plantation and garden
Wit: John H. Riggs, Joshua Cockram

HOLLAND NATHAN, Sr.　　　　　　　　　　L E f 109　　28 Apr 1801
　　　　　　　　　　　　　　　　　　　　L 2 p 10　　12 Dec 1803

Son: William Holland - "Holland's Addition" where testator lives, "Friend-
　　　　　　　ship", "Richard and Nathan", "Charles and Benjamin"
Children: Solomon Holland, Nathan Holland, Jr., Anna Smith, Deborah Smith,
　　　　　Susanna Holland, Sarah Brown
Ex: Solomon Holland
Wit: James Brooke, Jonathan Duley, Stephen Shaw

HOLLAND, SARAH　　　　　　　　　　　　　L I f 206　　11 Apr 1814
　　　　　　　　　　　　　　　　　　　　L 2 p 447　　21 Aug 1815

Sons: Nathan Holland, William Holland
Ignasious Waters (under age 21), son of Hazel Waters
Liones Holland, son of William Holland
Ex: William Holland
Wit: G. Howard, Abraham Dawson

HOLLAND, SUSANNA, planter　　　　　　　L B f 232　　　5 Apr 1781
　　　　　　　　　　　　　　　　　　　　L 1 p 209　　　9 Aug 1787

Daus: Hannah Dickerson, wife of Sarratt Dickerson; Ann Rickets, wife of
　　　Benjamin Rickets; Sarah Holland, wife of William Holland
Hrs. of dec'd daus: Rachel Cook and Susanna Warfel
Sons: Nathan Holland, Arnold Holland
Ex: Son Arnold Holland
Wit: Samuel White, Basil Brooke, Samuel R. White

HOLLAND, THOMAS, son of Benjamin   L B f 230   12 Aug 1786
                                                L 1 p 206   13 Feb 1787

Father and mother: (not named)
Brothers and sisters: Archibald and Benjamin Holland, Susanna Richards
Ex: Father Benjamin
Wit: Abraham Holland, Benjamin Williams, Joseph Clagett

HOLLAND, William of Frederick Co.   L B f 14   23 Sep 1769
                                                L 1 p 86   22 Jan 1781

Wife: Susanna Holland
Son: Nathan Holland - "Holland's Addition", pt. of "Charles and Benjamin"
Son: Arnold Holland - pt. of "Charles and Benjamin"
Daus: Hannah Dickerson, wife of Serratt Dickerson; Ann Ricketts, wife of
      Benjamin Ricketts; Rachel Cook, wife of John Cook; Sarah Holland,
      wife of William Holland; Susanna Warfield, wife of John Warfield
Ex: Son Arnold
Wit: Nathan Magruder, Samuel White, Jr., John Beall Magruder, Rector
     Magruder

HOLLAND, WILLIAM of Cassy (?)   L C f 148   30 Dec 1786
                                                L 1 p 299   14 Oct 1794

Wife: Sary Holland
Sons and daus: (not named)
Exs: William Holland of Nathan and son Nathan Holland
Wit: Joseph Waters, Nehemiah Holland, Joseph Hall

HOLMES, JOHN   L A f 40   9 Dec 1777
                                                L 1 p 36   5 Oct 1778

Wife: Isabella - "Snowden's Manor Enlarged" where testator lives
Sons: William, John, Basil, Josiah, Ely, Richard (youngest)
Daus: Betsy Estep, Nancy Holmes
Granddau: Nancy Estep
Ex: Wife Isabella
Wit: Richard Gartrell, John Barnes, Mary Rugloss

HOLMES, JOHN   L D f   3   11 Oct 1797
                                                L 1 p 381   9 Nov 1797

Wife: Mary Holmes
Wife's father: (not named)
Children: (not named - minors)
Ex: Wife Mary Holmes
Wit: John Clarke, Greenberry Griffith, John A. Brown

HOLMES, RICHARD   L B f 443   16 Aug 1791
                                                                     6 Oct 1791

Sister: Nancy Culver
Brother: John Holmes
Sister: **Betsey** Estep and her 2 youngest daus: Eleanor and Sarah Estep
Ex: William Culver
Wit: Ann Leatch, Polly Culver

HOPKINS, LEAVIN (ELEVEN)   L A f 37   4 Oct 1778
                                                   L 1 p 33   8 Jan 1779

Stephen - to be in care of Martaine Thomas until age 15
Ex: Friend, Martaine Thomas
Wit: John Moxley, Ahezriah Riggs, Berthewlomy Johnston

HOSKINSON, GEORGE   L I f 199   21 Mar 1815
                                                   L 2 p 433   3 Jun 1815

Son: Norris Hoskinson
Grandau: Elizabeth Hoskinson
Dau: Ann Hoskinson
Grandchildren: George B. Hoskinson, John N. Hoskinson, Hilleary Hoskinson,
               Elizabeth T. Hoskinson
Ex: Dau. Ann Hoskinson
Wit: Richard Beall, Leven Beall, John Beall

HOSKINSON, JOHN   L C f 221   8 Dec 1794
                                                   L 1 p 336   3 Nov 1795

Daus: Agnes Selby (eldest), Ruth Selby, Jane Summers, **Amelia Willson**
Sons: Elisha Hoskinson (eldest), Josiah Hoskinson, Nathan Hoskinson,
      Andrew Jackson Hoskinson (last two named are youngest)
Grandson: Josiah Browning
Ex: Andrew Jackson Hoskinson
Wit: Tyson Beall, Patrick Orme, Isaac L. Lansdale

HOULT, ANN   L A f 11   14 Jul 1777
                                                   L 1 p 11   25 Jul 1777

Husband: dec'd. (not named)
Daus: Elizabeth, Barbery, Rabeckah, Ann
Ex: Friends, Joseph Wilson, Robert Owen
Wit: Nathaniel Offutt son of Samuel, Mary Letton, Sarah Tomson

HOULT, RALPH "of Frederick Co. alias   L A f   5   26 Mar 1777
               Montgomery Co."   L 1 p   7   31 May 1777

Wife: Ann Hoult

70

Sons: Lawrence Owen Hoult, William Hoult - pt. of "Constant Friendship" and
                                             "Walker's First Survey"
Daus: Darkes, Elizabeth, Barbery, Rebecka, Ann
Ex: Wife Ann
Wit: Joseph Wilson, John Allison, Benjamin Allison

HOWARD, BAKER   L B f 421   25 Jul 1790
                                                          18 Aug 1790

Wife: Ann
Son: John - 222 a. land where testator now lives
Sons: Benjamin, Samuel
Daus: Hannah, Rebecca Howard, Eleanor
Exs: Jacob Howard and Thomas Howard
Wit: Townshend Dade, William Knott, Jr., Zephaniah Watson

HOWARD, HENRY of Thomas   L E f 334   30 Jan 1806
                                        L 2 p 85   16 Apr 1806

Wife: Sally Howard - land where testator lives purchased from Richard Thomas
Ex: Wife Sally
Wit: John Thomas 3rd, Samuel Thomas, Jr., Enoch Beall

HOWARD, THOMAS, Sr., planter, of Frederick Co. L B f 217   17 Dec 1775
                                                L 1 p 187   21 Jul 1786

Wife: Susanna Howard - "Gum Spring"
Sons: Greenberry Howard, George Howard, Jacob Howard, William Howard
Son: Thomas Howard - "Hard Struggle"
Daus: Susanna Howard, Priscilla Howard, Sally Howard, Sarah Viech, Sophia
      Murphy, Margaret Johnson
Exs: Wife Susanna and George Howard
Wit: Peter Hoey, Samuel Simmons of Samuel, John Johnson

HOWS, JOHN (indexed House)   L F f 446   8 Nov 1808
                                        L 2 p 204   23 Mar 1809

Wife: Mary Hows - use of dwelling plantation, "Addition to Brooke Grove", pt.
            of "Fair Hill", "Resurvey on Brooke Park", pt. of "Piney
            Grove" until son Reuben arrives at age 21
Sons: Reuben (under age 21), Nathaniel, Richard
Son: John Hows - use of pt. of "Ray's Adventure" until Reuben is age 21
Son-in-law: Charles Davis - use of land on which he now resides until Reuben
                is age 21
Daus: Loradia Davis, wife of Charles Davis; Lucrasia Penn, wife of Roby Penn;
      Mary Hows, Ann Hows
Grandchildren: Matilda and Perry Bowman
At the time son Reuben arrives at the age of 21, all property to be divided
  into 9 equal parts.
Ex: Brother Edward Hows
Wit: Charles Alexander Warfield, Ephraim Gaither of William, James Howse

```
HOWSER, MARTIN                            L H  f  20      22 Feb 1812
                                          L 2  p 322      30 May 1812
```

Youngest son: Philip Howser - 150 a. land where testator lives
Eldest son: William Pritchell Howser - remainder of land except 100 a.
Grandson: Christian Howser (under age 21) - 100 a. land
Grandchildren: Mary Buchanan Stephens, James Stephens
Dau: Eleanor Stephens
Exs: Sons William Pritchell Howser and Philip Howser
Wit: Thomas Scott, Jr., Kinsey Beall, Kinsey Gittings

```
HOWSER, MARY                              L F  f  14      26 Dec 1804
                                          L 2  p 128      29 Jun 1807
```

Son: Nathan Howser - 100 a. "Herbert's Chance"
Son: William Pritchall Howser - 100 a. "Dunghill"
Dau: Eleanor Stevens - 100 a. "Dunghill"
Granddau: Mary Buchanan Stevens
Son: Philip Howser - 100 a. "Dunghill" where testator now lives
Husband: Martin Howser
Wit: Richard West, Norman West

```
HUGHES, BENJAMIN                          L H  f   9       6 Jul 1811
                                          L 2  p 308      20 Feb 1812
```

Wife: Elizabeth Hughes
Youngest children: (not named)
Ex: Elizabeth Hughes and son Edward Hughes
Wit: Basil Waters, Greenberry Howard, Samuel Barber

```
HUNT, JAMES                               L C  f 222      19 Dec 1785
                                          L 1  p 338      28 Dec 1795
```

Wife: Ruth
Sons: James Hunt, William Pitt Hunt - pt. of "Brother's Industry", pt. of
                                      "Hopson's Choice", pt. of "Magruder's
                                      Industry" (now "Tusculum") and land in
                                      Halifax Co., Va.
Exs: Wife and sons
Wit: Patrick Magruder, John Wallace Douglass, Robert Douglass, John Wallace

```
HUNTER, HENRY                             L B  f  16       6 Oct 1779
                                          L 1  p  89      13 Feb 1781
```

Wife: Susannah Hunter
Minor children: (not named)
Dwelling plantation to be sold at public sale
Ex: Brother Daniel Hunter
Wit: Hezekiah Veatch, Jacob Stier, Daniel Ball

JAY, LYDDA (indexed Lydia)　　　　　　　　L M f 279　　　12 Apr 1820
　　　　　　　　　　　　　　　　　　　　　　　L 3 p 113　　　18 Nov 1820

Catholic Church at Barnestown
Granddau: Lydda Dillon
Dau: Mary Craddick
Ex: Friend, Charles Craddick
Wit: John Poole, Sr., Horatio Wilcoxon, Brooks Jones

JEFFERSON, BENJAMIN of Calvert Co.　　　　L B f 360　　　2 Jan 1788
　　　　　　　　　　　　　　　　　　　　　　　　　　　　　　　　　16 Aug 1788

Sons: Henry, Hambleton, Basil, Leonard, John
Son: William (under age 21) - legacy to be in care of his uncle Edward Wood
Dau: Violetta Jefferson
Exs: Sons Henry and Hambleton
Wit: Isaiah Boone, Robert Briggs

JOHNS, RICHARD of Georgetown　　　　　　　L C f 143　　　16 Jul 1794
　　　　　　　　　　　　　　　　　　　　　　　L 1 p 250　　　25 Jul 1794

Wife: (not named)
Son: Richard Henry Johns (under age 21)
Exs: Wife and Nicholas Lingan
Wit: Margaret C. Chene, William Deakins, Jr., C. Worthington

JOHNS, THOMAS　　　　　　　　　　　　　　　L C f 143　　　6 Oct 1793
　　　　　　　　　　　　　　　　　　　　　　　L 1 p 276　　　25 Jul 1794

Wife: dec'd.
Eldest son: Richard Johns - lot in "Beatty's Addition to Georgetown", land
　　　　　　　　　lying nr. mouth of Muddy Branch, island opposite,
　　　　　　　　　land in the pines
Youngest son: Leonard Hollyday Johns - "my mills and mill seat"
Daus: Margarett Crabb Johns, Sarah Johns - 2 lots with buildings in Georgetown
Brothers: Aquila Johns and Richard Johns - guardians to children until of age
Ex: Brother Aquila Johns
Wit: Thomas Cramphin, Brooke Beall, Jacob Richards, Aquila Johns

JOHNSON, BENJAMIN　　　　　　　　　　　　　L C f 151　　　25 Aug 1788
　　　　　　　　　　　　　　　　　　　　　　　L 1 p 306　　　10 Jan 1795

Wife: Rachel
Sons: Benjamin, John, Jonathan, James' hrs., Josias' hrs., Samuel, Resin
Daus: Maryann Johnson, Elizabeth Harriss, Rachel Wellman, Leurana Mullekin,
　　　　Jemimah Ryan
Exs: Sons Samuel and Resin
Wit: John L. Summers, John Dent Summers, John Nicholson

JOHNSON, LYDIA   L N f   1   30 May 1821
                                        L 3 p 145   11 Jul 1821

Grandsons: Reason Augustus Johnson, Thomas Johnson (under age 21)
Granddau: Mary Ann Johnson (under age 16)
Son: Samuel Johnson
Ex: Son Samuel Johnson
Wit: Thomas Anderson, Daniel Collins, Jacob Lowman, Sr.

JOHNSON, THOMAS   L N f 303   9 Jan 1823
                                        L 3 p 206   28 Jan 1823

Sons: Samuel, Reuben, Greenbury, Jeferson, Thomas, and Bazil Johnson
Daus: Mary Johnson, Priscilla Cross, Tabitha Mulican, Creasy Blowers,
    Margaret Warker
Ex: Son Reuben
Wit: James Brown of Thomas, James Brown of James, Henry Leeke

JOHNSON, THOMAS, Sr.   L C f 223   13 Jan 1796
                                        L 1 p 340   13 Feb 1796

Son: Thomas Johnson - remainder of land
Son: Richard Johnson - upper pt. of testator's dwelling plantation
Sons: John Johnson, William Johnson, Joseph Johnson
Granddau: Sarah (?) Ellis
Dau: Charity Mobley
Exs: Sons Thomas and Richard Johnson
Wit: Walter Carn, George Hardey, Philemon Plummer, Jr.

JONES, ABRAHAM   L N f 304   26 Oct 1810
                                        L 3 p 208   19 Feb 1823

Wife: Elizabeth Ann Jones - all property
States that they have no children
Ward and Nephew: Richard Abraham Harding - 250 a. of testator's farm and
                                           dwelling on south side of road
                                           from mouth of Monocacy to Balt.
Thomas N.H. Harding
Mary Elizabeth Harding (unmarried)
Ketturah Harding and her sister Mary Caroline Harding (both unmarried)
Ex: Elizabeth Ann Jones
Wit: Richard Beall, Abraham S. Hays, James E. Wilcoxon
Codicil dated 2 Feb 1823
Nieces: Mary Ann Belt and Sarah Elizabeth Jones, daus. of brother Horatio
Abraham Warfield, son of Alexander Warfield
Wit: C.T. Hempstone, William Hempstone, Richard Lyles, Sr., Daniel Duvall

JONES, ARIANNA   L F   f 204   9 Nov 1807
                                                L 2   p 163   8 Mar 1808

Sister: Susannah C. Jones - land nr. Rock Creek inherited from testator's
                              brother Henry
Sister: Eleanor Courts
Brother: Charles C. Jones - undivided 1/2 tract of land on Paint Branch
                            inherited from father
Nieces: Ariana Bruce, Susanna C. Jones
Wit: William Bayley, Elizabeth Dunlop, Henry Gaither

JONES, CHARLES, "RC"   L B   f 195   7 Mar 1785
                                                L 1   p 164   7 Sep 1785

Wife: Mary
Friend and nephew: Aaron Lanham - "Clagett's Purchase"
Sarah Jones, widow of late brother John Jones
Mary Jones, dau. of Sarah Jones
William Jones and Elizabeth Fowler, children of brother Edward Jones
Charles Jones, Edward Jones, Sarah Moore, Dorothy Adly, Mary Jones and Liddia
    Jones, children of brother John Jones
Ex: Wife Mary
Wit: Zephaniah Mockbee, Thomas Chappel, King English

JONES, CHARLES of "Clean Drinking Manor"   L D   f 141   9 May 1792
                                                L 1   p 426   6 Jul 1801

Daus: Sarah and Arraanna Jones - land where Norris Mitchel now lives
Dau: Sucky Courts Jones - land purchased from Henry Wilson and lot in
                           Georgetown
Dau: Henrietta Bruce
Son: Charles Courts Jones - "Clean Drinking Manor" and tract adjoining
                             purchased from William Beall and Jean Edmonson
Granddaus: Jean Love, Jane Bruce, Louisa Jones
Ex: Son Charles Courts Jones
Wit: Thomas Johns, Thomas G. Greenfield, Andrew Heugh

JONES, EVAN   L B   f 61   4 Nov 1781
                                                L 1   p 108   7 Oct 1782

Wife: Ann Jones
Sons: Nathan Jones and Evan Jones - "Bedfordshire Carrier"
Daus: Sarah Ball, wife of James Ball; Eleanor Tracey, Darcus Chambers
James Bonside owes testator tobacco for rent
Matthew Fields and his children by his wife Mary Fields, testator's dec'd. dau.
Ex: Evan Jones
Wit: Zachariah Offutt, William Loodge, Thomas Dyar

75

JONES, HANBURY   L 3 p 376   1817-1827

"A list of goods that I have given my children who have left me"
Brother-in-law John Poole is to charge children with goods as part of their
    portion of my estate
Children, beginning with the eldest: Susan Jones now Susan Anderson, Nathan
            V. Jones, Sarah Jones now Sarah L. Young, Mary Jones now Mary
            Piles, Ann V. Jones now Ann V. Willson, Priscilla P. Jones now
            Priscilla Fisher, Rebekah Jones, wife of John Piles; Elizabeth
            Jones, Isaac P. Jones, Hanbury Jones, William Jones, John Jones,
            Thomas L. Jones
(Note: The above is not a will.)

JONES, HENRY   L C f 318   2 Jan 1789
                                              L 1 p 369   21 Apr 1797

Sister: Ariana Jones
Ex: Sister Ariana Jones
Wit: Henry Townsend, Walter Clagett, Thomas Chesley

JONES, MARY, widow of the late Charles Jones L B f 444   8 May 1789
            of Rock Creek   15 Oct 1791

Friend: Aaron Lanham
Susanna Lanham Riley, wife of James Taylor Riley
Ex: Aaron Lanham
Wit: King English, Henry Jones, Thomas Chappel

JONES, MARY   L M f 286   4 Nov 1820
                                              L 3 p 124   3 Jan 1821

Sons: William Jones, John Jones, Evan Jones, Aquilla Jones
Dau: Priscilla Jones
Ex: Son John Jones
Wit: John Jones of Nathan, Laurance Lodge, Eleanor Jones

JONES, NANCY   L I f 207   19 Sep 1815
                                              L 2 p 448   14 Oct 1815

Grandchildren: Henry Jones (under age 21), Galen, John and Ann Jones,
                    children of dec'd son
Sons: John Jones, Brook, Evan Jones
Daus: Eleanor Jones and Ann Jones
Ex: Son John Jones
Wit: Aquilla Jones, Evan Jones, Jr., Sarah Benton

JONES, NATHAN   L H f 7   15 Dec 18
                                              L 2 p 306   25 Feb 1812

Wife: Nancy Jones - 1/3 of land where testator lives

Sons: John Jones and Evan Jones -- above land at wife's decease
Son: Brook Jones - land where he now lives
Daus: Eleanor Jones and Nancy Jones
Grandchildren: Henry Jones, John Jones, Galen Jones, Ann Jones
Exs: Sons John and Evan Jones
Wit: William Lodge, Thomas Clagett, John Herring, Sr.

JONES, SARAH   L I f 447   12 Jun 1811
                                         L 2 p 502   14 May 1816

Sons: Richard, Abraham, Walter, Joseph James Wilkinson, and Horatio Jones
Dau: Sarah B. Magruder, wife of John B. Magruder
Grandchildren: children of dau. Elizabeth Belt, wife of Carlton Belt
Granddaus: Sarah Jones, dau. of Joseph James Wilkinson Jones; Williminy and
            Sarah, daus. of John B. Magruder; Priscilla Jones, dau. of
            Richard Jones; Sarah Ann and Mary Belt, daus. of Elizabeth Belt
Grandson: Basil Jones, son of Benjamin W. Jones
Ex: Son Joseph James Wilkinson Jones
Wit: John Poole, Jr., Charles Willson, Thomas T. Williams, John Young

JONES, SUSANNA COURTS   L H f 18   23 Nov 1810
                                         L 2 p 319   29 Apr 1812

Brother: Charles Courts Jones
Barney Gray
Nieces: Maria Jones, Jane Bruce, Elizabeth Bruce
Samuel Forrest
Sisters: (not named)
Ex: Brother Charles Courts Jones
Wit: Thomas Cramphin, Henry Gaither, Augustus Daniel Sheele

JOSEPH, ANN   L C f   8   30 Jul 1792
                                         L 1 p 248   28 Nov 1792

Husband: Joseph Joseph
4 eldest children, by another husband: Elizabeth, Basil, William and Dorcas
4 youngest children: John, Ann Northcraft, Charlotte, Susannah
Ex: Husband Joseph Joseph
Wit: John Higdon, William Hocker

JOSEPH, CLEMENT   L D f 137   3 Jul 1798
                                         L 1 p 418   17 Aug 1798

Wife: Eleanor Joseph
Dau: Ann Joseph
Ex: Wife Eleanor
Wit: Zachariah Knott, Francis Knott, Joshua Pearre

JOYE, WILLIAM (nunc.)   L D f 549   18 Jan 1802
                                                                 14 Apr 1802

Daus: Helan and Susanna (both under age 16)
Son: Enos
Enos Joye was 16 yrs. of age 31 Oct 1801
Helan Joye was 13 yrs. of age 25 Sep 1801
Susanna Joye was 10 yrs. of age 9 Nov 1801
John Joye was 7 yrs. of age 11 Mar 1801
Wit: Samuel Belmear, Charles Williams
Probate states William Joye died about 18 Jan 1802

KELLY, THOMAS   L E f 110   6 Jan 1803
                                              L 2 p 12   25 Jan 1804

Wife: Hannah
Sons: Thomas Kelly, Joseph Kelly, Benjamin Kelly
Exs: Wife Hannah and son Thomas
Wit: Zachariah Macubbin, Thomas Rawlins, Elizabeth Rawlins

KEMP, PETER   L I f 216   7 Dec 1815
                                              L 2 p 470   30 Dec 1815

Wife: Sarah Kemp
John Kemp (under age 21), Jacob Kemp known as "Long Jake", and Peter Kemp,
   sons of "Short Jake" Kemp
Ex: Henry Culver
Wit: Tyson Beall, Burgess Culver, Thomas Beall

KLEIN, PETER of George Town   L C f 119   11 Aug 1793
                                              L 1 p 271   26 Oct 1793

Wife: (not named) - house and lot occupied by John Baltzer, Jr.
Sell house where testator lives
Ex: Daniel Reintzel, Anthony Reintzel
Wit: James Melvin, James Meem, Nicholas Hedges

KNEWSTAB, ROBERT W.   L B f 397   18 Apr 1789
                                                                 18 May 1789

Wife: Tomoson - pt. of "Joseph", purchased from Thomas Pack, on which testa-
                tor now dwells 120 a.
Ex: Wife Tomoson
Wit: William Pack, Greenbury Gaither, Simon Nicholls

KNEWSTEP, THOMASON   L F f 504   10 Sep 1792
                                              L 2 p 208   17 Apr 1809

Friend: John Holmes - land purchased from Thomas Pack by testator's husband

78

Husband: Robert Knewstep
Ex: John Holmes
Wit: Amon Riggs, Charles Legg, William Newhouse

KNOT, WILLIAM (indexed Knott)   L O f 168   10 May 1821
                                     L 3 p 288   8 Mar 1825

Sister: Mary Knot - dwelling place for life
Nephew: John T. Knot - dwelling place at Mary's decease
Nephew: Francis Knot - land where his father Phillip Knot now lives
Nieces: Daus. of Thomas Knot
Church at Barnestown
Ex: Nephew John T. Knot
Wit: John Poole, Sr., Joseph A. Murphy, Henry Wathen

KNOTT, MARY   L F f 505   15 Feb 1803
                                     L 2 p 210   8 Jul 1809

Eldest dau: Jane Knott
Second Dau: Mary Knott
Sons: William Knott, Thomas Knott, Phillip Knott, Zachariah Knott
Exs: Son Thomas Knott and dau. Jane Knott
Wit: John Clagett, Nathan Neighbours, Joshua Pearre

KNOTT, WILLIAM   L D f 547   25 Jul 1795
                                     L 1 p 494   7 Apr 1802

Wife: Mary
Son: William - pt. of "Conclusion" where Eleazer Watson now lives
Son: Thomas - pt. of "Conclusion" where he now lives, 44 a. land purchased
             from Barthon Warthen adjoining "Conclusion"
Son: Philip - pt. of "Fox Race Ground" and tract where testator now lives
Sons: Zachariah and Henry
Daus: Jane Knott and Mary Knott - 68 a. land due testator from Col. Francis
                       Deakins
Exs: Sons William, Thomas and Philip
Wit: Richard Hoggins, Jr., Henry Wathen, J. DuBois

KNOTT, ZACHARIAH   L M f 281   11 Feb 1820
                                     L 3 p 115   12 Dec 1820

Wife: Jane Knott - plantation where testator lives plus 40 a. purchased from
             John Belt
Children: Joseph, Stanislaus and Mary Ann Knott - above land at wife's dec.
Son: Stanislaus - 1/2 land with buildings on north side of road from mouth
             of Monocacy to Ellicott's Mills
Dau: Teresa Jones - other half of above lands
Son: Edward - 122 a. and house where he now lives
Children: Joseph, Caleb, Lewis, Stanislaus, Teresa Jones, Mary Ann Knott -

```
                    remainder of land where Edward lives adjoining lands of
                    Mr. Harding and Mrs. White
Son:   Caleb - 50 a. deeded testator by Francis Deakens and Francis Thomas;
            1 a. on south side of road in Barnesville
Children of son Leonard Knott, dec'd.:  Zephiniah Knott, Samuel Knott, Rosella
                                        Knott, Leonard Knott - 114 a. purchased from
                                        Jesse Burch and deeded by David Stewart
Children of dau. Catharine Offutt (minors) - 1/2 of 245 a. purchased from
                                        John Varnell and Greenbury Gaither
Dau:   Teresa Jones - other 1/2 of above land
Son:   Francis Knott - land purchased from Hebburn
Roman Catholic Church at Barnesville
Son-in-law Brooks Jones
Exs:   Wife Jane and son-in-law Brooks Jones
Wit:   Joseph A. Murphy, Leonard Hays, Jr., John T. Knott
Codicil dated 3 Nov 1820
Wife is now deceased, son Stanislaus Knott to be executor
```

LACKLAND, JAMES   L I f 185   9 Oct 1813
                                             L 2 p 404   14 Nov 1814

Sons: Eli Lackland, Dennis Lackland
Children: (not named)
Exs: Sons George L. Lackland and James C. Lackland
Wit: William Darne, Jr., Abraham Simmons, Nathaniel E. Magruder

LANCASTER, EDWARD   L O f 150   18 Jul 1819
                                             L 3 p 251   24 Sep 1824

Wife: (not named)
Sons: Edward Lancaster, William Lancaster, Charles Lancaster
Daus: Lily, Ann, Charity, Ally, Fanny, Rebecca
Son: Thomas Lancaster - plantation where testator lives, pt. of "Yorkshire",
                    pt. of "Resurvey on the Grove", pt. of "Resurvey on
                    part of James and Mary" - 159 3/4 a.
Granddau: Rebecca
Exs: Friend Isaac Lansdale, and son Thomas Lancaster
Wit: Thomas Gittings, James Lazenby, James Orme

LANE, JAMES B. of Leesburg, Va.   L L f 87   15 Aug 1818
                                             L 3 p 54   25 Aug 1818

Brothers: Hardage Lane, Harvey Lane
Brother-in-law: William Coleman
Sisters: Lydia Coleman, Elvira Edwards, Julia Swearinger
Episcopal Church in Leesburg
Exs: Brother-in-law William Coleman and Hardage Lane
Wit: William Darne, Norman West, John David, William Boswell, J.W. Coleman,
       Thomas W. Coleman

LANHAM, AARON   L C f 198   28 May 1792
                                             L 1 p 323   20 Apr 1795

Wife: Elizabeth
Sons: Walter, Hezekiah, Zadock and Aquila Lanham - land in Loudon Co., Va.;
                        pt. of "Clagetts Purchase"; pt. of "Labyrinth"
Daus: Elleanor, Elizabeth, Lethe, Mercy Ann - land in Frederick Co., Md.;
                        land in Loudon and Frederick Cos., Va.
Sell "Little Worth"
Ex: Wife Elizabeth and son Walter
Wit: Walter Clagett, Ninean Magruder, King English
Codicil dated 8 Apr 1795
Wit: William A. Nusbaum, Peter Becraft, Willy Janes

LANHAM, STEPHEN   L E f 336   25 Jun 1806
                                             L 2 p 90   9 Sep 1806

Wife: Susannah
Children: Archibald, Sarah, Jemimah, Thomas, Stephen, Leah, Maryann, Walter
           (under age 21), Samuel (under age 21), Margaret (under age 16),
           Ruth (under age 16)
Exs: Wife Susannah and James Alexander Shaw
Wit: James W. Perry, Basil M. Perry, John R. Bussard

LANHAM, SUSANNAH of Prince Georges Co. being L C f 322   19 Jun 1797
                  now in Montgomery Co.   L 1 p 376   28 Jul 1797

Son: George Horatio Lanham
Joseph Eden Priest
Granddau: Cassandra Humphrys
Daus: Mercy Ann Cretin, Elizabeth Smith
Exs: John Cretin of Harford Co., Md. and Robert Smith of Montgomery Co., Md.
Wit: John B. Magruder, Jeffry Magruder, John Adamson

LANHAM, ZADOCK   L L f 77   10 Aug 1814
                                             L 3 p 74   9 Jun 1818

Niece: Eloisa Ray
Brother: Aquila Lanham - land where testator's mother lives
Sisters: Eleanor Ray, Elizabeth Lanham, Marcia Ann Lanham
Ex: Brother Aquila Lanham
Wit: Thomas John Clagett, Jr., B.W. Flemming, Enoch Busson

LANSDALE, CATHARINE   L K f 237   19 Apr 1816
                                             L 2 p 533   10 Dec 1817

Granddau: Elenor Busey (unmarried)
Son-in-law: Adam Robb
Ex: Grandson John N. Robb
Wit: Henry Harding, Adam Robb

LASHLEY, ROBERT, planter   L A f 252   10 Aug 1779
                                            L 1 p 64   11 Mar 1780

Dau: Cesiah Lashley
Sons: John Lashley, William Lashley, Thomas Lashley, George Lashley
Wife: Lucy Lashley
Ex: Son George
Wit: George Hays, William Hays of William

LAZENBY, MARGARET   L M f 287   10 Jan 1810
                                            L 3 p 126   19 Jan 1821

Dau: Margaret Shaw, wife of William Shaw
Sons: Cephas Lazenby, James Lazenby
Exs: Sons Cephas and James
Wit: John Bonifant, James Bonifant

LAZENBY, ROBERT   L B f 209   3 Mar 1785
                                            L 1 p 174   14 Jun 1785

Daus: Anna Jones, Elizabeth Fairall
Sons: John, Robert, Elias, Thomas, Alexander, Henry, Joshua Lazenby
Wife: Martha Lazenby - dwelling house
Exs: Josiah Jones, John Lazenby
Wit: John Kelley, William Holmes, Basil Burton

LEACH, WILLIAM, Sr., planter   L B f 12   27 Aug 1779
                                            L 1 p 84   3 Jan 1781

Mary Leach, widow of son John Leach - pt. of "William and John"
Son: Thomas Leach - pt. of "William and John", pt. of "Resurvey of Orpus"
Son: William, Jr.
Daus: Martha Fields, Nancy Leach
Ex: Wife Martha
Wit: Thomas Kelly, John Suter, Benjamin Williams

LEE, JOHN, Sr.   L L f 99   7 Feb 1808
                                            L 3 p 17   6 Feb 1819

Daus: Sarah Moore, Darkey Hannes, Miliah Wilson
Grandsons: James Moore and John Star (both under age 21)
Sons: James Lee, John Lee, Daniel Lee
Margaret Wilson
Exs: Daniel Lee, James Lee
Wit: James Wallace, Zachariah Wilson, William Oliver

LEEKE, DINAH   L K f 237   23 Nov 1817
                                            L 2 p 532   6 Dec 1817

Mary Leeke

Step-mother: (not named)
Sister: Elizabeth Leeke
Wit: James Browne, John W. Leeke

LEEKE, ELIZABETH   L D f 588   25 Jun 1802
                                          L 1 p 508   18 Aug 1802

Daus: Mary Holland, Ann Brown, Lucy Moore
Granddaus: Elenor Deavor, Elizabeth Brown
Ex: Son-in-law James Brown
Wit: Philemon Plummer, Jr., Joseph Leeke of H.

LEEKE, HENRY   L A f 254   21 Sep 1779
                                          L 1 p 66   15 Mar 1780

1 acre of land to Hawlings River Chaple
Wife: Elizabeth Leeke
Son: Henry Leeke - pt. "The Resurvey of Leeke's Lott"
Son: Joseph Leeke - pt. "Gittings Hah-Hah", pt. "Leeke's Lott"
Son: Obed Leeke (minor)
4 daus: (not named)
Ex: Wife Elizabeth
Wit: Richard Green, Richard Macklefreash, Francis Gartrell

LEEKE, JOSEPH   L E f 136   30 Apr 1805
                                          L 2 p 66   2 Aug 1805

Wife: Casandrah
Daus: Elizabeth Leeke, Sarah Leeke, Mary Leeke, Ann Leeke
Son: John Waters Leeke
Ex: Wife Casandrah Leeke
Wit: Richard Green, Lloyd Dorsey, Benjamin Gartrell

LEEKE, JOSEPH, Jr.   L D f 11   30 Aug 1797
                                          L 1 p 395   26 Sep 1797

Wife: Elizabeth
Daus: Ann, Margaret, Elizabeth, Mary, Cassandra
Sons: Richard, Joseph, Samuel
Ex: Brother Samuel Leeke, also to be guardian of children while under age
Wit: Nathan Moore, William Stabler

LEEKE, Richard   L H f 19   7 May 1812
                                          L 2 p 321   29 May 1812

Brother: Samuel Leeke
Wife: Catherine Leeke
Ex: Friend William Booth of Baltimore
Wit: William Thomas, Samuel Leeke, Ann Leeke

```
LETTON, MICHAEL                                L L  f 117           26 Jun 1812
                                               L 3  p  47            3 Sep 1819
```

Grandson, Michael Hartly Letton, son of Brice Letton - 1/2 of land 230 a.
Grandson: Vanwick Michael Letton, son of Ralph Letton - 1/2 of land 230 a.
Grandson: Ninian Willett Letton
Sons: Caleb, John, Michael, Ralph, Brice
Daus: Tabitha Suter, Anna Maria Linsted, Sarah Smith, Ann Forseyth
Ex: Son Brice Letton
Wit: Lawrence O. Holt, James Beall of James, Willy Janes
Codicil dated 23 Aug 1819
Friends: William Willson, Isaac Riley and James B. Higgins - trustees to
         grandsons if fathers decease before they are of age
Dau-in-law: Harriot Letton, wife of Brice - land purchased from testator's
            dau. Tabitha Suter
Grandsons: Burton Summers Letton, Reuben Pike Letton
Wit: Adam Robb, Richard K. Watts, Willy Janes


```
LEWIS, DANIEL                                  L B  f 220            4 Sep 1781
                                               L 1  p 190           11 Jun 1787
```

Wife: Margaret
Son: Jeremiah Lewis - pt. of "Trouble Enought" and land on Bennet's Creek Run
Daus: Margaret Lewis, Drusiller Lewis
Son: David
Ex: Jeremiah Lewis
Wit: Alexander Beall, John Beall


```
LEWIS, JEREMIAH                                L N  f 298           23 Apr 1815
                                               L 3  p 198           31 Dec 1822
```

Daus: Rachel Watkins, Margaret Barber, Jane Windsor, Drusilla Browning
Sons: Jeremiah Lewis; Thomas Lewis; Levy Lewis, dec'd about 3 yrs.; Jonathan
      Lewis
Children of son Levy Lewis
Exs: Son-in-law Nicholas Watkins, son Jeremiah Lewis
Wit: John L. Trundle, Daniel Trundle, Levin C. Beall


```
LEWIS, JOSEPH                                  L O  f 152            6 Nov 1824
                                               L 3  p 254           19 Nov 1824
```

Wife: Mary Lewis
Sons: John W. Lewis, Joseph Lewis, Lewis D. Lewis, Nathan Lewis
Daus: Ann B. Lewis, Mary Lewis, Alice Lewis, Elizabeth Lewis, Maxainno (?)
      Lewis
Ex: William Burton
Wit: Thomas Waters, Richard Carr, Plummer Waters, Jr.

LEWIS, LEVIN, planter					L H f 24		31 Mar 1812
							L 2 p 328		11 Aug 1812

Wife: Rebeckah
6 children: (not named)
Exs: Wife and James Day
Wit: Jeremiah Watkins, Jonathan Browning, Zadock Browning

LINGAN, JAMES M.					L H f 23		7 Dec 1810
							L 2 p 326		6 Aug 1812

Arthur Shaaff, Roger B. Taney, Francis S. Key - testator's interest in
property of Henry Darnall of Frederick Co., dec'd., devised by him to
Henry Warring as per agreement, dated 12 Sep 1810, between testator and
Henry Warring
Wit: James Bowie Brookes, Thomas C. Nicholls, Henry Ball

LINTHICUM, ZACHARIAH					L F f 197		26 Jan 1805
							L 2 p 153		14 Jun 1808

Son: Ezekiah Linthicum - 200 a. including houses and plantation where
                         Frederick now lives
Son: Frederick Linthicum - residue of land and testator's dwelling plantation
Sons: John and Thomas Linthicum - have already been provided for
Sister: Jane Linthicum
Daus: Mary Magruder, Elizabeth Magruder, Sarah Macclefish
Exs: Sons Frederick and Ezekiah Linthicum
Wit: William Smith, John W. Warfield, Henry Jones

LODGE, JOHANNAH					L N f 224		31 Aug 1821
							L 3 p 178		23 Jul 1822

Daus: Elizabeth O'Neal, Johannah Lodge
Sons: William O. Lodge, Brook Lodge, John Lodge, Henry Lodge, Laurence Lodge
Ex: John Jones of Nathan
Wit: Evan Jones, Jr., Priscilla Jones, Sarah Benton

LODGE, JOHN						L N f 118		21 Mar 1822
							L 3 p 162		26 Mar 1822

Daus: Julian Lodge, Lucinda Russ Lodge
Exs: John Lansdale and Burgess Willett
Wit: Michael D. Gittings, William Sands, Laurence Lyddan

LOWE, LETITIA						L D f 305		1 Jan 1798
							L 1 p 454		13 Aug 1799

Niece: Mary Webb - testator's house and plantations for life

Nieces: Henrietta Montgomery, now living in Great Britain; Ann Casanave
Grandnephew: Benjamin Webb, son of Mary Webb - land after Mary's decease
Grandnieces: Polly Young, dau of Nicholas Young; Susannah Webb, Fanny Webb, Henrietta Webb and "unnamed" child of niece Mary Webb (all under age 21)
Brother: Notley Young
Ex: Notley Young
Wit: Daniel Brent, Patrick Braniff, Jane Murray

LUCKETT, VERLINDER   L D f 184   13 Jan 1799
                                           L 1 p 433   20 Jun 1799

Nephews: Francis William and William Francis Luckett (minors), sons of
         brother Leven Luckett - land inherited from testator's father
         David Luckett and his wife Susanna
Nephews: Luther Luckett, David Lawson Luckett and William Gipson Luckett
         (all under age 21), sons of David Luckett; Samuel Noland Luckett,
         son of brother John Luckett
Nieces: Juliett Luckett and Kitty Callander Luckett (both under age 16),
         daus. of David Luckett
Ex: David Luckett
Wit: Dorcas Stimston, Thomas B. Beall, Leonard Watkins

LUCKETT, WILLIAM   L B f 105   23 Oct 1782
                                           L 1 p 112   17 Jan 1783

Wife: Charity
Son: William Luckett - "Wheeler's Hope" in Prince Georges Co.
Son: John Luckett - "Gleaning" on an island in Potowmack River called Fair
              Island, pt. of "Georgi", pt. of "Accord"
Son: Thomas Hussy Luckett - "Beall's Goodwill"
Son: Levin Luckett - dwelling plantation called "Meredith's Hunting Quarters"
              and ferry boat
Daus: Virlinda Luckett, Susanna Luckett, Ann, Elizabeth, Eleanor
Sell "Ellis's Chance" and "Allisson's Adventure"
Exs: Wife Charity and son Levin
Wit: Zach. Harding, John Jacobs, Trueman Hilton

LUCUS, JOHN   L F f 512   7 Oct 1809
                                           L 2 p 221   12 Dec 1809

Wife: (not named) - dwelling plantation
Sons: William, Elisha, Amos (all under age 21)
Youngest son: John (under age 21)
Daus: Sarah, Matilda
Ex: Friend James B. Higgins
Wit: Ephraim Gaither of Wm., James Magruder, Clement Thompson

LYDDAN, PATRICK, Sr.   L I f 187   9 Aug 1814
                                              L 2 p 409   19 Mar 1815

Children: Timothy, Judas, John, Michael, Peter, Margaret, Bridget
Wife: Bridget Lyddan
Wit: John Bowie, William Edwards, John Connelly

LYNN, ELIZABETH   L E f 105   10 May 1790
                                              L 2 p   1   9 Sep 1803

Ex: Son David Lynn
Wit: Walter Cade Williams, William P. Williams

McATEE, FRANCIS X.   L F f 108   23 Feb 1807
                                              L 2 p 131   21 Aug 1807

Wife: Margaret McAtee - 207 3/4 a. land near Barnesville
7 children: George, John, William, Sarah, Charity, Nelly, Francis Xavier
Ex: Wife
Wit: Elisha Howard, Leonard Howard, George J. Judy

McATEE, SARAH   L N f 464   30 Jul 1823
                                              L 3 p 239   23 Sep 1823

Sisters: Elenor Gibbons, Elizabeth Pearce
Friends: Thomas Gittings, Henry Harding
Niece: Ann Sheckles, wife of Theodore Sheckles
Ex: Theodore Sheckles
Wit: Edward Harding, Elizabeth Shekells, Eleanor Pearce

McCARTHY, TIMOTHY of Little Falls of Potowmack L C f 116   1 Sep 1793
                  labourer for Potowmack Co.   L 1 p 268   9 Sep 1793

Friend: John Thomas, labourer
Wit: Florence McAuliffe, William Connor, Arthur O'Leary

McFARLAND, SAMUEL   L H f 15   4 Jan 1810
                                              L 2 p 314   25 Mar 1812

Wife: Margaret McFarland
Eldest dau. now alive: Margrett Boland
Son-in-law: George Boland
Granddau: Jeane Horner
2 youngest granddaus: Louisa and Mary Horner, daus. of Samuel Horner and wife
                     Mary McFarland
Youngest dau: Charlotte Matilda McFarland - all estate after wife's decease
Children of John Nickell, wife's only surviving brother
Children of Martha Cunningham, testator's only surviving sister

Nephew: Walter Cunningham, son of sister Martha
Ex: Wife Margarett McFarland
Wit: Benjamin Hersey, Thomas D. Allnutt

McKAY, WILLIAM   L C f 314   3 Nov 1796
                                              L 1 p 347   24 Jan 1797

Wife: Ann McKay
Daus: Ann Shaw, Margary Gun, Mary Boyd
Sons: William McKay, James McKay
Granddau: Ann Boyd
Grandchildren: Children of son William - legacies due testator in Scotland
Exs: Wife Ann; Andrew Boyd, merchant of Frederick Co.; Alex. Gun, merchant
     of Carrolina Co.
Wit: Joseph Jones, James Reat, Charles Neale

McMASTER, JOSEPH GARRISON of Jefferson Co., Va. L O f 161   9 Oct 1824
              now being sick in Brookeville,   L 3 p 277   12 Nov 1824
              Md.
Brother: John McMaster, Jr.
Nieces: Juliet McMaster, Mary McMaster, daus. of John McMaster, Jr.
John Weaver, son of Nancy Weaver
Nancy Weaver
William Starkey
Elizabeth Kinsey, wife of Joseph Kinsey of Montgomery Co., Md.
Ex: Brother John McMaster
Wit: Owen Summers, Samuel Cagleson, George Washington McCauley

MACCALLUM, JANE   L A f 237   13 Jan 1780
                                              L 1 p 63   8 Feb 1780

Ezebel Biggs, wife of John Biggs
Mary Glaze, dau. of Samuel
Samuel Glaze
Nathinal Glaze, son of Samuel
Ex: Son Samuel
Wit: James Beall, Basil Glaze, Jonathan Glaze

MACCATEE, WILLIAM   L K f 230   4 Oct 1805
                                              L 2 p 526   16 Dec 1817

Dau: Cloe - "in acknowledgement for her and her husband's services to me and
       my family", all property where testator lives
Sons: George, Francis
Lucy Maccatee, "who lives with me now"
Wife: Ellender, "altho in a very weak State of Health"
Son-in-law: Elisha Howard
Dau: Ann Elder
Roman Catholic Church - money to build a church if one is built within 6 years
             of testator's decease

Exs: Son George and son-in-law Elisha Howard
Wit: John Dubois, John Wailes, Thomas Howard

MACKATIE, ANN   L B f 218   4 May 1786
                                            L 1 p 203   5 Jul 1786

Daus: Lucy Mackatie, Elisabeth Clements Mackatie
"All my other children" (not named)
Wit: Thomas William Smithy, Mary Mackattee

MACKBEE, ALLEN   L C f 312   19 Apr 1796
                                            L 1 p 364   6 Oct 1796

Wife: Deborah Mackbee
Ex: Wife
Wit: John Wathen, Joseph Nicholson, Ephraim Gaither

MACKLAIN, JOHN   L B f 416   15 Mar 1790
                                                              9 Apr 1790

Wife: Priscilla - pt. of two tracts of land purchased from Thomas Stains
               being pt. of "Thomas Beall's Addition to Georgetown"
Children: (not named)
Ex: Wife Priscilla
Wit: Charles Beatty, William King, Peter Casanave, Henry Lucas

MAGRUDER, BASIL   L E f 133   25 Feb 1800
                                            L 2 p 61   17 May 1805

Brother: George Fraser Magruder of Frederick Co.
3 sisters: Susanna Warfield of Ann Arundel Co., Jemima Perry of Montgomery
        Co., Verlinder Clagett of Prince Georges Co.
Friend: Charles Gassaway, son of Nicholas Gassaway "on account of the strick
                Friendship and strong attachment I have for him -
                and in consideration of the many kindness and
                attentions I have received from him at all times
                for a number of years both on my Person or Business"
Ex: Charles Gassaway of Nicholas
Wit: Benjamin Edwards, Caleb Dorsey, Andrew Offutt, Joseph Burnside, John
     Chambers of Wm.

MAGRUDER, CATHARINE   L N f 90   5 Mar 1818
                                            L 3 p 156   11 Dec 1821

Sons: John Burgess Magruder, Robert White Magruder
Grandchildren: Wilson Lee Watkins, Joseph Watkins, Greenbury Watkins, Robert
            White Watkins, sons of Thomas Watkins; Julian Magruder, Green-
            bury Magruder, dau. and son of Greenbury Magruder; Levi Wade,
            Catharine Wade, John Wade, Samuel Wade, Gala Ann Wade, sons

and daus. of James Wade
Niece: Catharine Willett, dau. of Edward Willett
Son-in-law: Basil Magruder
Ex: Son John Burgess Magruder
Wit: Cephas Lazenby, Nathan Holland, Jr.

MAGRUDER, EDWARD   L L   f 126   6 Nov 1818
                                           L 3   p 68   9 Nov 1819

All land to be sold
Wife: Jane Magruder
Granddau: Elizabeth Magruder, dau. of Eli Magruder
Ex: Jane Magruder
Wit: Edward Hughes, Greenberry Griffith, Joseph Neel

MAGRUDER, HEZEKIAH   L E   f 339   26 Jul 1798
                                           L 2   p 98   17 Nov 1806

Wife: Susanna
3 children: Daniel Magruder, George Magruder, Ann Hardin
Grandsons: Alexander Magruder, Hezekiah Magruder
Grandchildren: Hezekiah, Theodorus, Josias Hardin and Violander, children
               of son Daniel by his 1st wife Sarah Berry
Exs: Sons Daniel and George Magruder
Wit: Walter Clagett, Joseph S. Belt, Leonard Mackall

MAGRUDER, JANE   L B   f 404   7 Aug 1783
                                                              4 Jul 1787

Son: Archibald
Ex: Son Archibald
Wit: Zech. Magruder, James Doull, John Baker

MAGRUDER, JOHN   L B   f 98   8 Sep 1782
                                           L 1   p 120   1 Nov 1782

Wife: (not named)
Sons: Ninean, Edward, Archibald, James
Daus: Elizabeth, Eleanor, Jane
Ex: Archibald
Wit: Elizabeth Magruder, James Doull, Ninian Magruder

MAGRUDER, JOSEPH   L C   f 115   31 Jul 1793
                                           L 1   p 263   7 Sep 1793

Wife: Catherine - pt. of "The Finish of Trouble Enough", pt. "Bedfordshicarior"
Sons: Joseph Magruder, John Burgess Magruder, Greenbury Magruder, Robert White
      Magruder - land in Alleghany Co., Md. called "The Cove"

Son: Philip Magruder - land in "Beatty's Addition to Georgetown"
Son: Basil Magruder - "The Trap"
Daus: Elizabeth Magruder, Margaret Magruder, Ann Magruder, Catherine Magruder
Exs: Wife Catherine and friend William Offutt Magruder
Wit: Ninean Willett, Henry Childs, Ozias Offutt

MAGRUDER, LUCY   L C f 221   30 Jul 1795
                                            L 1 p 334   10 Sep 1795

Dau: Lucy Berry
Son: George Beall Magruder
Other children: (not named)
Granddaus: Ann Wilson, Lucy Wilson
Ex: Son George Beall Magruder
Wit: Jo. Boone, John B. Kerby

MAGRUDER, MARY, widow   L B f   4   20 Sep 1780
                                            L 1 p 78   14 Oct 1780

Sons: Ninian, William Jr.
Daus: Annie, Rebecca, Priscilla, Mary
Ex: Son Ninian
Wit: James Doull, William Offutt, Jr.

MAGRUDER, NATHAN, planter   L B f 239   17 Jan 1781
                                            L 1 p 218   25 Apr 1786

Son: Isaac Magruder - land where testator lives
Sons: Isaac Magruder, John Beall Magruder, Jeffry Magruder - tracts of land
    on Rock Creek, "Magruder's Farm", "Addition to Turkey Thicket", "The
    Ridges", "The Mistake", pt. of "Charles and Benjamin" to be divided
    into 3 parts
Daus: Elizabeth Magruder, Rebekah Magruder, Sarah Magruder, Verlinda
    Magruder, Susanah Tawnyhill
Son: Nathan Magruder of Frederick Co. - "Resurvey on Well's Invention" in
                              Frederick Co.
Ex: Son Jeffry
Wit: Samuel White, Basil Brooke, Arnold Holland

MAGRUDER, NATHANIEL , son of Alexander   L D f 124   28 Nov 1793
                                            L 1 p 401   28 May 1798

Son: Walter Magruder - pt. "Grubby Thicket" of 51 a. purchased from Joseph
                    Benton who purchased it from Robert Peter; plantation
                    where he now dwells
Son: Aquila Magruder - plantation where testator now dwells
Daus: Elizabeth Hawkins, Lethe Talbott
Granddau: Hariot Magruder
Ex: Son Walter Magruder
Wit: Samuel Br. Magruder, Joseph Benton, Ninian Magruder, Richard Blacklock

MAGRUDER, RACHEL (nunc.)   L I   f 31   14 Jul 1814
                                         L 2   p 289   1 Aug 1814

Sister: Mary Ann Magruder
Mother-in-law: Mrs. Eleanor Magruder
Mira Magruder, dau. of Thomas Magruder
Wit: Benjamin S. Bohrer, Elizabeth Bealmear, Eleanor Magruder, Mary Ann
     Magruder
She died in the home of her mother-in-law "where she had dwelt for many years"

MAGRUDER, REBECCA of Prince Georges Co.   L C   f 270   24 Feb 1796
                                                     L 1   p 360   2 Jun 1796

Sister: Rachel Magruder
Brother: John Bowie Magruder
Wit: William Smith, William Waters

MAGRUDER, ROBERT POTTINGER   L N   f 221   31 Jul 1822
                                       L 3   p 174   12 Aug 1822

Wife: Elizabeth Magruder
Nephews: Robert P. Magruder, Jonathan W. Magruder, Zadock Magruder, William
       Magruder, Robert Read, Zadock Cook, Nathan Cook, Nathaniel M. Waters,
       Horace Waters
Brother: Zadock Magruder, dec'd.
Nieces: Elizabeth Read, dau. of dec'd. sister; Rachel Bealmear, dau. of
      Elizabeth Bealmear; Luranna Green, dau. of Elizabeth Bealmear
Sisters: Elizabeth Bealmear, Rachael Dorsy, Nancy Waters
Friend: Richard Henderson, son of Mrs. Lydia English
Richard Henderson's sisters: Sarah and Jennett
Children of friend David English: Charles English, John English, Lydia
                                      English, Jane English, Eliza Ann Beall
                                      English
Sons of half brother, William Bowie, dec'd.: William Bowie, Charles Bowie
Exs: Wife Elizabeth and nephew Jonathan W. Magruder
Wit: Roger Perry, Richard J. Orme, Perry Wade

MAGRUDER, SAMUEL, son of Ninian   L B   f 240   27 Mar 1784
                                         L 1   p 220   3 Jul 1786

Wife: Margaret - dwelling plantation consisting of "Magruder's Purchase"
               originally pt. of "Friendship"; pt. of "Addition to
               Magruder's Purchase", pt. of "Resurvey of the Additions
               to Magruder's Purchase"
Son: Samuel Brewer Magruder - "Resurvey on the Addition to Magruder's Purchase"
Daus: Elizabeth Offutt, wife of William Offutt; Ann Clagett, widow of Henry
      Clagett
Eldest son: Ninian Beall Magruder
Son: Joseph Magruder

Grandchildren: Elizabeth, Samuel, Verlinda, Rebecca, Sarah and Zachariah
            Williams; Samuel Clagett, son of Ann
Sell pt. of "Resurvey on the Addition to Magruder's Purchase", "Mill-Use",
"Beall's and Magruder's Honesty"
Exs: Ninian Beall Magruder, Joseph Magruder, Samuel Brewer Magruder
Wit: Hezekiah Magruder, Edward Magruder, Archibald Magruder, Thomas Flint

MAGRUDER, SAMUEL, Sr. of Prince Georges Co.,   L A f 81   30 Jan 1739
              planter   L 1 p 48   9 Feb 1779

Wife: Eleanor - dwelling house and 220 a. adjoining
Son: Elias - land at Upper Marlboro
Sons: Alexander and Josias - store house at Nottingham and land
Son: William - Mills
Sons: Samuel and Zachariah
Daus: Eleanor, Lucey, Elizabeth Spencer
Ex: Wife Eleanor
Wit: John Clagett, Joshua Busey, A. Magruder

MAGRUDER, SAMUEL B.   L L f 96   15 Apr 1818
                                                L 3 p 71   20 Nov 1818

Wife: Eleanor Magruder - dwelling house and 1/3 of land
Son: Walter Magruder - land
Sons: James Magruder, Samuel Magruder, Ninian Magruder
Mill to be sold unless son Walter buys it for $500
Dau: Charlotte Beall
Thomas Watkins - to pay $1,000 for 60 a. of land
Ex: Son James Magruder
Wit: John B. Magruder, John Wallace, Thomas M. Clagett

MAGRUDER, SAMUEL JACKSON   L C f 114   29 Oct 1789
                                                L 1 p 262   7 Sep 1793

Sisters: Margaret Magruder, Ruthey Magruder, Elizabeth Magruder
Wit: Samuel Br. Magruder, Robert Douglass

MAGRUDER, SAMUEL WADE   L C f   6   21 Mar 1792
                                                L 1 p 245   18 Sep 1792

Wife: Lucy
Sons: Levin Magruder, Charles Magruder - "Piney Luck"
Sons: George Beall Magruder, Patrick Magruder - land in Georgetown where
              testator formerly lived, "Hawkins and Beatty's Addition",
              land above Georgetown and land in Marlboro in P. G. Co.
Sons: Warren Magruder, Lloyd Magruder, Thomas Contee Magruder - remainder
              of land
Daus: Sarah Willson, Lucy Berry
Exs: Wife Lucy and son Levin
Wit: Thomas Beall of George, Samuel Davidson, Thomas Flint

```
MAGRUDER, THOMAS of Falls of Potomac        L B  f 200      17 Jan 1785
                  of Fairfax Co., Va.       L 1  p 170      23 Apr 1785
```

Nephews: George Fraser Warfield, William Burrett Magruder
Brother: Basil Magruder
Friend: Richard Thompson of Georgetown
Exs: Basil Magruder, William Burrett Magruder, Richard Thompson
Wit: Benjamin Becraft, Jr., Walter Smith, W.A.G. Cornish


```
MARQUESS, ANN                               L D  f 584      17 Jun 1802
                                            L 1  p 504      27 Jul 1802
```

Daus: Eleanor Porter, Deborah Marquess, Anne Marquess, Elizabeth Marquess
Mary Knight
James Marquess
Exs: Joseph Harriss, George Hays
Wit: Alexander Pearre, Jr., William Murphy, Jr., Aquila Murphy


```
MASON, RICHARD                              L B  f 221      17 Oct 1787
                                            L 1  p 191      11 Nov 1787
```

Wife: Ann Mason
Son: Magruder Mason
Other sons: (not named)
Daus: Selby Mason, Verlinda Mason, Leannah Mason, Frances Mason
Exs: Selby Mason and Leannah Mason
Wit: Nicholas Hocker, Mordecai Moore, Thomas Knott


```
MEDLEY, JOHN BAPTIST                        L'F  f 188      22 Jul 1803
                                            L 2  p 143      26 Feb 1803
```

Wife: Mildred Medley
Son: Basil Medley (under age 20) - land on south side of road from mouth of
                                   Monocacy to Georgetown
Son: Thomas Medley (under age 20) - land on north side of said road
Exs: Wife Mildred and brother-in-law Peter Bowie
Wit: Levin Beall, Hanbury Jones, Hugh S. Dunn


```
MELTON, RAPHAEL (indexed Milton)            L I  f 448      15 May 1816
                                            L 2  p 500      11 Jun 1816
```

Children in Kentucky: Joseph, Henrietta, Alexander, Elizabeth, and Mary Ann
                     Melton
Eleanor Mitchell, Anne Mitchell, Rachel Mitchell alias Eleanor Melton, Anne
   Melton, Rachel Melton - 2/3 estate in Montgomery Co.
Sarah Mitchell - 1/3 estate
Ex: John Augustus Chiswell
Wit: Dennis Lackland, Joseph Chiswell, John A. Howard

MILES, JOSEPH of Georgetown	L C f 225	31 Oct 1795
	L 1 p 342	28 Feb 1796

Wife: (not named)
Joshua Mudd and George Castograve of Charles Co. - land for which testator
                                                   holds their bond
Children: (not named)
Granddau: Tracy Miles
Exs: Sons Henry and Edward Miles
Wit: Christian Kurtz, Walter B. Walter, Benjamin White

MOCKBEE, NINIAN	L H f 27	30 Jun 1812
	L 2 p 329	 9 Feb 1812

Wife: Mary Mockbee
Dau: Nancy Smith
Milla Lowe
Anna Lowe
Fanny Buxton
3 children: Ninian Mockbee, Jr., Cordelia Mockbee, Martha Mockbee
Ex: Wife Mary Mockbee
Wit: James M. Lingan, Zachariah Williams, Zachariah Waters

MOCKBEE, ZEPHENIAH	L E f 128	31 Jan 1805
	L 2 p 51	 7 Mar 1805

Sister: Rejoice Mockbee
Son: Zepheniah Mockbee, afflicted (under age 21)
Sons: Hezekiah and Alphud Mockbee
Exs: Sons
Wit: Thomas Fletchall, Henry Jarboe

MOCKEBEE, ALFRED	L H f 37	18 Jan 1813
	L 2 p 345	 9 Feb 1813

Rhodalph Maginnis
Ex: Rhodalph Maginnis
Wit: Joseph Soaper, Henry Stallings

MOORE, LEVIN, planter	L G f 236	15 Oct 1810
	L 2 p 259	15 Feb 1811

Nephew: Benjamin Moore
3 single sisters: Keziah Moore, Priscilla Moore, Elizabeth Moore
Brother: James Moore
Exs: Sisters Keziah and Elizabeth Moore
Wit: William Blanchard, Isaac Riley

MOORE, WILLIAM   L B   f 420   9 Apr 1790
                                                           10 Aug 1790

Wife: Mary
Sons: Zedekiah and Horatio
Daus: Elizabeth and Hariet
Exs: Wife Mary, Zachariah Moore, George Moore, George Baurne
Wit: Edward Burgess, John Ray, Thomas Leach

MULLICAN, DORCAS   L D   f 130   9 Jun 1798
                                        L 1   p 408   21 Jul 1798

Brothers: Basil, William
Sister: Elizabeth
Sister-in-law: Teresa
Ex: Brother Basil
Wit: James Northcraft, William Burns, Francis McAtee

MULLIKIN, BASIL   L E   f 12   13 Sep 1802
                                        L 1   p 538   31 Jan 1803

Wife: (not named)
Nephew (also referred to as cousin): Basil Mullikin, son of John and Sarah
      Mullikin - pt. of "Addition to Brooke Grove" where testator now lives
Cousin: Margarett Ryney
Richard Beall, son of Lawson
William Mullikin, son of John and Ann Mullikin
Sell tract which is pt. of "Gittings Ha-Ha" purchased from John Dells
Ex: Richard Green
Wit: James Holland, Benjamin Gartrell, Philemon Plummer

MULLIKIN, JOHN   L A   f 26   13 Jan 1778
                                        L 1   p 22   21 Mar 1778

Wife: Ann
Sons: Basil, Willey - "Chestnut Ridge" where testator lives
Daus: Elizabeth, Darcus
Wit: William Traill, Edward Northcraft, Francis Culliam

MULLIKIN, RACHEL   L H   f 317   20 Feb 1804
                                        L 2   p 358   12 Oct 1813

Nephew: Stephen Penn
Niece: Ruth Griffith
Ex: Basil Griffith
Wit: Philemon Plummer, Thomas Davis, Philemon Plummer, Jr.

MULLIKIN, WILLIAM of Prince Georges Co.   L A   f 27   9 Jan 1767
                                                 L 1   p 23   21 Mar 1778

Wife: (not named)
Son: William - land where testator lives
Son: John - land bought of John Rile on Sinnack Creek
Son: Bassel
Granddau: Mary Moble
Exs: Sons William and John
Wit: William Magruder Selby, Joshua Bennett, Nathan Selby, James Selby

MULLOY, ELIZABETH   L O   f 150   29 Apr 1823
                                                 L 3   p 249   18 May 1824

Sisters: Agness Prater, Uphen Clagett, Martha Ricketts, Jane Riggs
Brothers: James Willson, Robert Willson
Ex: Brother Robert Willson
Wit: Joseph Poole, Richard Poole, Overton Williams

MURDOCK, JOHN of Georgetown   L B   f 423   29 Apr 1788
                                                                   27 Aug 1790

Son: William and his wife and children
Brother: Addison Murdock
Friends: John Thomas Boucher, Robert Peter
Dorothy Barber - 100 a. to include houses where she now lives and plantation
         of James Collins
John (under age 21), son of Dorothy Barber
Elizabeth (under age 18), dau. of Dorothy Barber
Mary (under age 18), 2nd dau. of Dorothy Barber
Exs: Addison Murdock, John Thomas Boucher, Robert Peter
Wit: Brooke Beall, William Robertson, Thomas Beall of Geo., Elisha O. Williams

MURPHY, CHARLES of Frederick Co.   L B   f 11   17 Sep 1780
                                                 L 1   p 82   18 Dec 1780

Wife: Mary
Children in order of birth: Josue, Deborah, William, Cassandra, John
Guardians of children: James Offutt, Sr. and John Flemming
Ex: Wife Mary
Wit: Ninian Tannehill, King English

MUSGROVE, JOHN   L B   f 207   5 Jun 1785
                                                 L 1   p 172   8 Aug 1785

Son: Amos
Children: (not named)
Exs: Son Nathan Musgrove and Richard Ijams
Wit: Anthony Holland, Benjamin Gaither, John Scrivenor

NEEDHAM, WILLIAM   L F f 195   30 Jul 1806
                                            L 2 p 150   1 Jun 1808

Son: William Abington Needham - "King Cole" in Washington Co., Md. devised
                               testator by Sarah Needham, dec'd., widow of
                               testator's brother John Needham
Children of dau. Sarah Ann
House-maid: Ann Bogler
Brother: Richard Needham, late of Staffordshire, England, dec'd.
Son: John Needham
Daus. of sister Sarah Heugh, dec'd.
Ex: Son William Abington Needham
Wit: Upton Beall, Robert Wallace, Lewis Beall

NICHOLLS, NAOMA (indexed Nicholas)   L I f 30   19 Apr 1814
                                            L 2 p 388   17 Jun 1814

Sisters: Prissilla, Polly Stonestreet, Sena Clements
Brothers: Westly Nicholls, Cephas Nicholls, Samuel Nicholls
Father: Samuel Nicholls, dec'd.
Mother: (not named - living)
Wit: William Childs, Edward W. Gatton, Z. Gatton

NICHOLLS, PRISCILLA, Sr.   L L f 106   14 Aug 1816
                                            L 3 p 29   13 Jul 1819

Husband: Samuel Nicholls, dec'd.
Sons: Samuel Nicholls, Cephas Nicholls
Daus: Priscilla, Polly Stonestreet, Pegga, Aseaner Clements
Ex: Jesse Leach
Wit: John Braddock, Nathan Brown, Robert Willett, Jesse Leach
Codicil dated 15 Apr 1817
Wit: Jesse Leach, Eliza Leach
Codicil dated 8 Oct 1818
Changes ex. from Jesse Leach to Cephas Nicholls
Wit: Jesse Leach

NICHOLLS, THOMAS   L E f 14   20 Jun 1802
                                            L 1 p 543   6 Jun 1803

Sons: Isaiah Nicholls, Benjamin Nicholls, Edward Nicholls, Daniel Nicholls
Grandchildren: Helen Beall, Thomas Beall, Norman Beall, Priscilla Beall
Daus: Elizabeth Beall, Cassandra Nicholls, Rebeccah Harding
Exs: Sons Isaiah and Edward
Wit: Basil Mockbee, Benedict Green, Francis Green

NICHOLUS, JOHN   L N f 112   10 Jul 1820
                                            L 3 p 171   8 Mar 1822

Benjamin Oden

Daus: Ann Nicholus, Nancy, Marget, Mealey, Elleonor
Sons: John, James, Asa, Phillip, Elisha
Grandson: William Nicholus, son of Phillip Nicholus
Ex: Greenbury Howard
Wit: Joseph Neel, Arthur Dillehay, G. Howard

NIXON, ELIZABETH   L E f 328   24 Sep 1804
                                    L 2 p 73   30 Jan 1806

Brothers: Hugh Nixon, James Nixon - "Poor Stony Hill" in Prince Georges Co.
Sister: Mary Becraft - "Poor Stony Hill" in Prince Georges Co.
Sister: Amy Howard - pt. of "Friendship"
Brothers: Jonathan Nixon, Richard Nixon
Ex: Brother Richard
Wit: William Buchan, Thomas Rhoades, George Upton

NIXON, JONATHAN   L D f 136   22 Oct 1794
                                    L 1 p 422   7 Mar 1799

Son: Hugh Nixon - "The Farm" where he formerly lived and 10 a. of "The
            Resurvey on the Farm"
Son: James Nixon - remainder of "Resurvey on the Farm" and 60 a. "Poor
            Stony Hill" in Prince Georges Co.
Son: Jonathan Nixon
Dau: Mary Becraft
Daus: Elizabeth Nixon, Amey Nixon - plantation where Joshua Nixon formerly
                                    lived
Son: Richard Nixon - "Friendship Enlarged" where testator lives
Exs: Sons Hugh and Richard Nixon
Wit: Josha W. Selby, Andrew Scholfield, John Needham

NORRIS, BENJAMIN, planter   L B f 233   16 Jan 1786
                                    L 1 p 210   28 Apr 1786

Son: William Norris - dwelling plantation which is pt. of "Hopewell"
Daus: Mary Norris, wife of George Norris; Eleanor Jarrat, wife of William
      Jarrat, blacksmith
Grandsons: Benjamin, William, John and Thomas Ray Jarrat, sons of William
Exs: Son William Norris and son-in-law William Jarrat
Wit: Alexander Pearre, Nathan Harris, John Edwards

NORRIS, GEORGE   L B f 407   28 May 1789
                                                        4 Jul 1789

Wife: Mary
Eldest son: William - his dwelling plantation and land
Son: George - testator's new dwelling plantation and remaining land
Sons: Solomon, Thomas John, Benjamin

Daus: Charlotte, Darcus, Mary Anne
Exs: Wife Mary and son William
Wit: George B. Hays, Nathan Harris, Jesse Harris

NORRIS, WILLIAM of William, planter   L C f 219   11 Nov 1796
                                              L 1 p 370   15 Feb 1797

Wife: Elizabeth Margaret Norris - dwelling plantation
Son: William Norris Silver
Daus: Susannah Norris Silver, Eleanor Norris Silver
Ex: Wife
Wit: Lenox Martin, Peter McNamara, James Barnett

NORRIS, WILLIAM of Belmont Co., Ohio   L H f 309   15 Oct 1807
                                              L 2 p 346   10 Aug 1812

Wife: Mary
Dau: Sarah Martin
Son: Otho Norris
Children: Mary Ann, Luther, Benjamin, William, Ann Mariah, Eliza
Exs: Wife and Notley Hays
Wit: Sterling Johnston, Joseph Bell, Thomas Lawson

NORTHCRAFT, RICHARD, planter and farmer   L B f 409   9 Sep 1789
                                                                   24 Oct 1789

Sons: Erasmus, Edward
Son: James (under age 21) - land where testator now lives called "Molls
                Rattle" and "Resurvey on Molls Rattle" 150 a.
Son: Hezekiah - pt. of "Resurvey on Buxton's Delight 100 a., pt. of "Lyby"
           33 1/3 a., pt. of "Resurvey on Molls Rattle" 70 1/2 a.
Children: Elizabeth, Casandra, James, Parmelia, Mary, Catrine, Hezekiah
Exs: Friends Zachariah Waters and James Trail Jr. son of James
Wit: Zachariah Waters, William Waters, Basil Waters

NUGENT, JOHN   L I f 214   2 Aug 1815
                                              L 2 p 466   12 Dec 1815

Acknowledges himself to be father of children of Fanny, a black woman, viz:
   Evan, Betsy, Polly, Sally. Daus. disinherited if they marry a black man.
Ex: Ephraim Gaither, son of William
Wit: Thomas Davis, Philemon Plummer, Jr., Andrew Graff

ODEL, BARUCK   L B f 404   9 Dec 1788
                                                                    9 Jun 1789

Wife: Margaret - 1/3 land
6 children: (not named) minors - 2/3 land
Ex: Wife Margaret

Wit: James Hunt, Walter S. Greenfield, William P. Hunt

OFFUTT, ALEXANDER					L B f 215		7 Jan 1786
							L 1 p 185		8 Feb 1786

Children: Cassandra, Jane, Martha, Rachell, James Duell
Ex: James Perry, uncle of 5 children above and their guardian
Wit: George H. Offutt, Thomas Scott, Richard Wootton

OFFUTT, ELEANOR						L H f 21		2 Nov 1811
							L 2 p 324		27 Jun 1812

Son: Alexander Offutt - ex. to handle his 1/8 share
Other 7 children: Andrew Offutt, Basel Offutt, Aaron Offutt, Charles Offutt,
		Rachel Clagett, Mary Clingan, Eleanor Offutt
Ex: Son Basel Offutt
Wit: William Darne, Jr., Joseph Clagett, John H. Clagett, William Roberts

OFFUTT, ELIZABETH					L G f 404		29 Jan 1810
							L 2 p 295		13 Jan 1812

Daus. of Jane Wheeler
3 daus: Sarah Offutt, Margett Austin, Elizabeth Thrift
Sons: Samuell Offutt, James Doull Offutt
Children: William Mockbee Offutt, Sarah Offutt, Rezin Offutt, Margett
	Austin, Nathaniel Offutt, Elizabeth Thrift, Alexander Offutt,
	Jane Wheeler, dec'd., Baruch Offutt
Exs: Sons Alexander and Baruch Offutt
Wit: William Offutt Magruder, Colmore Offutt

OFFUTT, HEZEKIAH					L B f 394		16 Nov 1788
									10 Feb 1789

Wife: Sarah - plantation where testator now lives
Children: Hannah, Elizabeth, Thomas Odle, Brooke Burgess, Jane, Humphrey
	Burgess Offutt
Ex: Wife Sarah
Wit: John Dent, Richard Gatton, Martin Houser

OFFUTT, JAMES						L D f 584		20 Jul 1802
							L 1 p 506		11 Aug 1802

Wife: Rebecca Offutt
Sons: William Offutt, Zadok Offutt, Ozias Offutt - pts. of "Clewerwall",
				"Hensley", "Addition to Hensley"
Daus: Jane Offutt, Velinder Beatty, Rebecca Offutt, Mary Offutt
Children of dau. Elizabeth Jones, dec'd.
Children - "Fair Dealing" on the Potomack River
Ex: Son Ozias Offutt

Wit: Hilleary L. Fisher, Kinsey Gittings, Jesse Wade, James Wade

OFFUTT, MORDECAI BURGESS   L I   f 19   18 Feb 1810
                                    L 2   p 368   7 Mar 1814

Daus: Jane Thrift, wife of Absalom Thrift; Mary Offutt; Clarissa Offutt;
       Elizabeth Wade, wife of John Wade; Rebecca Jones, wife of Charles O.
       Jones; Cassandra Offutt, wife of George W. Offutt; Verlinda Offutt,
       wife of Baruch Offutt; Sally Cartenhour, wife of John Cartenhour
Son: Colmore Offutt
2 youngest daus., Mary and Clarissa to live with Jane and Absalom Thrift
Exs: Baruch Offutt and Absalom Thrift
Wit: Thomas Scott, Jr., Thomas Scott, Sr., Richard West

OFFUTT, NATHAN of Lower District of Frederick   L A   f 18   7 Jan 1777
              Co. alias Montgomery Co.   L 1   p 16   22 May 1777

Wife: Mary Offutt - "Newtown" where testator now lives, "Barron Hill"
Sons: Thomas Burgess Offutt (minor), George Washington Offutt
Daus: Cassandra, Molly, Debby (all under age 21)
Ex: Wife Mary
Wit: Middleton Smith, Ninean Beall Magruder, Henry Clagett

OFFUTT, SAMUEL C.   L G   f 386   25 May 1811
                                    L 2   p 272   17 Jul 1811

Father: (not named) dec'd.
Mother: Margaret Offutt
Brother: Zephaniah Burgess Offutt - testator's claim against estate of the
                                    late Hannah Offutt
Brother: Zachariah Offutt
Sisters: Lucy B. Knott, wife of Leonard Knott; Catherine C. Offutt
Ex: Brother Zephaniah B. Offutt
Wit: Charles Evans, Cephas Fleming

OFFUTT, SARAH, widow   L A   f 217   23 Jun 1779
                                    L 1   p 61   1 Nov 1779

Nephews: Midleton Beal, son of Robert; James Offutt; Josias Beall, son of
          Josias; George Offutt
Nieces: Valinder Dent, Lucy Offutt, Betsy Offutt, daus. of William
Ex: George Offutt
Wit: James Doull, Alexander Offutt

OFFUTT, THOMAS, Sr.   L D   f 292   22 Oct 1799
                                    L 1   p 436   13 Dec 1800

Son: Thomas Hussey Luckett Offutt - 120 a. pt. of "William and James"

Son: Thomas Wootton Offutt - 128 1/2 a. land where testator's father
formerly lived
Son: Thomas Levi Offutt (under age 21) - 122 1/2 a. pt. of "Addition to
William and James" purchased from Mrs. Sarah Offutt
Daus: Charity Bryan, Nancy West, Rebecca Neale, Elizabeth Lewis Sugars,
Serena Milema Offutt (under age 21), Rachel Scott
Granddau: Elizabeth Luckett Scott (under age 21)
Ex: Son-in-law John Bryan
Wit: Richard West, Samuel West, Joseph Roberts

OFFUTT, WILLIAM, Jr.	L B f 219	14 Jul 1786
	L 1 p 189	29 Sep 1786

Wife: (not named) - use of dwelling plantation
Sons: James, Elisha, Baruch - "Clewerwall"
Son: Samuel - 200 a. "As good as we can Get" land where he now lives
Sons: Alexander, Rezin, William
Son: Nathaniel - land in Bedford Co., Va.
Daus: Jane, Sarah, Margett, Elizabeth
Ex: Wife
Wit: Walter Smith, Charles Wooton, William Offutt Magruder

OFFUTT, WILLIAM, III	L H f 3	1795
	L 2 p 299	23 Aug 1810

Wife: (not named)
Son: James Offutt - 1/2 of pt. of "William and James" and addition to same
Son: Ozgood Offutt - other 1/2 of above land where testator lives
Son: Thomas Offutt, Jr. - "James's Park", "The Young Man's Folly"
Granddaus: Elizabeth Luckett, dau. of Ozgood Offutt; Mary Ann; Sarah West,
dau. of Thomas
Grandson: Fielder, son of George H. Offutt
Children: Thomas, James, Elizabeth
Exs: Sons James Offutt and Thomas Offutt, Jr.
Wit: John Hawkins, B. Ward, James Wade, Samuel Magruder, William Offutt of
James, Thomas H.L. Offutt
Codicil dated 23 Apr 1795
Son: Ozgood
Wit: John Hawkins, B. Ward

OFFUTT, ZACHARIAH	L I f 202	3 Jun 1815
	L 2 p 439	2 Aug 1815

Married sister: Lucy B. Knott
Brother: Zepheniah B. Offutt
Exs: Brother Zepheniah B. Offutt and sister Catherine C. Offutt
Wit: William Trail, Abraham S. Hays

OFFUTT, ZEPHENIAH   L C f 226   14 Jan 1796
                                                                    23 Feb 1796

Wife: Margaret - land devised testator by his father Samuel Offutt
Brothers: Mordecai Burgess Offutt and Hezekiah Offutt
7 children: Rezin Beall Offutt, Elizabeth Chew Offutt, Lucy Burgess Offutt,
            Samuel Chew Offutt, Zachariah Offutt, Zepheniah Burgess Offutt
            (under age 21), Catharine Christie Offutt (under age 18)
Refers to legacy left by Robert Beall to testator's son Rezin Beall Offutt
Ex: Wife Margaret
Wit: George Culp, Zachariah Offutt, Thomas Clagett

OGDON, BENJAMIN, late of Charles Co.,   L C f 110   7 Feb 1793
               now of Montgomery Co.   L 1 p 252   15 Feb 1793

Eldest son: Henry Ogdon
Second son: Benjamin Ogdon
Step-children: (not named)
Ex: Friend, John Addamson
Wit: Edward Burgess, William Fulks, Rachel Oden

OLIVER, CHARLES (nunc.)   L C f 33   10 Mar 1790
                                                                    16 Mar 1790

Brother: William
Sister: Nelly
Lewis Stephens
Brothers and sisters: (not named)
Wit: Henry Hooper Wheeler, Ann Hall

O'NEAL, MARGARET   L N f 291   23 Jul 1819
                                                 L 3 p 183   13 Nov 1822

Sister: Sharlotte Layton - house and lot where testator now lives
Children of Sharlotte Layton
Nieces: Ann Cook, Ann Fiffe
Brother: William B. Hungerford
Children of William B. Hungerford
Exs: Friends, William Wilson of John and Edward Burgess
Wit: John H. Riggs, John Adams, Washington Gloyd

O'NEALE, HENRY   L K f 232   16 Oct 1817
                                                 L 2 p 529   14 Nov 1817

Sisters: Eleanor Jamison, Mary Ann O'Neale
Money for repairs to Barnesville Church known as St. Marys
Cousin: Ann O'Neale, who lives with testator
Nephew: Laurence Jamison
Francis Jamison
Exs: Sister Mary Ann and Francis Jamison

Wit: James Redmond, Thomas F.W. Vinson

O'NEALE, JOHN   L B f 201   1 Apr 1785
                                                    L 1 p 171   2 Apr 1785

Sons: Joseph, Barton
Wife: (not named)
Daus: Mary, Jannet
Ex: Wife
Wit: Thomas Higdon, Randal Tucker

O'NEALE, JOHN   L L f 85   22 Feb 1815
                                                    L 3 p 87   12 Aug 1818

Wife: Eliza Henrietta
Dau: Ellen
Children: (not named)
Ex: Francis Jamison
Wit: R.B. Taney, Michael Taney, Jr., Thomas William Morgan

O'NEALE, SARAH, widow of William O'Neale   L I f 35   27 Feb 1812
                                                    L 2 p 394   5 Nov 1814

Son: Alexander Adams
Son-in-law: Richard West
Exs: Alexander Adams and Richard West
Wit: Jesse Leech, John Fleming, John Braddock

O'NEILL, BERNARD   L I f 212   21 Jun 1815
                                                    L 2 p 462   2 Dec 1815

Wife: Barbara O'Neill
Daus: Mary O'Neill, Elizabeth Diggs, Eleanor Diggs, Mary Diggs
Trustees: Francis Jammison, Joseph Smith
Exs: Wife Barbara O'Neill and daus.
Wit: William Vyrmeer, Abraham S. Hays

O'NEILL, ELIZABETH   L F f 208   26 Aug 1807
                                                    L 2 p 169   29 Aug 1808

Mother: Susan Waring, dec'd. - her will dated 21 May 1800 and codicil dated
                16 Apr 1804
Husband: Bernard O'Neill - use of all property devised testator by above will
Daus. of husband: Mary O'Neill and Elizabeth O'Neill
Wit: R.K. Waters, C.H.W. Wharton

105

ORME, LUCY   L C f 181   12 Jan 1795
                                                    L 1 p 318   31 Jan 1795

Dau: Eleanor Orme - brick house and lot in Georgetown
Son: Alpheous Beall
Dau: Masey Williams
Granddaus: Lucy Williams, Harriet Williams, Eleanor Williams, Ruth Williams,
           Patty Williams, Nancy Deakins, Tabythey Deakins
Sell other house in Georgetown
Ex: Son-in-law Benjamin Williams
Wit: John Beall, Levi Beall, John Deakins

ORME, MOSES   L B f 68   4 Dec 1781
                                                    L 1 p 100   12 Feb 1782

Wife: Priscilla - tract "Shawfields" known by name "Discovery"
Son: James Orme - above land at mother's decease
Son: Moses Orme - "Taylor's Pasture" in Prince Georges Co.
Son: Samuel Taylor Orme - "Taylinton" in Prince Georges Co. and "Discovery"
Dau: Mary Burns - "Carrolinor"
7 youngest daus: Ursulla, Verlinder, Rebecca, Harriot, Eleanor, Priscilla,
                 Charlotte
Exs: Wife Priscilla and son Samuel Taylor Orme
Wit: Clement Beall, Peter Becraft, Henry Davison

OWEN, EDWARD   L I f 39   8 Nov 1814
                                                    L 2 p 401   13 Jan 1815

Dau: Nancy Smith, wife of James Smith - pt. "Batchelor's Forest" of 86 3/4 a.
Granddaus: Rachel Ann Smith and Octavia Owen Smith, daus. of James Smith
Son-in-law: James Smith
Ann Beall, dau. of Samuel Beall
Nancy Owen Crafford, dau. of Robert B. Crafford
Sister: Eleanor Crafford
Wife: Rachel Owen
Ex: Wife Rachel Owen
Wit: Nathan Holland, Jr., John Bowie, Walter C. Williams

OWEN, JOSHUA   L E f   6   2 Dec 1802
                                                    L 1 p 526   6 Jan 1803

Wife: Mary Owen
Sons: Singleton Owen, John Candler Owen, Daniel Owen
Dau: Rosanna Owen
Ex: John Candler
Wit: Archibald Orme, Alexander Campbell, John Harper, Daniel Candler

106

OWEN, ROBERT   L A f 175   11 May 1779
                                            L 1 p 53   4 Jul 1779

Sons: Edward, Robert and Washington Owen (all under age 21) - lands on
                                          Rock Creek
Son: Washington Owen - dwelling plantation
"Shepherd's Hard Fortune" where testator's father lived to be sold
Wife: Mary Owen
Daus: Elinor, Ann, Elizabeth, Mary and Octavia (minors)
Exs: Wife Mary and son Edward
Wit: Martha Williams, Joseph Hall, Richard Brooke

PACK, HARRIET   L N f 289   Not dated
                                            L 3 p 185   29 Oct 1822

Aunt: Elenor Young
Elenor Young, dau. of John Young
Ex: Aunt Elenor Young
Wit: Aeneas Belt, Joseph J.W. Jones

PACK, THOMAS, Sr.   L E f 122   10 Jan 1802
                                            L 2 p 39   6 Nov 1804

Wife: Christena Pack
8 children: Richard Pack; William Pack; Thomas Pack; Zadock Pack; Nathan
            Pack; Eleanor Holland, wife of Archibald Holland; Rachel
            Greenwell, wife of Barnabas Greenwell; Elizabeth Loveless,
            wife of Zadok Loveless
Ex: Wife Christena Pack
Wit: John Harding of Edw., Benjamin Nicholls of Thos.

PAGNO, NICHOLAS   L I f 35   3 Apr 1799
                                            L 2 p 395   7 Dec 1814

Wife: (not named)
William Benson and Ninean Benson, sons of William Benson
Sarah Benson, dau. of William Benson
Ex: William Benson, son of William Benson
Wit: Thomas Davis, Ephraim Gaither, Nathan Musgrove

PEARCE, BENJAMIN NOTLEY of Georgetown   L B f 452   4 Jul 1790
                                                              12 May 1792

Henry Culver Pearce, eldest son of testator's brother John Pearce, dec'd.
Wife: Katherine Pearce - land
Ann Pearce "otherwise called Ann Keagen" - land at wife's decease
Eldest son of Henry Culver Pearce (not named)
Exs: Wife and Ann Pearce
Wit: George French, Kenneth Thomson, John M. Garett

PEARCE, MARGRATE   L B f 202   24 Apr 1785
                                                L 1 p 163   30 May 1785

Son: John Baptist Pearce - dwelling plantation
Son: William Gale Pearce
Exs: John Baptist and William Gale Pearce
Wit: Aeneas Campbell, Simon Reeder, John Medley

PEARRE, ALEXANDER, Sr.   L E f 123   24 Dec 1800
                                                L 2 p 41   6 Nov 1804

Son: Alexander Pearre - testator's home plantation called "Rome"
Children: Joshua Pearre; James Pearre; Alexander Pearre; Eleanor (Nelly)
           Arnold, wife of David Arnold; Nancy Arnold, wife of Peter Arnold
Exs: Sons Joshua, James and Alexander Pearre
Wit: William Murphy, Joseph Benton, Jr., John White

PEERCE, HENRIETTA   L N f 337   3 May 1823
                                                L 3 p 224   5 Jun 1823

Son: William Peerce - dwelling plantation
Sons: Walter Peerce, James Peerce
Granddau: Rachel Daws
Ex: Son William Peerce
Wit: Cephas Lazenby, James Lazenby, John Bowie

PEERCE, HENRY C.   L I f 23   6 Mar 1812
                                                L 2 p 375   2 May 1814

Wife: Elizabeth Peerce - plantation where testator lives which is pt. of
                          "Elizabeth's Delight", lands adjoining on the N.W.
                          side of the Northwest Branch
Daus: Anne Higdon of Kentucky, Verlinder, Eleanor Peerce, Terecy Peerce in
       Kentucky
Granddau: Virlinder Higdon
Son-in-law: Peter Higdon
Eleanor Joy
Sons: William C. Peerce (under age 21), Leonard Peerce in Kentucky
Wife's sister: Sarah Macketee
"Wife's children" to live with her (states there are 3)
Sons: John and Ignatius Peerce - land on east side of Northwest Branch
Exs: Wife Elizabeth Peerce and son John Peerce
Wit: Joshua Nelson, Samuel Cecil, John Cecil

PEERCE, RACHEL   L H f 11   Sep 1811
                                                L 2 p 310   15 Nov 1812

Son: William Peerce - "St. Winnexburgh" where testator now lives
John Stone Frazer, Jr.

Granddaus: Cinthia Frazer, Rachel Frazer, Cleopartra Frazer
Exs: Son William Peerce and son-in-law John S. Frazer, Jr.
Wit: Arn Dyer, Sr., James Orme, William Culver

PELLY, HARRISON   L E f   4   6 Sep 1802
                    L 1 p 518   17 Sep 1802

Wife: Mary Pelly
Gerard Jarvis
Jane Clark and Thomas Clark, her son
Zadock Jarvis, son of Gerard
Exs: Wife Mary and Gerard Jarvis
Wit: Har. Lane, Zadock Magruder, Jr., Joseph Lufflin

PENN, ZACKEAS   L D f 569   2 May 1801
                    L 1 p 496   18 Apr 1802

Brother: Robey Penn - pt. of "Penn's Inheritance" where he now lives
Mother Elizabeth Penn and sister Elizabeth Penn - pt. of "Penn's Inheritance"
                                                 where testator lives
Sister: Elizabeth Penn - "Addition to Ray's Adventure"
Ex: Sister Elizabeth Penn
Wit: Edward Burgess, Sr., Charles Penn, Lodowick Davis

PERRY, CHARLES   L L f 97   17 Oct 1807
                    L 3 p 15   9 Feb 1819

Wife: Priscilla
Sons: Thomas Perry, Roger Perry
Daus: Ruth Worthington, Elizabeth Magruder, Lidia Henderson, Rebecca Pollard
Exs: Sons Roger and Thomas Perry
Wit: Upton Beall, Nathan Holland, Jr., Solomon Holland

PERRY, JAMES   L B f 168   3 Jul 1784
                    L 1 p 149   14 Dec 1784

Wife: Hanner Perry - "Pint Lookout"
Son: John Perry - pt. of "Hope Improved" where he lives
Sons: James Perry, Basil Perry, Thomas Perry, Francis Perry - lands
                                           adjoining "Hope Improved"
Daus: Peggy Perry, Marry Perry, Nancy Perry, Rachel Perry, Lydia Perry,
      Betsy Perry
Exs: Wife Hanner and son John
Wit: Charles Penn, Abraham Sheckell, Nicholas Ray

PERRY, JAMES   L D f 539   4 Feb 1802
                    L 1 p 483   10 Feb 1802

Wife: Rachel Perry

Sisters: Rachel West, Ann Hilleary
Nieces: Jane Beall, Martha Wade
2 daus. (under age 16) of niece Cassandra Wayman, dec'd.
Friends and relatives: John Willson and Richard Wootton - at decease of
wife Rachel Perry, land called "Joseph's Goodwill"
and "Wickhams Park" willed testator by his dec'd.
father; also, "Little Park" deeded testator by
Thomas Nickolls and "West part of Discontent"
deeded testator by Richard Wootton
Wit: Archibald Orme, Zachariah Dowden, Aquilla Gatton
Codicil dated 8 Feb 1802
Wit: Charles Williams, Greenbury Gaither, Zachariah Gatton, Sr.

PERRY, JEMIMA   L H f 28   19 Mar 1811
                                                 L 2 p 330   3 Sep 1812

Granddaus: Anne Waters Perry, Jemima Magruder Perry
Grandson: Elias Waters Perry
Friend: Dr. John Bussard
Ex: Friend Dr. John Bussard
Wit: Charles Clagett, Mary Clagett, Sarah Ann Clagett

PERRY, JOSEPH, planter   L D f   6   Dec 1795
                                                 L 1 p 385   8 Oct 1797

Wife: Jemima - 1/2 dwelling plantation, 1/2 land bought from James Beall and
           his son Alexander Beall, 1/2 of "Littleworth"
Son: Basil Magruder Perry - above land at mother's decease, 1/2 dwelling
                             plantation, "Piss Ant Hills" and resurvey of it
Dau: Mary Gaither
Daus: Jane Beall, Margaret Hillary - land in Monococy
Son: James Wilson Perry - tract "Content" being pt. of "Bear Garden Enlarged",
               also, "Bear Garden" and "Deer Park"
Son-in-law: John Gaither - 200 a. land in Kentucky
Grandson: James Wilson Gaither - 200 a. land in Kentucky
Grandson: Joseph Hillary - 200 a. land in Kentucky
Sons: James Wilson Perry, Basil Magruder Perry - remainder of the 2,000 a.
                                                     in Kentucky
Granddau: Mary Beall
Exs: James Wilson Perry, Basil Magruder Perry
Wit: Thomas Edmonston, Robert Orme, Alexander Edmonston

PERRY, PRISCILLA, relict of Charles Perry   L O f 170   25 Jul 1822
                                                 L 3 p 293   31 Mar 1825

Desires to be buried beside her husband
Granddau: Priscilla Douglass, late Priscilla Pollard
Daus: Ruth Worthington, Elizabeth Magruder, Lydia English, Rebecca Pollard
Friend: Robert P. Magruder
Children of Rebecca Pollard

Children of sons Roger and Thomas J. Perry
Ex: Robert P. Magruder
Wit: Upton Beall

PERRY, ZADOCK   L B f 449   7 Jan 1792
                                                                  15 Mar 1792

Wife: Ann
7 children: John Perry, Elisha Perry, Jeremiah Perry, Collen Perry, Stephen
            Perry, Levi and Sarah Perry
Exs: Wife Ann and Francis Osbourn
Wit: Lawrence O'Neale, Zadock Magruder, Richard Shekell

PETER, DAVID of Georgetown   L H f 32   30 Nov 1812
              District of Columbia   L 2 p 337   8 Dec 1812

Wife: Sarah Peter
Son: William - corner lott on Bridge and Congress Sts.
Son: Hamilton - corner lott on Water and High Sts.
Youngest son: James - house and lott next to last above
Daus: (not named)
Exs: Wife Sarah Peter, Capt. George Peter, Leonard H. Johns
Wit: Thomas Sims, Richard Johns, Thomas Peter

PETER, JAMES of Georgetown, District of   L F f 350   19 Jun 1808
              Columbia, County of Washington   13 Sep 1808

Brothers: David Peter of Georgetown, Robert, George
Mother: (not named)
Sister: Margaret Dick
Wit: None - Richard A. Bowyer and Richard Smith swore to handwriting as
           that of James Peter

PETER, ROBERT of Georgetown, Washington Co.,   L F f 329   10 May 1802
              and District of Columbia   L 2 p 180   29 Nov 1806

Sons: Thomas (now married to Miss Custis), Robert, David, George, James
         (under age) - all land out of Georgetown and City of Washing-
         ton except "Clagett's Purchase"
Wife: (not named) - dwelling house in Georgetown
Friends: Benjamin Stoddart, Uriah Forrest, Thomas Beall of George
Dau: Elizabeth Dunlop - lot and house in Georgetown already conveyed to her
Dau: Margaret Dick - pt. of "Clagett's Purchase"
Son: Alexander S. Peter - inheritance to be in care of friends John Peter,
                 Thomas Beall of George and Dr. John Weems
Debtor: Mrs. Broomly, formerly Mary Smith
John Peter

111

Cassandra Chew and daus. Harriot Bruce and Mary Broomly - lot with improvements where she now lives
Exs: Sons Thomas, Robert and David Peter; son-in-law James Dunlop
Wit: John Dunlop, J.M. Jackson, William Pierpont Richardson
Codicil dated 18 Oct 1804
Son: Alexander S. Peter - to have debts paid until "he shall become reformed from Drunkiness"
Friend: John Peter is "lately dead" and replaced as trustee by testator's son Thomas
Wit: George King, John Thompson, Henry Tuell
Codicil dated 22 May 1805
Son: Alexander S. Peter - annuity raised
Dau: Margaret Dick - lands in Montgomery Co. bought from Philip B. Key adjoining "Clagett's Purchase"
Grandchildren: Robert Dick, son of Margaret Dick; Elizabeth and James Dunlop
Wit: John Thompson, Henry Tuell, J. Thompson
Codicil dated 19 Aug 1805
Son: Alexander S. Peter - 20 pounds in full, but brothers and sisters and mother are to keep him from charity
Grandchildren: Jane and Elizabeth Peter, daus. of David Peter
Wit: John Thompson, J. Thompson, Henry Tuell
Codicil (nunc.) 8 Nov 1806
Wit: J. Weems, Eliza Honburg, Ariana French
A court case arose over will and codicils. Verdict found for defendant 15 Oct 1807

PETER, ROBERT of Washington County, District of Columbia	L G f 237 L 2 p 265	23 Jun 1809 15 Nov 1809

Mother: (not named)
Sisters: Mrs. Margaret Dick, Elizabeth Dunlop
Nephew: Robert Dick (under age 21)
Children of Elizabeth Dunlop: George, Henry, Mary, Helen
Brother: David Peter - house rented to Mr. David M. Ershire inherited from testator's father
William, son of David Peter - above house at age 21
Cousins, daus. of John Peter, dec'd.: Mary Peter - lot 16 square 29
    Elizabeth Peter - lot 16 square 32
    Janet Peter - lot 10 square 37
    Ann Peter - lot 8 square 41
    above lots in City of Washington
Brothers: Thomas Peter, George Peter
Exs: Thomas and David Peter
Wit: George Peter, Elisha W. Williams, John Hoye

PETERS, JOHN S.	L E f 110 L 2 p 11	16 Aug 1802 3 Jan 1804

8 children: Mary Medley, Charles Gilbert Peters, Elizabeth Peters, Rachel Peters, Ruth Peters, John Peters, Liney Peters, Phebe Peters (some of children are minors)

Ex: Elijah Medley
Wit: Edward Phelps, Edward Anderson, John Clark

PIGMAN, MATTHEW, planter   L B   f 133   27 Dec 1783
                                                  L 1   p 129   28 Jun 1784

Wife: Dorcas
Sons: John "that is now absent", Joshua
Son: Ignatius - pt. "Charley Forest" and dwelling plantation
Daus: Philenia, Sarah - "Philenia and Sarah", pt. "Pleasant Plains of
                        Damascus"
Ex: Ignatius
Wit: Mat Myler, Jasper Peddicoart, Bazel Windsor

PILES, JANE, widow of Leonard Piles   L F   f 511   9 Nov 1809
                                                  L 2   p 219   6 Dec 1809

Dau: Nancy Miles
Son-in-law: John Douglass
6 grandchildren: Samuel, Jane, Elizabeth, John, Mary Ann, Rebecca Douglass
                 (all minors), children of dec'd. dau. Sarah Douglass, wife
                 of John Douglass
Children: Francis Piles, Richard Piles, Jane Piles, Mary Batson, Elizabeth
          Mullican, Leonard Piles
Exs: Sons Francis and Leonard Piles
Wit: John Aldridge, Colmore Williams

PLEASANTS, MARGARET of Goochland Co., Va.   L G   f 161   25 Aug 1806
           Quaker   L 2   p 249   20 Oct 1806

Brothers: James Brooks Pleasants, William Henry Pleasants
4 sisters: Deborah Stabler, Mary Stabler, Sarah Pleasants, Henrietta M.
           Pleasants
Ex: William Henry Pleasants
Wit: Isaac W. Pleasants, Mary Pleasants, Thomas Nucols
Codicil dated same day
2 nieces: Elizabeth Ann and Margaret Pleasants

PLEASANTS, THOMAS of Goochland Co., Va.   L G   f 157   31 Dec 1803
           Quaker   L 2   p 251   18 Jun 1804

Sell land in Virginia - 600 a. on fork of James River, Fluvania Co.; 500 a.
                        on Little My-Chunk Creek, Fluvania Co.; 159 a. on
                        Little Byrd Creek, Goochland Co.; 20 a. on Genneh's
                        Creek and 226 a. on same creek, Goochland Co.; testa-
                        tor's 1/3 pt. of 157 a. including mill nr. mouth of
                        Wreck Island Creek, Buckingham Co.
Sell land in Maryland - pt. of "Brooke Piney Grove", "Fair Hill", etc.

Daus: Henrietta and Margaret Pleasants - 60 a. on Seneca Creek, pt. of "Brooke's Addition", "Dickerson's Delight" and "Brother's Content"
Daus: Deborah and Mary Stabler - mill on Patuxent tract where George Gue lives as tenant called "Addition to Brooke Grove" of 190 a., "Brooke's Addition" on Hawlings R. a little below Gaither's Mill
Sons: James Brooke Pleasants and William Henry Pleasants - land on which testator lives and ½ of mill called "Beaverdam Mill"
Dau: Deborah Stabler - land where she now lives of 390 a. of "Snowden's Manor Enlarged"
Dau: Mary Stabler - 255 a. on Patuxent R. mostly in A.A. Co. where Joshua Penn lives as tenant and pt. "Brooke's Addition" and 150 a. of "Brooke's Addition", "Dickerson's Delight", and "Brother's Content"
Dau: Sarah Pleasants - 400 a. where Elizabeth Leeke lives as tenant
Dau: Henrietta Pleasants - 400 a. on Seneca Creek pt. of "Brooke Piney Grove", "Fair Hill', etc. where Joshua Pigman lives as tenant
Dau: Margaret Pleasants - 400 a. on Seneca Creek next to Henrietta's land
The poor belonging to Cedar Creek Monthly Meeting
Niece: Mary Younghusband
Mother: Mary Pleasants
Sister: Jane Hunnicutt
Exs: 2 sons James Brooke Pleasants and William Henry Pleasants; 2 sons-in-law William Stabler and Edward Stabler
Wit: James Bryden, Micajah Crew, John Webber, Margaret Crew

PLUMMER, PHILEMON   L M f 272   21 Feb 1818
                                        L 3 p 102   15 Sep 1820

Sons: Philemon Plummer, Joseph Plummer, William Plummer
Dau: Sarah Anderson, wife of Stephen Anderson
Grandchildren: daus. of son George Plummer (not named); Philemon Plummer, son of Joseph; Philemon Plummer, son of William; Philemon Anderson, son of Sarah; children (not named) of dau. Nancy by her 1st husband John Moore
Grandson: William Plummer, son of John - dwelling plantation
Elenor Joseph, "a poor old woman" - support while she lives in testator's dwelling
States some heirs live out of state
Ex: Grandson William Plummer, son of John
Wit: Thomas Davis, Nathan Musgrove, Sr., Frederick Gaither
Codicil dated 29 Aug 1820
Wit: Thomas Davis, Frederick Gaither

POOLE, JOHN, planter   L I f 439   14 Jul 1804
                                        L 2 p 484   30 Jan 1816

Son: John Poole - all land

4 daus (now living): Elizabeth, wife of Hanbury Jones; Ann, wife of Francis
                     Piles; Priscilla; Rebecca
Ex: Son John Poole
Wit: Hugh S. Dunn, Thomas Fletchall, Zedekiah Swann

PORTER, CHARLES   L F   f 509   16 Aug 1809
                                            L 2   p 217   21 Oct 1809

Sons: Nathan, Denton S., David and Edward Porter
Son-in-law: John Riddle
Grandson: David Shook
Wife: Polly Porter
Children (minors) of dau. Frances Lodge, wife of William B. Lodge
Children (minors) of dau. Charlotte Heeter, wife of George Heeter
Ex: Son Nathan Porter
Wit: George Ray, William Fulks

PRATHER, BENJAMIN   L A   f 31   30 May 1778
                                            L 1   p 28   30 May 1778

Wife: (not named)
Massy
Wit: John Gaither, Alexander Mason, Samuel Israel Godman, Zephaniah Prather,
     Nicholas Hanker

PRATHER, JOHN, planter   L C   f 313   8 Sep 1795
                                            L 1   p 345   19 Nov 1796

Son: Thomas Prather
Daus: Sarah Linthicum, Mary Duvall
Ex: Samuel Brooke
Wit: Nathan Musgrove, Philemon Plummer, Jr., Thomas Davis

PRATHER, MARY   L E   f 138   4 Aug 1805
                                            L 2   p 70   24 Aug 1805

Dau: Eleanor Craycraft
Sons: William Prather, John Prather
Wit: James Sherlock, Beal Ayton

PRITCHETT, THOMAS   L A   f 49   19 Jan 1778
                                            L 1   p 46   21 Mar 1778

Children: Elias, Charles, William, Ruth West, Elizabeth West, Mary, Liddy
Son: William - land where testator lives
Ex: Friend William O'Neal
Wit: John Crabb, William M. Offutt, Abraham Benjamin

QUARY, NICHOLAS   L B f 373   13 Oct 1788
                                                            15 Dec 1788

Wife: Margaret - 1/3 land
Sons: Daniel and Henry - all land at wife's decease
5 daus: Mary Ann March, Christiana Shingler, Catharine March, Elizabeth
        Humbert, Susanna Tice
Ex: Wife Margaret
Wit: Archibald Orme, Oswald Clements, John Golden

RAWLINGS, JAMES   L E f 116   10 Apr 1804
                                         L 2 p 27   16 Jun 1804

Children: Sarah Howard, Mary Berry, James H. Rawlings, Benjamin Rawlings,
          Richard Rawlings - land in Spotsylvania Co., Va. and land which
                       came to testator from his wife
Brother: Benjamin Rawlings
Granddau: child of Edward and Mary Berry (minor)
Ex: Sons James H., Benjamin and Richard Rawlings
Wit: Obed Swearingen, John Hobbs, Ely Godman

RAWLINS, JOHN   L B f 163   15 Aug 1784
                                         L 1 p 146   12 Nov 1784

Wife: Mary - pt. "Final Conclusion"
Sons: Thomas, John (under age 18) - pt. "Final Conclusion"
Daus: Ann, Priscilla, Elizabeth, Sarah, Mary Eloner and Mary Rawlins
Exs: Wife Mary and son Thomas
Wit: John Suter, Basil Adamson, Calvert Petty

RAY, JAMES   L F f 107   7 May 1807
                                         L 2 p 129   31 Jul 1807

Wife: Mary Ray
Friend: Robert Briggs
Granddau: Mary Ray Riley - house and lot in Rockville
Dau: Ann Riley
Margaret Cocklan "who lives in my family"
Exs: Wife and son-in-law Camden Riley
Wit: Edward Willett, Sr., William O'Neale, Jr., Absalom Remington

RAY, JOSEPH   L 3 p 107   12 Sep 1820

Affadavit of Revolutionary War Service
Resident of Montgomery Co., 65 years of age
Service: enlisted 1776 as Pvt. in Co. commissioned by Capt. Benjamin Price
         2nd Md. Reg. commissioned by Col. Gunby
         discharged in fall of 1783
         fought in Battles of Camden, Monmouth Plaines, Eutaw Springs
         wounded in left knee in later battle

RAY, MARY   L D f 140   24 Dec 1794
                                                    L 1 p 425   9 Feb 1799

Sisters: Margaret Pritchett, Rebecca Ray - use of tract "The Charles and
                                                         Thomas"
Nephew: Samuel Busey, son of Joshua Busey - above tract at sisters' decease
Nephew: Josiah Ray, son of John Ray
Niece: Ann Ray, dau. of brother John Ray
George Washington Busey
Mary Sheir
Ex: Nephew Samuel Busey
Wit: William Digges, David Parker, John Chappell

REED, MATTHEW   L D f 538   14 Jul 1801
                                                    L 1 p 482   30 Jan 1802

Wife: Eleanor Reed
Children: Alletha, William, Ruth, Mahala, Eleanor
Wit: Caleb Darby, Samuel Riggs, Jesse Herbert

REEDER, FRANCIS   L B f 447   14 Dec 1791
                                                                    24 Jan 1792

Simon Reeder, Sr. of Charles Co.
3 youngest brothers: John, Hezekiah and Henry
Francis McAtee
Margaret McAtee
Ex: Francis McAtee
Wit: William McAtee, John H. Wathan, Greenbury Howard

REID, JAMES   L L f 94   3 Oct 1818
                                                    L 3 p 13   27 Oct 1818

Wife: Elizabeth Reid
Sons: Henson, Thomas, Robert, Zachariah, Leven and James Reid
Daus: Patty Howel, Anna Reid, Margaret Reid
Exs: Wife Elizabeth and son Hanson
Wit: G.W. Harwood, William S. Chilton, Thomas H. Phillips

REID, JOHN of Frederick Co.   L K f 227   8 Jul 1811
                                                    L 2 p 523   15 Jul 1811

Wife: Ann
Sons: George Nelson, William Perry, John Alferd, Joseph, Archibald Anderson
      and Thomas
Daus: Eastor, Ann, Mary (all minors)
Ex: Wife Ann
Wit: Henry Smoltzer, George Butt, Jo. Swearingen

117

RHOADES, NICHOLAS of Frederick Co. L A f 256   5 Nov 1767
                                    L 1 p 67   15 Mar 1780

Sell pt. of "None Left"
Wife: Jane Rhoades
Sons: John Rhoades, Elisha Rhoades, Nicholas Rhoades
Exs: Wife Jane and son Elisha
Wit: William McKay, Joseph Knight, William Knight

RICHARDS, JACOB   L I f 208   26 Dec 1814
                                    L 2 p 450   17 Oct 1815

Wife: Marian - farm where testator lives
Son: George - 1/2 of farm with dwelling after wife's decease
Daus: Elizabeth Willson, Catharine Adams, Eleanor Richards, Christina
      Richards, Mary Richards - other 1/2 of farm
Exs: Wife and son-in-law Benjamin Adams
Wit: John Bowie, William Huddleston, Truman Greenfield

RICKETTS, ANTHONY, Sr. (nunc. written by   L C f 143   4 Feb 1793
                       Benjamin Ricketts) L 1 p 288   8 Apr 1794

Wife: Mary Ricketts
2 youngest sons: Zadok and Gerard
Wit: Solomon Holland, John Linthicum

RICKETTS, BENJAMIN, Sr.   L B f 372   16 Nov 1787
                                                 13 Aug 1788

Son: Benjamin Ricketts - "Banks Venture" and "Green Marsh"
Son: Jacob Ricketts - plantation where testator now lives
Grandson: Robert Ricketts, son of Jacob - above plantation at decease of Jacob
Dau: Martha Ricketts - 52 a. "Ricketts' Folly"
Grandson: Jacob Elliott
Daus: Druzilla Ricketts; Mary Ricketts, wife of Anthony Ricketts
Ex: Son Benjamin
Wit: Zadock Magruder, Benjamin McDugle, Thomas Reade

RICKETTS, MARTHA   L L f 79   5 Feb 1818
                                    L 3 p 77   13 Apr 1818

Sons: Merchant Ricketts, Benjamin Ricketts
Daus: Drusilla Easton, Sally Ricketts, Rhoda Ricketts
Father: Benjamin Ricketts - willed testator land "Ricketts Folly"
Wit: Willy Janes, Arnold T. Winsor, Jonas Pasley

RICKETTS, RICHARD   L L f 127   11 Nov 1819
                                                   L 3 p 70   16 Nov 1819

Wife: Elizabeth Ricketts
Ex: Wife Elizabeth Ricketts
Wit: C.H.W. Wharton, Edward Digges, Francis Hutchinson

RIDGWAY, ROBERT   L B f 51   9 Jun 1781
                                                   L 1 p 94   20 Jul 1781

Wife: Sarah Ridgway
Sons: Isaac, Jeremiah
Dau: Sarah
Exs: Wife Sarah and son Isaac
Wit: Lechd. (?) Magruder, William Beall Magruder

RIGGS, AMON   L N f 120   27 Nov 1818
                                                   L 3 p 160   15 Apr 1822

Wife: (not named)
Children: (not named)
3 grandchildren: children of dec'd. son Charles
Son: John Riggs - place where he now lives
Son: Henry Riggs
Exs: Sons John and Henry
Wit: Howard Griffith, John Griffith, Edward Burgess

RIGGS, EDMUND   L B f 132   24 Nov 1783
                                                   L 1 p 128   11 Apr 1784

Wife: Ruth Riggs
Sons: James Riggs, Greenberry Riggs, John Riggs
Daus: Elizabeth Leech, Verlinder Caton
Exs: Ruth and son James
Wit: Newton Chiswell, Charles Clagett, Lawrence Owen

RIGGS, JOHN   L F f 206   28 Oct 1797
                                                   L 2 p 165   14 Sep 1808

Kinswoman: Mary Griffith, dau. of Benjamin Griffith
Kinsmen: John Hammond Riggs, Reuben Riggs
Ex: John Hammond Riggs
Wit: Thomas Davis, Nathan Musgrove, Philemon Plummer, Jr.
Codicil dated 2 Oct 1798
Wit: Thomas Davis, Nathan Musgrove

```
RIGGS, SAMUEL                              L I  f  26        7 Jun 1813
                                           L 2  p 381       15 Jun 1814
```

Wife: deceased
Son: Thomas Riggs - 200 a. land purchased from Henry Griffith, 100 a. pt. of
        "Bordley's Choice"
Son: Reuben Riggs - 222 1/2 a. where he now lives which was deeded by Isaac
        and Hannah Briggs 8 Dec 1797
Son: George Washington Riggs - 504 a. land purchased from David Lynn which
        is pt. of "Dublin" and "Resurvey on Dublin"
Son: Romulus Riggs - 176 a. land deeded by George and Deborah Chandlee
Son: Remus Riggs - all of "Bordley's Choice" that testator owns except that
        given son Thomas
Son: Elisha Riggs - surveying instruments in addition to land already deeded
Daus: Polly Griffith, wife of Henry Griffith; Henrietta Gaither, wife of
        Daniel Gaither; Julia Riggs
Grandchildren: Amelia Dorsey Griffith; Samuel Riggs Gaither; Amelia Dorsey
        Riggs, dau. of George Riggs; Samuel Riggs, son of George
        Riggs; Samuel Riggs, son of Romulus Riggs; Amelia Dorsey
        Riggs, dau. of Romulus Riggs; Samuel Riggs, son of Reuben
        Riggs; Ann Riggs Gaither; Samuel Riggs, son of Thomas Riggs
Exs: Sons Thomas and Remus
Wit: Thomas Davis, John H. Riggs, James Holland

```
RIGGS, THOMAS                              L D  f   5       28 Dec 1794
                                           L 1  p 384       30 Oct 1797
```

Delilah Plummer, wife of George Plummer
Ex: George Plummer
Wit: John H. Riggs, John Penn, Richard Price, Johnsey Plummer

```
RILEY, GEORGE                              L I  f 195        Not dated
                                           L 2  p 425        9 May 1815
```

Wife: Mary Riley
Daus: Sarah Martha Camden Riley, Tabitha Ann, Mary George
Wit: None - Camden Riley, Isaac Riley and John Busey attest to handwriting
    as that of George Riley

```
RILEY, HUGH                                L E  f 333        4 Aug 1805
                                           L 2  p  82       29 Mar 1806
```

Sons: James Riley, Amos Riley, Benjamin Riley
Son: George Riley - land in P. G. Co.
Son: Isaac Riley - land purchased from Honore Martain and that from Edward
        Owen
Son: Camden Riley - 450 a. where testator lives which is pt. of "Dann"
Daus: Dorcas Williams, Sarah Nicholls, Eleanor Riley, Esther Beall
Dau: Martha Riley - lot #112 in "Beattys and Hawkins Addition to Georgetown"
Dau: Mary Riley - lot #108 in "Beattys and Hawkins Addition to Georgetown"

3 single daus: Eleanor, Martha, Mary - tract testator bought from Richard
                                      Wootten, trustee for hrs. of Daniel
                                      Henry
Ex: Isaac Riley
Wit: Richard Blacklock, Philip Yost, Basil Greenfield, Thomas Blacklock

ROBERTS, ANN   L F f 199   8 Mar 1805
                                       L 2 p 156   14 Jun 1808

Free negros
All estate to negro Henne Prather
Wit: Edward Tillard, Henry Poole, Hezekiah Ward

ROBERTS, BILLINGSLY   L B f 431   9 Nov 1790
                                                         7 Jan 1791

Wife: (not named) - lease to plantation where we now live
Sons: Richard in Kentucky and John - 300 a. "Camels Choice" on north fork of
                                                Holson River
Sons: Henry, Joseph, James and William - 900 a. in Kentucky
Daus: Margaret Duley, Ann Saubrage
All Children: Richard, Eleanor and John Roberts; Sarah Benton; Cassandra,
              Henry, Joseph, Mary, James and William Roberts
Exs: Wife and son John
Wit: John Hawkins, James Offutt of Wm., John Dent

ROBERTS, WILLIAM   L I f 438   21 Jan 1816
                                       L 2 p 482   30 Jan 1816

Sisters: Darcas Roberts, Ann Harper, Drusilla Saffle
Niece: Maryann Saffle
Ex: Friend, William Darne
Wit: William Coleman, John Candler, Nathan Soper, John Doud

ROBERTSON, BENJAMIN   L E f 106   29 Jul 1803
                                       L 2 p   2   8 Oct 1803

Sons: Thomas Robertson, Benjamin Robertson
Wife: Sarah Robertson
Dau: Priscilla Ford Robertson
Ex: Wife Sarah Robertson
Wit: Elias Owen, Paul Summers

ROBERTSON, SAMUEL   L I f 200   30 May 1815
                                       L 2 p 438   5 Jun 1815

Sell land
Exs: Friends, William Robertson and Aaron Offutt
Wit: Richard J. Orme, Benjamin Lyon, Joshua Howard

SAFFELL, MARY, planter L B f 244   29 Jun 1785
                        L 1 p 224   10 Apr 1787

Sons: Charles, Joshua, William, Samuel and James Saffell
Daus: Sarah, Ann and Elizabeth
Grandson: Hezekiah Saffell
Ex: Charles Saffell
Wit: John Kelley, Benjamin B. Kelley, Clement Green

SAFFELL, SAMUEL of Frederick Co., planter L A f 3   25 Nov 1776
                                           L 1 p 4   28 May 1777

Sons: John, Joshua, Samuel, Charles, William, James
Daus: Ann, Elizabeth, Sarah
Wife: Mary - lands
Ex: Wife Mary
Wit: Robert Dawe, Benjamin B. Kelley, Griffith Davis

SCHOLL, FREDERICK   L I f 197   18 Apr 1815
                        L 2 p 428   24 May 1815

Wife: Catharine Scholl
Daus: Catharine Griffith, Margarett Scholl
Son: Mountjoy Scholl
Ex: Wife Catharine Scholl
Wit: William Willson of John, James Hawkins, Otho Willson

SCOTT, GUSTAVUS   L D f 435   Not dated
                        L 1 p 462   4 Feb 1801

Eldest son: John C. Scott - "Strawberry Vale" devised to testator by his
                            brother William
Son: Gustavus Hall Scott - land in Fairfax and Stafford Cos., Va.
Son: William B. Scott - land in Fauquier and Loudoun Cos., Va.
Son: Robert Scott - land in Alleghany Co., Md.; land in Va.; land on
                    Panther's Creek in Kentucky
Daus: (not named) - $10,000 each
Residue of estate in trust for daus. by exs.
Exs. to be trustees and guardians to all children under age 21
Exs: Thomas J. Bullitt, Nathaniel Crawford, John Threlkeld, Uriah Forrest
Wit: Sarah Scott Brown, Sophia Bullitt, Matilda Cole, Antje Hortulanus

SCOTT, THOMAS   L M f 276   21 Jan 1819
                        L 3 p 108   14 Oct 1820

Wife: Margaret Scott
Granddaus: Sarah Scott, dau. of Thomas Scott, Jr.; Elizabeth Offutt, dau. of
           William Scott; Eliza Scott, dau. of Amos Scott
Sons: Amos Scott, Thomas Scott, Jr., William Scott

Dau: Elizabeth West, wife of Norman West
Son-in-law: Norman West
Children of Elizabeth West
Sister: Sarah Allen
Exs: Thomas Scott, Jr. and William Scott
Wit: Richard Key Watts, Nicholas Clopper, Thomas B. Offutt

SCRIVENOR, ELIZABETH wife of John   L D   f 536   7 May 1799
                                                     L 1   p 478   8 Jan 1802

Husband: John Scrivenor - "Resurvey on Brandy"
Daus: Hanny Spates, Elizabeth Collins, Peggy Hickman, Sally, Polly
Sons: Levy, Reason, William
Wit: Basil Beckwith, Martin Fisher, John Douglass

SCRIVENOR, JOHN   L H   f 31   30 Nov 1812
                                             L 2   p 334   10 Dec 1812

Wife: Sarah Scrivenor
Grandson: John Scrivenor
Children: Sarah Scrivenor, William Scrivenor, Hennelretta Spates, Mary
          Scrivenor, Elizabeth Collins, Rezin Scrivenor, Margaret Hickman
Exs: Son William Scrivenor and John Douglass
Wit: Ezekiah Linthicum, Martin Fisher

SEAGAR, JOHN   L B   f 203   26 May 1781
                                             L 1   p 156   12 Apr 1785

Eldest dau: Sarah Ducker - pts. of "Buxton's Delight", "William and John",
                  "Thomas and John" where testator lives
Youngest dau: Sophia
Ex: Nathaniel Ducker
Wit: John Watts, Walter Fryer, Ninean Mockbee

SEAR, ISRAEL   L E   f 330   26 Jul 1805
                                             L 2   p 77   11 Feb 1806

Wife: Mary Sear
Son: John Thompson Sear
Daus: Mary Sear and Hester Sear - "former wife's clothes"
Children: John Thompson Sear, Betsy Sear, Hester Sear, Lawson Sear, Josiah
          Sear
Ex: Wife Mary Sear
Wit: Joshua Sear, Hezekiah Veatch

SEAR, JOSHUA   L I   f 193   18 Apr 1815
                                             L 2   p 421   8 May 1815

Brothers: Elias, Israel, William

Brother: Hezekiah - all land provided Anderson Cowley remain for the
             time he rented it
Nephew: John, son of Israel
Virlinda Ashon
Ex: Friend, Abraham Jones
Wit: James Cooley, Thomas A. Cowley, William Adlum, Abraham Jones

SEAR, WILLIAM   L E f   8   26 Aug 1802
                                        L 1 p 527   1 Feb 1803

Son: Joshua Sear - pt. of "Progress", "The Slipe"
Daus: Priscilla, Rebecca
Sons: Israel Sear, Elias Sear, William Sear, Hezekiah Sear
Grandson: Thomas Sear
Dau: Mary - pt. of "Progress" including house, pt. of "The Slipe"
Ex: Son Joshua Sear
Wit: Hezekiah Veatch, John Veatch, Solomon Veatch

SEARCY, WILLIAM (indexed and signed Searsey)   L I f 201   22 Feb 1815
                                               L 2 p 435   19 Jun 1815

Wife: Nancy Searcy
Gerrat Hickman (minor)
Greenberry Hickman
Brother: Robert Searcy - land on Grayson Co., Ky. on Rock Creek
Ex: Wife Nancy Searcy
Wit: Benjamin Poole, Colmore Williams, Dennis Lackland

SEEDERS, BENNETT, Sr.   L E f 13   17 Dec 1802
                                        L 1 p 540   3 Mar 1803

Wife: Ruth
5 youngest children: Mary, Anne, William, James, Samuel
Exs: Wife Ruth and son Henry
Wit: William Holmes, Archibald Mason

SEGWICK, ELISHA   L F f 200   10 May 1808
                                        L 2 p 158   14 Jun 1808

Priscellar Keeth
Wit: John Darby, John Hopwood, Jr.

SELBY, JOHN   L H f 313   28 Jun 1813
                                        L 2 p 352   4 Sep 1813

Son: John Eversfield Selby (unmarried) - 100 a. laid off in testator's
                   dwelling plantation which is pts. of "Bear
                   Garden" and "Deer Park"

Dau: Elenor Bowie Selby - remainder of above 2 tracts including
                      dwelling house
Dau: Sarah Selby - "Eversfields Addition"
Son: Walter Bowie Selby
Daus: Esther Orme, wife of Archibald Orme; Susannah Brian, wife of William
      Brian; Margaret Jones, wife of William Jones
Ex: Friend, Robert Edmonston
Wit: James Beddo, Zachariah Downs, John S. Wilson, Richard M. Downs

SELBY, THOMAS, Sr., planter   L C f 111   1 Nov 1783
                                      L 1 p 257   28 May 1793

Wife: Rebekah Selby
Sons: Thomas, Sachariah, Richard - pts. of "Charles and Johns Choice" and
                                   "Fellowship"
Daus: Elenor, Rebekah, Leurana, Verlindar
Exs: Wife Rebekah and son Sachariah
Wit: Robert Dawe, Benjamin Grey, William Grey, John Adamson, Joseph Catron

SELF, JOHN   L D f 442   14 Mar 1797
                                      L 1 p 471   22 May 1801

Dau: Polly Self
Son: William Self
John Hickman, Sarah Hickman, Richard Hickman, children of Elizabeth Hickman
Ex: Elizabeth Hickman
Wit: Thomas B. Beall, Jesse Wade, Nancy Hickman

SHAW, WILLIAM   L A f 177   4 Jun 1779
                                      L 1 p 55   30 Jul 1779

Wife: Rebecca
Sons: William, Robert, Adamson Tanihill and Hessisah Shaw (all minors)
Dau: Rebecca Shaw (minor)
Thomas Austin - legacy for education
Ex. and trustee to children: Wife Rebecca
Wit: Allen Bowie, Jr., Edward Garrott

SHEPHEARD, FRANCES   L I f 451   30 Jul 1816
                                      L 2 p 509   18 Sep 1816

Sister: Mary Burne
Nancy Wilson, dau. of Hezekiah Wilson
Son: Thomas Shepheard
Eldest son: Wadworth Shepheard
Ex: Son Thomas Shepheard
Wit: Ezek. Linthicum, William Dawson, Wilson Burn

SHERLOCK, JAMES					L C f 323		22 Mar 1797
								11 Jul 1797

Son-in-law: James Lawson - "Trouble Enough" and "Mount Prospect"
Ex: James Lawson
Wit: Richard King, King English, William Ratrie

SIMMONS, ABIGAIL				L B f 235		29 Dec 1785
								L 1 p 213		8 Feb 1786

Daus: Margaret Simmons, Elizabeth Simmons, Mary Dawson, Deborough Burket,
	Eleanor Hays, Sarah Sheckles
Sons: Isaac Simmons, James Simmons, George Simmons
Heirs of son Samuel Simmons, dec'd.
Ex: Step-son Samuel Simmons
Wit: Simon Reeder, Frederick Sprigg

SIMMS, CATHERINE				L E f 126		31 Dec 1804
								L 2 p 49		24 Jan 1805

Husband: deceased
Sons: Ignatius (under age 21), Elexious, William, Thomas and Walter Simms
Daus: Mary Clark, Henrietta Clark, Ann Roads
Grandsons: Francis Simms, Joseph Simms
Valinda Jarbo
Reverand Plunkett
Granddau: Ann Simms
Exs: Son Walter Simms and son-in-law Robert Clark
Wit: Nathaniel Wilson, Henry Baggerly, Walter Beall

SIMPSON, SOLOMON				L E f 119		6 Sep 1804
								L 2 p 35		30 Oct 1804

Niece: Dorcas Davis (under age 16), dau. of Richard and Esther Davis -
	money paid testator by Solomon Davis, adm. of Richard
	Davis, dec'd., being Dorcas Davis' share
Wife: Dorcas Simpson - testator's dwelling plantation
Brother: James Simpson - 1500 a. in Kentucky
Nephew: Allen Simpson
Nieces: Esther Trundle, wife of Basil Trundle; Harriot Davis, dau. of
	Richard Davis, dec'd.
Nephews: Eli Davis, Richard Davis, Solomon Davis
Solomon Simpson Selby - lot and improvements in Charlesburgh, Mont. Co.
Nancy Barruch, wife of George Barruch
Exs: Wife Dorcas and nephew Solomon Davis
Wit: Alexander Whitaker, George Hoskinson, Sr., Hugh S. Dunn

SLATER, ANNA					L I f 190		28 Dec 1814
								L 2 p 416		4 Apr 1815

Niece: Sarah Robertson "who has lived with me from her infancy"

Jonathan Prout, son of William and Sarah Prout
Niece: Elenor Lyon
Ex: Gerard Brooke
Wit: Basil Brooke, Eden Beall

SMALLWOOD, DIRECTOR (female)   L H f 33   27 Dec 1812
                                   L 2 p 340   22 Jan 1813

Granddau: Jain Smallwood, dau. of son William T. Smallwood - 119 3/4 a. land
          on which testator lives called "Conjurer Out Done"
Dau: Susanah Pemmet Cloud
Granddaus: Susanah Pemmet Cloud, Artemesia Cloud, Emsey Cloud, Naoma Cloud,
           Artemisa Roberts, Susanah Pemmet Roberts
Grandsons: Trammall Hickman Cloud, Sampson Smallwood
Dau: Elizabeth Roberts, wife of James Roberts
Son: Sampson T. Smallwood
Son: William T. Smallwood - all testator's islands in Potomack River and
     tract "Smallwood's Entrenchment"
Ex: Son William T. Smallwood
Wit: Richard Gatton, Alexander Adams, Zachariah Gatton, William Darne, Jr.
Codicil dated 12 Jan 1813
Wit: William Darne, Jr., Alexander Adams, Richard Gatton

SMALLWOOD, SAMPSON TRAMMELL   L I f 446   23 May 1812
                                   L 2 p 499   9 Apr 1816

Elizabeth Shelton
Ex: Friend, William Darne, Jr.
Wit: Mordecai B. Offutt, Thomas B. Offutt, George W. Offutt

SMITH, DAVID   L D f 299   30 Jan 1800
                                   L 1 p 444   4 Mar 1800

Wife: Sarah Smith
Granddau: Susanna Collins
Ex: Wife Sarah
Wit: John Chappell, William B. Chappell, Joseph Atkins

SMITH, IGNATIUS   L C f 311   30 Jan 1795
                                   L 1 p 362   10 Sep 1796

Sons: Leonard Smith, Benjamin Smith
Wit: Elizabeth Doyle, Samuel Wesley, James Doyle

SMITH, JAMES "now a resident of   L B f 388   1788
          Montgomery Co."   13 Feb 1789

Wife: Sicilly (Sicillia) Smith

127

Joseph "my free Mulatto" - 104 a. "Jumhoyle"
Ealse, mulatto - 80 1/4 a. pt. "Jumhoyle"
David, mulatto
Exs: Wife, Martin Fisher, Zachariah Gatton
Wit: Martin Fisher, Charles Allison, John Gaskins

SMITH, MIDDLETON   L A f 20   2 Jul 1777
                                          L 1 p 18   19 Feb 1778

Wife: Rebecka Smith - "Outlet" and "Strong Beer"
Ex: Wife Rebecka
Wit: Robert Beall, Sr., William Murphy, John Dent

SNELL, ELIZABETH widow of George   L F f 506   26 Nov 1802
                                          L 2 p 213   12 Jul 1809

Godson: Zachariah Warfield
Brother: William Scrivenor, dec'd.
Ex: Godson Zachariah Warfield
Wit: Charles Beaven, Mordeca Iams, Brice J. Gassaway

SOAPER, BASIL, Sr.   L O f 159   28 Feb 1825
                                          L 3 p 274   30 Apr 1825

Son: Basil Soaper - pts. "Busey's Adventure", "Beall's Addition", "Mercy's
                Inheritance" containing 45 a.
Son: Ignatius Soaper - 106 a. pt. "Mercy's Inheritance"
Son: Samuel Soaper - pts. "Mercy's Inheritance", "Resurvey on Content",
                "This or None" containing 100 a.
Daus: Mercey Buxton, Priscilla Ward, Susanna
Son: John Soaper and his children
Granddau: Priscilla Browning
Ex: Samuel Soaper
Wit: Charles Mackelfresh, Asa Hyatt, Christopher Zeigler

SOAPER, JOHN   L G f   3   20 Oct 1809
                                          L 2 p 229   12 Dec 1809

Wife: Ruth Soaper
2 children: Nelson B. Soaper, Mary Ann Soaper - land in Ohio Co., Kentucky
Ex: Samuel Soaper
Wit: Samuel Browning, Nathan Browning, Samuel Hobbs

SOLLARS, ROBERT   L E f   5   22 Sep 1802
                                          L 1 p 520   23 Nov 1802

Wife: Ann Sollars - land where John Hambleton lived, house and lot in
                Barnesville bought from Leonard Hays
Ex: Wife Ann

Wit: William Bennett, Daniel Jarrett, John C. Mackubin

SOPER, CHARLES, Sr., planter   L C f 317   19 Nov 1794
                                       L 1 p 366   11 Mar 1797
Wife: Sarah
Son: Barton Soper
Children: (not named)
Ex: Wife Sarah
Wit: William Holmes, Zachariah Downs, Thomas Cross

SOPER, NATHAN   L N f 290   2 Aug 1822
                                       L 3 p 186   14 Nov 1822
Wife: Ann Soper - house and lot in Darnes Town
Sister: Amelia Langford
States he has no children
Ex: Wife Ann
Wit: William Darne, James Hawkins, Robert Soper

SPARROW, JONATHAN   L F f   1   22 Nov 1806
                                       L 2 p 102   9 Feb 1807
Children: Sollomon, Fardonando, William, Thomas, Priscilla and Charlotta
           Sparrow
John Read Free, a boy who now lives with testator
Ex: Friend, Alexander Adams
Wit: Ozias Offutt, Benjamin Sedgwick

SPARROW, THOMAS   L B f 451   20 Feb 1792
                                                        21 Mar 1792
Wife: Ann
Children: Margaret Bawlding, Thomas, Ann, Aquilla Sparrow
Exs: ⁀Wife and George H. Offutt
Wit: John Dent, James Fleming, Jonathan Sparrow

SPENCER, ELIZABETH   L E f 13   25 Mar 1803
                                       L 1 p 541   28 Apr 1803
Nieces: Ann Ward, Maryann Ward
Sister: Ann Wimsett
Father: Joseph Ward, dec'd.
John Burke
Ex: John Burke
Wit: Levi Veirs, Elijah Veirs

SPRIGG, ELIZABETH   L G f 402   17 Jan 1808
                                                       L 2 p 293   30 Dec 1811

Daus: Eleanor Stallings, Mary Lawman, Elizabeth Markham, Lucy McAtee
Granddau: Lucy Lawman
Sons: John Sprigg, Rezin Sprigg
Cousin: Clemment Pearce, dec'd.
Ex: Son John Sprigg
Wit: Bissett Weeks, Joshua Pearre, Leonard Wathen

SPRIGG, JAMES   L A f 47   2 Apr 1778
                                                       L 1 p 44   14 May 1778

Wife: Elizabeth
Oldest dau: Eleanora Sprigg
2nd dau: Mary Sprigg (minor) "weak and helpless"
Children: John, Rezin, Elizabeth, Lucy, Margaret
Ex: Wife Elizabeth
Wit: Frederick Sprigg, Richard Owens

STABLER, WILLIAM, Quaker   L E f 335   1 Dec 1805
                                                       L 2 p 89   31 May 1806

Wife: Deborah Stabler
Exs: Wife Deborah Stabler and Friends Caleb Bently and Roger Brooke
Wit: Gerard Brooke, Basil Brooke, Roger Brooke

STALLINGS, JOSEPH, Sr.   L C p 323   24 Mar 1791
                                                       L 1 p 378   10 Aug 1797

Wife: Elizabeth Stallings
Children: (not named)
Ex: Wife
Wit: Robert Beall, Zadok Bloyce

STONE, JOHN of Georgetown, Innkeeper   L D f 133   27 Jul 1798
                                                       L 1 p 413   16 Apr 1798

Estate to be equally divided among family by law
Ex: Wife and Dr. Charles Beatty
Wit: John T. Mason, Ignatius Nowton, Charles Tilley, Zachariah Tilley

STONER, JACOB, blacksmith   L B f 15   26 Oct 1780
                                                       L 1 p 88   6 Feb 1781

Wife: Margaret Stoner - dwelling plantation which is pt. of "Hunting Hills"
Ex: Wife Margaret
Wit: John Suter, James Hadley, James Moore of Arch.

STORY, HENRY (nunc.)   L C f 111   9 Aug 1792
                                              L 1 p 254   13 Mar 1793
Free slaves
Wit: Abraham Cox, Mary Palmore, Mary Cox

STRAUSE, HENRY of Washington Co.   L L f 113   6 Jan 1819
                                              L 3 p 38   7 Aug 1819
Sell all property in Washington Co.; if necessary part in Montgomery Co.
Wife: Christiana
Children: George, Henry, Eliza, Rebecca and youngest child Hiram (all under
     age 21) - land in Montgomery Co.
Ex: Wife Christiana
Wit: Otho Lawrence, O.H. Williams, A.M. Waugh
Codicil dated 26 Mar 1819
Exs: Wife Christiana and Matthew Murray
Wit: same as above

SUMMERS, DENT of Frederick Co., Md.   L G f   1   28 Sep 1802
                                              L 2 p 225   3 Dec 1809
Sons: Hosekeah, Paul, James, Zadock, John, Walter Dent Summers
Daus: Maryan Hardey, Sarah White, Margaret Hoskins
Exs: Sons Hosekeah and Zadock Summers
Wit: William Morsell, Philemon Griffith, William Morsell, Jr.

SUTER, JAMES   L I f 215   2 Nov 1815
                                              L 2 p 468   23 Dec 1815
Wife: (not named)
Daus: Mary Taylor, Elizabeth Christiman
2 sons: Nathan Suter, Alexander Suter
Ex: Friend, Adam Robb
Wit: Henry Harding, William Magrath, Adam Robb

SUTER, JOHN of Georgetown   L C f 178   14 Jul 1784
                                              L 1 p 316   23 Nov 1794
Wife: Sarah Suter - house and lot in Washington Square 5, N 12
Sons: Robert Suter (minor), Alexander Suter, John Suter, Jr.
Daus: Margret Suter; Volendar Smith, wife of Alexander Smith
"Earnhill" and pt. of "Pines" in Mont. Co. and land in Allegany Co. to be
     sold and money divided
Exs: Wife Sarah Suter and son John Suter
Wit: Thomas Beall of George, J. Thompson, Samuel Huff

SWANN, THOMAS TURNER   L B f 139   9 May 1783
                                             L 1 p 135   14 Jun 1783

Sister: Ann Swann
Wit: Daniel Veirs, William Veirs, Maddox Dyson

SWEARINGEN, THOMAS   L C f 147   31 Jul 1794
                                             L 1 p 296   15 Oct 1794

Wife: Mary Swearingen
Sons: John, Daniel, Obediah, Samuel, Van (minor), Hezekiah (minor), and
      Josiah (minor)Swearingen
Son: William Swearingen - land in Frederick Co. on Bennett Creek called
                           "Trouble Enough" conveyed to testator by Alex.
                           Beall
Daus: Eleanor Ferrell, wife of James Ferrell; Mary Willcoxson, wife of
      George Willcoxson; Ruth Burriss, wife of Charles Burriss; Elizabeth
      Willcoxson, wife of John Willcoxson
Ex: Son Elemelick Swearingen
Wit: Charles Beckwith, Michael Letton, Richard Allison

TALBOTT, JAMES   L D f 10   27 Nov 1797
                                             L 1 p 392   28 Dec 1797

Wife: (not named)
Children: (not named)
Father: Thomas Talbott
Sons: Wilson Talbott, Benjamin Talbott - minors to be reared by testator's
                                         father
Wit: Thomas Morton, George Norris, Thomas Talbott

TALBOTT, THOMAS   L G f 154   19 Jun 1810
                                             L 2 p 247   4 Sep 1810

Son: Benjamin Talbott - 52 a. "Ray's Adventure"
Sons: Thomas and Paul Talbott - remainder of land where testator lives and
                                that part where testator's son James Talbott
                                formerly lived
Daus: Elenor Norriss, Elizabeth Cowley, Rebecca Norriss, Sarah Talbott,
      Catherine Reid, Ann Cawood
Dau: Sarah - Lot N in Mt. Carmill, Mongahalia Co., Va.
Granddau: Ann Reid, dau. of Catherine Reid
Elenor Cawood (minor)
Exs: Sons Benjamin and Thomas Talbott
Wit: David Trundle, Henry Jones, James Trundle

TAYLOR, MARGARET of Georgetown   L A   f 287   9 Apr 1780
                                          L 1   p 72   26 May 1780

Rebecca Bayly (under age 16), dau. of William Bayly, Jr.
Dau: Teresa
Son: John Taylor
Benjamin Williams
Ex: Thomas Beall, son of George Beall
Wit: Lucy Orme, Richard Thompson, James Orme

TAYLOR, WALTER   L B   f 236   24 Jan 1786
                                          L 1   p 215   6 Mar 1786

Wife: Mary Taylor
2 daus. by former wife
Son: Henry Taylor
William Cohaghan
Susannah Newell
Wit: John Baker, Thomas Smithy

THOMAS, HEZEKIAH   L G   f 145   1 Jan 1810
                                          L 2   p 235   2 Jun 1810

Wife: (not named)
Daus: Elizabeth; Margarete Higgins, Wife of Joshua C. Higgins; Mary Riggs,
        wife of Reuben Riggs
Grandchildren: Emily Jane Higgins, George W. Higgins, Richard T. Higgins,
               Joshua Higgins
Exs: Sons-in-law Joshua C. Higgins and Reuben Riggs
Wit: John Burgess, Jasper Peddicoard, Ephraim Gaither of Wm.

THOMAS, RICHARD, Quaker   L E   f 340   28 Nov 1806
                                          L 2   p 100   15 Dec 1806

Sons: Richard Thomas, Jr. and William Thomas
Grandchildren: Samuel Thomas, Jr., John Thomas 3rd, Sarah Thomas, Henryetta
               Thomas, Elizabeth Thomas, Mary Howard, children of dec'd.
               son Samuel Thomas
Dau: Elizabeth Johnson
Grandchildren: Thomas and Sarah Robertson, children of dau. Mary Robertson
Grandchildren: Sarah, Elizabeth, Ann, Thomas, Samuel, Hannah and Lidia
               Gilpin, children of dec'd. dau. Sarah Gilpin
Grandchildren: Richard Brooke, John Thomas Brooke, Elizabeth Brooke,
               children of dec'd. dau. Margaret Brooke
Exs: Sons Richard Thomas, Jr. and William Thomas
Wit: John Thomas, Joseph P. Plummer, John Sullivan

THOMAS, SAMUEL   L B f 135   28 Jan 1780
                                            L 1 p 131   14 Oct 1783

Son: Evan Thomas
Ex: Son Evan
Wit: Jeremiah Orme, Richard Jones, Elizabeth Culver

THOMESON, CHANEY   L A f 152   20 Mar 1779
                                            L 1 p 52   25 Mar 1779

Dau: Elizabeth Thomeson - to be in care of Mr. Edward Smoote until age 16
Brothers: John Hilton, James Hilton, Jonothan Hilton
Sister: Cloe Hilton
Father and Mother: (not named)
Brethern: Jane Willson, John Willson, Jonathan Willson, Thomas Willson,
           Samuel Willson, Dorothey Willson, Cloe Hilton
Ex: Father John Hilton, Sr.

THOMPSON, AGNESS   L D f   9   24 Oct 1797
                                            L 1 p 393   20 Dec 1797

Sons: John Thompson, James Thompson
Dau: Rebecca Fling
Ex: Son John Thompson
Wit: John Fenwick, Joseph Smalwood

THOMPSON, ZACHARIAH, Sr.   L N f 466   24 May 1823
                                            L 3 p 241   23 Feb 1824

Daus: Harriott Thompson, Cordelisa Thompson - 150 a. "Hutchcraft's Range"
                                       including dwelling house
Son: Evan Thompson - remainder of "Hutchcraft's Range", lot in Damascus
                      adjoining lot where he now lives
Son: Zachariah Thompson, Jr. - 135 3/4 a. pts. of "Hope Improved", "Raye's
                      Adventure" and "Trouble Enoug"; lot in
                      Damascus
Dau: Elizabeth Winsor
Grandchildren: Zachariah Thompson Winsor, George Washington Winsor, Elenor
                Ann Winsor, Lozanser Baten Winsor, children of Elizabeth
                Winsor (all under age 21)
3 grandchildren: children of dau. Amelia Anderson
Ex: Son Evan Thompson
Wit: Henry Griffith of L, Middleton Davis, Edward Burgess

THRASHER, WILLIAM, planter   L D f 439   1795
                                            L 1 p 467   22 Jan 1801

Wife: Margaret
Dau: Mary Tracy, wife of Philip Tracy

134

NEPHEW: Thomas James, son of Daniel James
Children: John, William, Elizabeth, Sarah and Margaret Thrasher
Ex: Wife Margaret
Wit: Benjamin Gittings, Daniel Lee, Josiah Beans

THRELKELD, HENRY of Frederick Co.   L B f 81   23 Feb 1764
                                    L 1 p 116   23 Jun 1782

This will annuls the one made before his marriage
Wife: Mary
Son: John Threlkeld (minor)
Brother: Thomas Threlkeld
Uncle: Henry Daken
Sister: Susannah Hewetson and her children
Ex: John Threlkeld
Wit: Elizabeth Tarvin, John Tarvin, Martha Russell

THRELKELD, JOSEPH, V.D.M. of Prince Georges Co. L B f 119   6 May 1769
                                                 L 1 p 126   29 Apr 1783

Wife: Jane
Dau: Sarah, born Aug. 23, 1768
Ex: Wife Jane
Wit: Robert Bradly, Robert Whitaker, William White

THUILLAIR, JOHN   L B f 417   14 Mar 1790
                                                 13 Apr 1790

Children of brother Charles Thuillair, Blegier in Picardee
Children of brother-in-law John Baptist Veauxblead, merchant in Picardee
                                                                in France
Exs: William Hickman and Peter Bowie
Wit: Thomas B. Beall, William Rayman, John B. Pearce

TIPIT, ELEANOR (indexed Trippett)   L E f 132   9 Jan 1805
                                     L 2 p 59   13 May 1805

Daus: Eleanor Tipit; Mary Herbert, wife of James Herbert; Margaret Herbert,
      wife of Elisha Herbert; Ann Madden, wife of John Madden; Kasiah
      Newman, wife of William Newman; Mary Magdaline Tipit, wife of Nelson
      Tipit
Sons: John Tipit, Joseph Tipit
Ex: Dau. Eleanor Tipit
Wit: Edward Willett, Sr., William Willson

TOMLINSON, HENRY   L O f 158   12 Jan 1825
                                     L 3 p 269   29 Mar 1825

Land to be sold

Wife: (not named)
Children: (not named)
Exs: Antony Taylor in Bucks Co., Pa.; Otho Magruder in Mont. Co., Md.
Wit: William Talbott, Lloyd Magruder, Thomas S. Watkins

TOPPING, JAMES L B f 325 29 Oct 1786
 L 1 p 230 3 Nov 1787

Wife: Margaret Leadsom Topping, dec'd.
Dau: Judith Leadsom, commonly called Judith Topping, dau. of Margaret
 Leadsom and James Topping
Ex: Judith Topping
Wit: Francis Clements, Micheal Cookendorfer, Hannah Cookendorfer
Codicil dated 19 Sep 1787
Friend: Dr. John Parham, son of Dr. Frederick Parham of Charles Co., Md.
Wit: William Digges, Micheal Cookendorfer

TRAIL, ANN L F f 192 28 Dec 1807
 L 2 p 147 23 Apr 1808

States she made this will shortly after her marriage with her present husband
Husband: William Trail
Dau: Esther Trundle - guardianship of 3 youngest daus.
Sons: Aeneas Belt who "does not appear at all times to be of sound mind",
 Alfred Belt, Tilghman Belt, Lloyd Belt
3 youngest daus: Ann Campbell Belt, Elizabeth Belt, Henne Ann Campbell Belt
Children: Lloyd Belt, Esther Trundle, Ann Campbell Belt, Elizabeth Belt,
 Henne Ann Campbell Belt - 54 a. where testator lives
"Now pregnant" but supposes "from my infirm state that I shall not be
 delivered"
Exs: Son-in-law Daniel Trundle and son Alfred Belt
Wit: William Hempstone, Thomas Veatch, Sr., John Young

TRAIL, DAVID, Sr. of Frederick Co., planter L B f 64 5 Mar 1775
 L 1 p 106 10 Dec 1781

Wife: Margaret
Son: David Trail - "Locust Thickett" in Frederick Co.
Son: Basil Trail - "Roses Delight" in Frederick Co. and "Younger Brother"
Daus: Massa, Cassandra, Darkus
Ex: Son David
Wit: John Hilleary, Joseph West, Sr., Abraham Holland

TRAIL, JAMES L D f 138 11 Mar 1783
 L 1 p 420 18 Mar 1798

Wife: Rachel
Son: James Trail - 126 3/4 a. "Resurvey on Younger Brother" where he now
 lives

Son: Archibald Trail - 60 a. "Back Head" where testator now dwells,16 3/4 a.
"Pleasant Fields" purchased from William Benson,
27 1/4 a. "Resurvey on Younger Brother", 23 a. pt.
of "Trail's Addition"
Son: Ozbern Trail - 100 a. pt. of "Father's Good Will", 27 a. pt. of
"Trail's Addition"
Dau-in-law: Frances Trail, widow - 100 a. of "Father's Good Will" where
she now dwells
Grandchildren: James Trail, William Trail, Edward Trail, Nathan Trail -
above land at her decease or remarriage
Daus: Eloner Lee, Jean West, Sarah Buckston, Cassandra Ford, Rachel Cybert,
Margary Fryer
Exs: Wife Rachel and son James
Wit: Edward Burgess, Lodwick Yost, Basil Trail

TRAILE, JAMES, Sr.   L N f 314   6 Feb 1823
                                      L 3 p 218   8 Apr 1823

Wife: Mary Ann Traile
Daus: Eloner Buxton, Mary Ann Buxton, Rachel Ricketts, Julyl meriah
Ricketts, Susaner Basel, Frances Ricketts
Sons: Ashford Traile, Nathan Traile, James Traile, Edward Northcraft Traile,
Notly Traile
Ex: Son Edward
Wit: Benjamin Gray, James E. Jones, Zadoc M. Cooke, Nathan Cooke

TRUNDLE, RUTH   L G f 149   3 Feb 1810
                                      L 2 p 240   7 Jun 1810

Husband: deceased
Granddau: Drusilla Lewis Trundle Wilcoxon (minor), dau. of Levi Wilcoxon
and Letha Wilcoxon, dec'd.
8 children: David Trundle, John Trundle, Daniel Trundle, James Trundle, Otho,
Hezekiah Trundle (minor), Charlotte Belt, Elenor Jones
Ex: Son David Trundle
Wit: Hezekiah Veatch, Hezekiah Wilson, Joseph G.W. Jones

TRUNDLE, THOMAS, Sr.   L C f   7   18 Jul 1791
                                      L 1 p 246   11 Sep 1792

Wife: Hannah Trundle
Daus: Hannah Barnes, Rachel Trundle, Ameli Wilson
Son: Thomas Trundle (unmarried)
Ex: Wife Hannah
Wit: Zadock Harris, James Shaw, Charles Selby

TRUNDLE, THOMAS   L C f 150   8 Oct 1793
                                      L 1 p 305   9 Feb 1795

Wife: Rechell Trundle

137

Sons: Basiel, Thomas, Daniel
Son: Evan - "Trundle's Inheritance" to be sold to purchase better land
Daus: Massey Trundle, Rechell Trundle, Delilah Trundle
Exs: Wife Rechell and son Basiel
Wit: Aeneas Campbell, N. Stone, Samuel Edwards

TURNER, SAMUEL	L F f 445	18 Dec 1807
	L 2 p 203	22 Mar 1809

Granddaus: Elizabeth Turner Magruder, Nancy Turner Magruder
Children: Thomas Turner, Samuel Turner, Arie Anna Turner
Grandchildren: children of dau. Sarah Magruder
Exs: Thomas Turner and Samuel Turner
Wit: Dennis Lackland, Bennett Clements, Richard Wootton

UPTON, GEORGE	L H f 17	13 Feb 1812
	L 2 p 317	29 May 1812

Wife: Elizabeth Upton
Sons: Filmon Upton, Darcy Upton, George Upton
"All my children"
Exs: Wife Elizabeth Upton and son Filmon Upton
Wit: Richard Nixon, Thomas Cecil

UPTON, TILGHMAN	L I f 195	1 Mar 1815
	L 2 p 424	29 Apr 1815

Brothers: Theador Upton, George Upton - "Half our Work", 1/2 "The Farm",
          pt. "Resurvey on the Farm"
Sisters: Leah Upton, Ann, Jimminor
Exs: Walter Prather and Theador Upton
Wit: Walter Prather, Richard Speaks, Richard Cecil

VEATCH, NINIAN	L D f 17	10 May 1785
	L 1 p 400	5 May 1798

Sons: John Veatch, Solomon Veatch
Dau: Jemima Fraim Veatch
Exs: Sons John and Solomon
Wit: Nathan Veatch, Hezekiah Wilson, William Draper

VEATCH, SILAS	L E f 335	30 Oct 1800
	L 2 p 87	11 Jun 1806

Son: Orlando Veatch - all property
Wife: Elizabeth Veatch
Daus: Kesiah, Susannah
"All of my children ... now reside out of the State of Maryland, some living
  in Kentucky and some on the northwest side of the Ohio..."

Trustee: Friend, Hezekiah Veatch
Wit: Hendery Allison, Thomas Fletchall, John Fletchall

VEATCH, THOMAS, Sr.   L L   f 120   3 Aug 1819
                                 L 3   p 56   31 Aug 1819

Wife: deceased
Mrs. Lucy Rigney
Sons: Hanson Veatch, Thomas Veatch, Elijah Veatch of North Carolina
Daus: Barsheba Wilson, Mary Trundle
Grandchildren: Elizabeth Ann Veatch, Ann Jenkins Veatch, Alexander Contee
               Hanson Veatch
Son: John T. Veatch - guardian of grandchildren
Ex: Friend, Leonard Watkins
Wit: G.W. Harwood, John Beard, Otho Trundle
Codicil dated 19 Aug 1819
Revokes appointment of Leonard Watkins as ex. and names son-in-law John L.
    Trundle
Wit: John Harwood, Otho Trundle, Henry Harwood

VEIRS, DANIEL   L B   f 226   23 Apr 1787
                                L 1   p 200   9 Jun 1787

Sons: John Veirs; Elisha Veirs; Nathan Veirs (under age 21)
Daus: Mary, Sarah, Ruth
Ex: Son John
Wit: William Veirs, Daniel Whelan, Elijah Veirs

VEIRS, WILLIAM   L G   f 391   25 Jun 1811
                                L 2   p 280   7 Nov 1811

Wife: Mary - 262 a. dwelling plantation including pt. "William and Mary and
       Daniel's Inheritance" and other tracts
Sons: Levi Veirs, John Mason Veirs - above plantation at mother's decease
Son: Hezekiah Veirs - 140 a. plantation where he now lives adj. John Dyson's
Son: Solomon Veirs - 136 1/4 a. plantation where he now lives
Son: Elijah Veirs - 116 a. including residence where he now lives, where
                Archibald Mullican formerly lived
Son: William
Grandchildren: Dau. Dorothy Hanly's Dyson children for their mother's part;
               children of dau. Pheby Thomas for their mother's part;
               William, son of dau. Nancy Clarke; Polly, dau. of son Edward
               Veirs; Daniel, son of Solomon Veirs; Mary, dau. of son
               William Veirs
Son: Edward - negro he "carried with him to KenTucky"
Daus: Nancy Clarke, Dorcas Fletchall
Ex: Son Levi Veirs
Wit: Lawrence Allnutt, William Vinson, James Allnutt

WADE, ABIGEL   L H f 16   3 Dec 1808
                                                      L 2 p 356   17 Sep 1813

Sons: William Wade, Jessee Wade, John Wade, James Wade
Dau: Ann Wade
Ex: Son James Wade
Wit: Kinsey Gittings, Norman West

WALLACE, JAMES   L O f 165   7 Aug 1824
                                                      L 3 p 283   28 Jan 1825

Son: James - 100 a. of testator's dwelling plantation which testator's
              father James Wallace of Wm. purchased and 250 a. adjoining
              land of testator's dec'd. brother William Wallace; 4 a. of
              island in Potomac called "Fishmarket"
Son: William - 100 a. of above land if he "be restored to his reason" and
              be capable of handling his own affairs
Dau: Mary - 100 a. adjoining her brother's
Dau: Elizabeth - 70 a. remaining land as far as the public road
Dau: Eleanor Young - 40 a. on other side of public road; William's 100 a.
              at his decease
Grandchildren: Solon Young, Mary Young, Kitty Ann Anderson, Elizabeth
              Anderson, Eleanor P. Anderson
Ex: Son James
Wit: James W. Anderson, Charles Wallace, John Wallace

WALLACE, WILLIAM   L E f 332   17 Jan 1806
                                                      L 2 p 80   2 Mar 1806

Dau: Eleanor Wallace - property
Children: William Wallace, James Wallace, Charles Wallace, Robert Wallace,
          John Wallace, Mary Anderson, Ann Anderson, Eleanor Wallace
Granchildren: Fanny Wallace, dau. of son Alexander Wallace; William M.
          Wallace, son of Alexander Wallace
Wit: Walter Greenfield, Basil Greenfield, James Wallace

WALLICK, CHRISTIAN   L I f 449   7 Jun 1816
                                                      L 2 p 505   26 Jun 1816

Wife: Ann Wallick, now pregnant
Dau: Mary, 9 mos. old
Exs: Wife Ann Wallick and Henry Winsor
Wit: James Hawkins, Eden Edmonston, John Shaw

WALTER, GEORGE, planter   L B f 199   16 Mar 1785
                                                      L 1 p 169   12 Apr 1785

Daus: Elizabeth, Sarah, Rebecca, Ann (minor)
Son: Thomas

Nephew: Hepzibah
Ex. and guardian to children: Brother David Walter
Wit: William Hickman, Mark Elliott, William Chaney

WARD, EDWARD   L M f 131   16 Jul 1819
                                              L 3 p 92   21 Mar 1820

Granddaus: Matilda, Sarah, Pollyann, Milla, daus. of dau. Milla Poole -
             3 3/4 a. pt. of "Ward's Inheritance"
Son: Asa Ward (now 4 yrs. past age 21) - 126 3/4 a. lands conveyed testator
       by William Cecill and Henry Poole being pts. of "Resurvey on
       "Wildcat Spring", "Chance" and "Widow's Purchase"
Sons: Esra and Asa - 354 1/2 a. pts. of "Ward's Inheritance" and "The
         Principal"; Esra to get the pt. where he now lives;
         Asa to get the pt. where testator lives
Sons: Amos Ward, John Ward
Grandchildren: Silas Ward and Sarah Moran Ward, children of son Robert Ward
Daus: Sarah Layton, Casander Winemiller
Exs: Son Asa Ward and son-in-law Ashur Layton
Wit: Basil Soaper, Sr., Christopher Ziegler, Basil Soaper, Jr., Samuel Soaper

WARD, JOSEPH   L B f 22   18 Aug 1780
                                              L 1 p 91   19 Feb 1781

Wife: Anne Mary Ward
Daus: Elizabeth, wife of William Spencer; Ann Ward; Mary Ann
Sons: Benjamin Ward, Joseph Ward, John Ward
Ex: Wife Anne Mary Ward
Wit: Aeneas Campbell, Patrick Aughterbony, Bennet Greenwell, Jonathan
     Goldsburry

WARD, ROBERT   L G f 387   22 Aug 1811
                                              L 2 p 275   2 Sep 1811

Wife: Sarah Ward - lands and dwellings
Son: Silas Ward
Dau: Sarah Ward
Exs: Wife Sarah Ward and Ashford Laton
Wit: Isaac Riley, Philip Edelen, Richard Hoggins, Jr.

WARD, SARAH B.   L L f 83   11 May 1818
                                              L 3 p 84   11 Jun 1818

Dau: Sarah Moran Ward - 1/2 lands to include dwelling plantation
Son: Silas Ward - other 1/2 of land
Brothers: Andrew Moran, Zachariah Moran
Ex: Brother Zachariah Moran
Wit: Henry Fister, Jr., Samuel Soaper, John Evey

WARFIELD, JOHN WORTHINGTON   L G f 233   14 Dec 1802
                                    L 2 p 261   11 Mar 1811

Wife: Mary Warfield - "Mount Airy" where testator lives
Son: Arnold Warfield - "Warfield's Vine Yard"
Son: Alexander Warfield - pts. "Mitchel's Range","Gravelly Hill" and "The
                        Gap Filled Up"; "Mount Airy" at wife's decease
Daus: Arra Cooper if she does not marry again, Nancy Stevens, Sarah Day
Exs: Sons Arnold and Alexander
Wit: Upton Beall, Solomon Holland, Thomas P. Willson, Charles Willson

WARMAN, STEPHEN   L D f 297   26 Apr 1799
                                    L 1 p 442   14 Aug 1799

Son-in-law: John Vinson - 100 a. "Hickery Hills" in Arnurland Co. (Anne
                        Arundel Co.), Md.; 1200 a. in Cantuckey called
                        Military lands; lands in Virginia
Son: Thomas Warman, dec'd.
Ex: John Vinson
Wit: Zadock Magruder, Jr., John M. Read, William Vinson

WARREN, GEORGE, planter   L B f   5   21 Jan 1780
                                    L 1 p 79   17 Oct 1780

Wife: Mary
Sons: Thomas, John, George
Daus: Mary, Ally (both unmarried)
Ann Thompson
Mary Queen
Exs: Wife Mary and son John
Wit: John Dowden, Peter Hoggins, Ninian Clagett

WATERS, BENJAMIN   L O f 153   16 Nov 1822
                                    L 3 p 256   15 Feb 1825

Wife: Hannah Waters - dwelling and other houses where testator now lives
                    which is pt. of "Beall's Manor"
Children: Polly Edmonston, Benjamin Waters, Freeborn Garretson Waters,
          Nancy Allison, Aqualina Perry - remainder of testator's pt. of
                    "Beall's Manor"
Dau: Lucretia Edmonston, wife of Eden Edmonston - 300 a. "Cowpasture" nr.
          Clarksburg which they now rent
Son: Benjamin Waters - land in Prince Georges Co. which testator inherited
                    from his sister Charity Waters; remainder of land in
                    Prince Georges Co. after claim of William Waters' hrs.
Grandchildren: Nancy Waters Brown, Jamima Magruder Perry, Elias Waters Perry,
          Perry Andrew Lycurgus Bussard, Milton Mortimer Bussard
Sell pts. of "Snowden's Manor Enlarged", "Browning's Folly" and lot purchased
    from Daniel Bussard adj. the Female Lancaster Schoolhouse in Georgetown, D.C.
"Unfortunate sister" - Rachel Donaldson

Ex: Benjamin Waters
Wit: B. Gilpin, George L. Lackland, Somerset R. Waters

WATERS, ELIZABETH   L I f 433   24 Dec 1814
                                            L 2 p 474   30 Jun 1815

Step-son: Horace Waters - Lot #2 square 83 in Washington, D.C. (formerly
            "Hamburgh")now in the name of Henry Hilleary, Jr.
Wit: Basil Waters, Baker Waters, Zachariah Waters

WATERS, HANNAH, wife of Benjamin   L P f 315   29 Jan 1825
                                             L 3 p 416   19 Aug 1825

Children of testator's husband: Benjamin Waters, Jr. of Alexandria; Freeborn
                                G. Waters of Baltimore; Ann Allison of Richmond, Va.
Hannah Ann Edmonston, dau. of Eden Edmonston and granddau. of Benjamin Waters
Husband: Benjamin
Exs: Benjamin Waters, Jr. and Freeborn G. Waters
Wit: Abraham Dennis, Thomas Hill, Burgess Culver, Andrew Brown, Eli H. Duvall

WATERS, JAMES   L I f 198   18 Jul 1813
                                             L 2 p 430   27 May 1815

Nephew and nieces: Joshua Hickman, Jr., Margaret W. Strider and Mary Hickman
                    - 55 a. pt. of "Forrest"
Brother: Hendry Allison
Nephews: Alpheus Allison, Hendry Allison, Jr., James Allison
Ex: Joshua Hickman, Jr.
Wit: G.W. Harwood, William Burns, James Trundle

WATERS, JOSEPH, Sr.   L M f 129   30 Dec 1819
                                             L 3 p 89   18 Jan 1820

Son: Adamson Waters - 110 a. dwelling plantation
Son: Azel Waters - 105 a. of land
Grandchildren: Hrs. of son Joseph Waters, Jr. and his wife Mary Waters -
                106 a. land after decease of Joseph, Jr.
Granddau: Deborah Shank
Daus: Rosetta Holland, Casander Waters, Mary Holland
John Barns
Ex: Son Adamson Waters and William Holland
Wit: Greenberry Howard, Greenberry Griffith, Henry Winsor

WATERS, MARY   L C f 112   17 Mar 1792
                                             L 1 p 259   11 Jun 1793

Son: Ignatius Waters
Dau: Elleanor Waters

Wit: Samuel White, Nathan Holland, Isaac Smith

WATERS, RICHARD	L G f 144	20 Feb 1805
	L 2 p 232	26 May 1810

Wife: Margaret Waters - dwelling house and 132 a. land
Daus: Ann S. Waters (under age 16) and Betsy Belt
Sons: Richard R. Waters, Somerset Waters, Nacy Waters (all under age 21)
Ex: Wife Margaret Waters
Wit: Betsy Plummer, Lucetta Dorsey

WATERS, RICHARD, Sr.	L C f 317	23 Dec 1794
	L 1 p 367	10 Apr 1797

Son: Nacy Waters - "Back Pond" on Seneca Creek
Son: Richard Waters - 400 a. dwelling plantation; "Lucky Range" nr. Luke's Cabbin Branch
Granddaus: Amelia, Anna, Katy, children of son Azel Waters, dec'd. - 60 a. "Timber Creek" on Ten Mile Creek
Granddau: Rosetta, dau. of dau. Deborah
Dau: Betsy Plummer - 20 a. pt. of "Waters's Conclusion" next to "Gartrell's Good Will"
Dau: Deborah
Children of son Joseph Waters, dec'd.
Ex: Son Nacy Waters
Wit: John Belt, John Chambers, Thomas Knott

WATERS, SAMUEL	L B f 1	13 Apr 1780
	L 1 p 75	10 Oct 1780

Son: Josephas Burton Waters - "Waters Luck" where James Fosset now lives, surveying instruments
Son: Plummer Waters
Grandson: Thomas Waters, son of Plummer Waters - pt. of "Maiden's Fancy"
Dau: Cresay Waters - pt. of "Maiden's Fancy"
Daus: Mary Williams, Sarah Waters, Susannah Waters, Rebekah Waters (minor), Artridge Waters (minor), Ann, Elizabeth Cheney
Testator's father John Waters gave pt. "Water's Purchase" to testator's sister Elizabeth Waters
Exs: Son Josephas Burton Waters and dau. Cresay Waters
Wit: Thomas Beall, Jacob Aldridge, Benjamin Owens, Jr., John Aldridge

WATERS, THOMAS	L I f 436	7 Apr 1809
	L 2 p 478	2 Jan 1816

Nephew: Thomas Waters, son of Plummer Waters - 580 a. "Waters' Purchase", 150 a. of which was bought from hrs. of Samuel Waters, dec'd.; 40 a. "Waters' Lott"
Ex: Nephew Thomas Waters, son of Plummer Waters
Wit: Henry Dever, John Wilson, William Burton, Richard Waters

WATERS, WILLIAM   L 0 f 159   3 Nov 1820
                                          L 3 p 272   9 Apr 1825

Nephew: Thomas Waters, son of Plummer - 100 a. plantation where testator
             formerly lived which is pt. of "Maiden's Fancy"
             partially in Prince Georges Co. and partially in
             Montgomery Co.; 39 3/4 a. "William Waters' Lot" in
             Prince Georges Co. adjoining "Maiden's Fancy"
Ex: Nephew Thomas Waters
Wit: Benjamin Roby, John Wilson, Michael Murphey

WATERS, WILLIAM, Sr., planter   L B f 222   30 Jan 1788
                                          L 1 p 193   13 Mar 1788

Wife: Mary Waters
Eldest son: Zachariah Waters
2nd son: William Waters
3rd son: Basel Waters - "Conclution", "Maiden's Bower" and "Panthers Range"
Daus: Sarah Holland, Anna Waters, Nancey White
Dau: Elloner Waters - 75 a. dwelling plantation
Son: Ignatius Waters - dwelling plantation, "Charles and Benjamin",
             "Edmonston's Refuse", "Honesty the Best Policy",
             "James Brooke's Reserve", "Magruder's Court"
             totaling about 800 a.
Sell "Chance" and "What You Will" on Seneca
Exs: Wife Mary and son Zachariah
Wit: Charles Warfield, Roger Brooke, Samuel Riggs

WATERS, ZACHARIAH   L 0 f 169   3 Jul 1819
                                          L 3 p 290   16 Mar 1825

Wife: Anna Waters
Son: Baker Waters - pt. "Conclusion" conveyed to testator by his father,
             including dwelling house; pt. "First Bit Enlarged"
Son: Tilghman Waters - pts. "First Bit Enlarged", "Waters Prospect",
             "Addition to Waters Prospect", "Conclusion",
             "Resurvey on Richard's Fancy", "William and Mary"
             including mills
Dau: Courtney Waters - 500 a. in Randolph Co., Va.
Ex: Son Baker Waters
Wit: William Willson of John, Thomas Anderson, Jonathan W. Magruder

WATHAN, LEONARD   L B f 75   23 Aug 1782
                                          L 1 p 110   18 May 1782

Wife: Ann - dwelling plantation
Sons: Barton, Gabriel, Henry, Willfred and Benedict Wathan
Daus: Monica Wathan, Ann Statia Wathan
Exs: Wife Ann and sons Barton and Gabriel
Wit: Walter Karrick, Zachariah Knott, Jane Knott

WATTERS, GODFREY L G f 396   24 Aug 1811
                  L 2 p 285   12 Nov 1811

Sell all of estate
Mary Beall - 1/4 provided she continues to live with me; also, use of house,
    firewood and cows, etc. until sold
Basil Watters - 1/4 part
Sarah Hariman and Mary Watters, daus. of Walter Watters - 1/4 part
Trustees of Methodist Chartered Fund in Philadelphia for the use of the
    Methodist Society - 1/4 part
Ex: Zachariah Watters
Wit: Amon Riggs, Charles Miles, Samuel Soaper

WAYMAN, CHARLES   L E f 330   3 Jan 1805
                  L 2 p 56   25 Feb 1806

Sister: Dorcas Harriss
Nieces: Ann, Deborah and Mary Harriss, daus. of Dorcas Harriss
Wit: Jesse Harriss, Hezekiah Veatch

WELSH, BETSY   L D f 144   4 Dec 1795
                  L 1 p 428   Not probated

Nephew: Ephraim Davis - 160 a. plantation where testator now lives left by
            her mother; pt. of "Gaither's Meadow"
Nieces: Betsy Burgess, Jenny Burgess, Nancy Burgess, Peggy Burgess - land
            bought from testator's uncle, Edward Gaither
Nephew: Thomas Davis, son of brother Ephraim Davis, dec'd. - "Sapling Range"
Brother: Amos Davis, dec'd.
Nephews: Thomas Davis, Amos Davis (minors), sons of brother Amos Davis
Nephew: Thomas Griffith, son of sister Sarah Griffith
Ex: Thomas Davis, son of Ephraim Davis
Wit: Ephraim Gaither, Charles Alexander Warfield, Nathan Musgrove

WELSH, HAMUTAL   L I f 434   15 Nov 1811
                  L 2 p 475   18 Jul 1815

Grandchildren: Caroline Elenor Riggs (under age 16), Sarah H. Riggs and
                Samuel Riggs, children of Thomas Riggs
Grandson: John Hammond Riggs
Ex: Grandson John Hammond Riggs
Wit: Thomas Davis, John Bowie, James Dwyer
Codicil dated 15 Feb 1813
Wit: Thomas Davis, Elizabeth Davis

WEST, SAMUEL   L A f 43   13 Oct 1777
                  L 1 p 40   10 Feb 1778

Wife: Sarah
Sons: Richard, Samuel, William, Normond - land

Land on Seneca which Benjamin Holland rents may be sold
Exs: Wife Sarah and son Richard
Wit: Thomas Peak, James Jordan, Elender Peak

WHARTON, JESSE of St. Mary's Co.   L C f 268   20 Feb 1787
                                          L 1 p 352   21 May 1796

To be buried at Catholic Chaple nr. Mr. Edmund Plowden's
Wife: Ann Wharton
Son: Charles Henry Waring Wharton (under age 21)
In case of mother's decease, uncle Marsham Waring to be guardian of Charles
Wit: John White
Codicil dated 23 Feb 1788

WHEELER, ELIZABETH of Waterford, Loudoun L M f 479   31 Aug 1818
                   Co., Va., widow   L 3 p 140   14 Sep 1818

Cousins: Elen Powell, Fetney Powell, Dr. Charles Edwards
Friends: Henrietta Conn; Leanna Conn; Kezia Addams; Mary McCabe, wife of
         Dr. McCabe; Esther Addams, wife of Williams Addams; Ann Henry;
         Rev. Nicholas Willis
Methodist Society
Exs: Friends, Robert Braden and Henrietta Conn
Wit: W. Addams, A. Addams

WHELAN, REBEKAH (nunc.)   L C f 144   9 Jun 1793
                                          L 1 p 289   10 Jun 1794

Son: Otha - his aunt to take care of him until he comes of age
Wit: George Heyden, Robert Wilson

WHITE, BENJAMIN   L N f 114   9 Feb 1822
                                          L 3 p 166   15 Apr 1822

Wife: Rebecca White - land for life
Son: Stephen N. White - 175 a. "Wolf's Cow" and "Fertile Plains"
Son: William White - 100 a. "Hanover", 3 a. "Albany" where tanyard is
Son: Benjamin White - 100 a. "Wolf's Cow"
Son: Joseph White - pts. of "Albany", "Wolf's Cow" and "Liberty" where
                    testator lives
Dau: Elizabeth White - 50 a. "Wolf's Cow"
Dau: Anne Dawson, who lives in Kentucky
Exs: Sons Joseph White and Stephen N. White
Wit: Elijah Veirs, James M. Dawson, John Waters

WHITE, JOSEPH   L H f 29   15 Feb 1811
                                          L 2 p 332   13 Nov 1812

Wife: (not named)

147

Son: Thomas Clagett White
Dau: Harriot White - 1 a. purchased from George B. Magruder
Ex: Son Thomas Clagett White
Wit: James Wallace, Thomas M. Clagett, Thomas Clagett

WHITE, NATHAN SM.   L N f 315   11 Oct 1817
                     L 3 p 221   19 May 1823

Wife: Peggy White - dwelling plantation
2nd son: Nathan S. White
3rd son: Stephen White
Son: Benjamin White
Daus: Eleanor White, Sarah White
Ex: Son Nathan S. White
Wit: Anthony Livers, Richard Gott, Robert T. Dade

WHITE, SAMUEL   L D f 15   12 Dec 1797
                     L 1 p 398   1 Jan 1798

Rachel Liezear - to continue with family and manage for them
Samuel Beall White
Grandson: Samuel White (minor)
Joseph White Clagett, Samuel Beall White - guardians to grandson Samuel White
Ex: Samuel Beall White
Wit: Nathan Holland, Jeffrey Magruder, Jonathan Duley

WHITE, SAMUEL BEALL L B f 430   15 Mar 1790
                                  14 Dec 1790

Wife: Nancy White, possibly with child
Wife's brothers: Basil Waters and Ignatius Waters
Children of uncle Guy White
Ex: Basil Waters
Wit: Nathan Holland, Roger Brooke, Arnold Holland

WIGHTT, TRUMAN   L B f 66   23 Nov 1781
                     L 1 p 104   21 Dec 1781

Brother: Samuel Wheeler
Sister: Ann Wheeler
John Hanson Wheeler
Ex: Clement Wheeler
Wit: Clement Brooke, Thomas Shelton, Hendery Allison

WILCOXON, JESSE   L H f   5   16 Nov 1811
                     L 2 p 307   13 Mar 1812

Wife: Elizabeth - pt. of "Buck Lodge" where testator lives
Son: Jesse Wilcoxon

Son: Horatio Wilcoxon - land at wife's decease
Son: James E. Wilcoxon - pts. of "Woolf's Cow" and "Buck Lodge"
Son: William Wilcoxon - adjoining land
Son: Thomas Wilcoxon - pt. of "Dan" on east side of road from William
           Glaze's school house to Newport Mills
Daus: Deborah Magruder, Maryelenor Higgins, Ruth Wilcoxon, Ann P. Clagett
Exs: Wife Elizabeth Wilcoxon and son Horatio Wilcoxon
Wit: Nicholas Lowe Dawson, Brooks Jones, William Dawson

WILCOXON, WILLIAM   L E f 111   21 Sep 1803
                                          L 2 p 14   14 Feb 1804

Wife: Rebeckah
Sons: Josiah, Amos, Rezin
Daus: Elizabeth, Rachel, Ann
Ex: Wife Rebeckah
Wit: John Howse, John Chamber, Charles Davis

WILCOXON, WILLIAM, Sr.   L G f 235   6 Feb 1811
                                          L 2 p 264   3 Apr 1811

Benjamin Taylor, Sr.
William J. Johnson
Ex: William J. Johnson
Wit: Thomas Leatch, Sr., Hillery Williams, Hezekiah Veatch

WILLETT, ANN   L J f 22   1 Jun 1810
                                          L 2 p 373   9 Apr 1814

Sons: John Willett, Edward Willett, Robert White Willett, Burgess Willett,
      Oratio Willett
Daus: Ann Colley, Mary Willett, Caterine Jones, Sarah Leech
Granddaus: Ann Jones, Leah Leech
Grandsons: Robert Willett, son of Edward Willett; Gaylon Jones
Brother: James Fleming
Wit: Edward Willett, Sr., Jonathan Granger

WILLETT, WILLIAM   L B f 204   8 Feb 1785
                                          L 1 p 154   4 Apr 1785

Son: Edward Willett - 1/2 tracts "Scotland", "Addition to Scotland", pt.
       "Resurvey on Black Oak Thicket"
Six other children: (not named)
Exs: Brother Ninian Willett and son Edward Willett
Wit: Leonard Robinson, William T. Chambers, William Tracey

WILLIT, GRACE   L C f   5   21 Jul 1787
                                        L 1 p 244   15 Aug 1792

Son: John Litton's hrs.
Dau: Johanna Hall
Son: Michael Litton
Granddau: Elizabeth Richard, dau. of William Richard
Grandchildren: children of Michael Litton
Son-in-law: Benjamin Summers
Exs: Michael Litton and grandson John Litton Summers
Wit: James Beall, Richard Allesson

WILLIAMS, BARBARA   L B f 436   17 Jan 1791
                                                        16 Mar 1791

Son: Walter Caid Williams - 2 a. lot
Son: Thomas Owen Williams
Son: William Prather Williams - land on head of Captain Johns Branch of
                                 Potomac
Granddau: Sarah Clagett
4 daus: (not named)
Daus: Martha and Barbara Williams - estate bequeathed them by William
                                     Williams, dec'd.
Ex: Son Thomas Owen Williams
Wit: George Robertson, Archibald Beall, Samuel Beall

WILLIAMS, CHARLES   L B f 197   9 Sep 1785
                                        L 1 p 166   29 Sep 1785

Wife: Sarah
7 children: Clement Williams, John Williams, Sarah More, Lucy Gathrel,
             Elizabeth Hobs, Ann Selby, Mary Beall
Exs: Sons Clement Williams and John Williams
Wit: Valentine Myers, William Tomlinson, Evan Thomas

WILLIAMS, ELISHA O. of Georgetown,   L F f 326   11 Dec 1805
                     District of Columbia L 2 p 175   21 Jan 1806

Wife: (not named)
7 children: (not named - minors)
Exs: Leonard H. Johns, John K. Smith and wife (probate shows Harriet Williams)
Wit: Zachariah Williams, Helen Steuart, Leonard Mackall
Codicil dated 11 Dec 1805
Brother: Thomas O. Williams - 100 a. pt. of "Resurvey on Partnership"
                               devised testator by his father
Wit: Jeremiah Williams, Helen Steuart, Leonard Mackall
(Note: Will probated in Washington, D.C.)

WILLIAMS, ELIZABETH   L K f 223   17 Oct 1814
                                              L 2 p 521   19 Aug 1817

Sister: Jean Linthicome
Stepdaus: Elizabeth Magruder Simmons, Verlinda Thomas, Margaret Scott,
           Sarah Briggs
Jacob Williams Thomas
Stepson: Zachariah Williams, Sammuel Williams
Niece: Elizabeth Evans and her dau. Eliza Evans
Sarah Ann Magruder
Elizabeth Ann Williams
Elizabeth Ann Briggs
Ex: Abraham Simmons
Wit: Zachariah Muncaster, Samuel W. Simmons

WILLIAMS, JACOB   L E f 118   13 Dec 1802
                                              L 2 p 32   1 Sep 1804

Wife: Elizabeth Williams
Son: Zachariah Williams - "Williams' Range" and "Addition to Williams' Range"
Daus: Margaret Williams, Sarah Williams, Elizabeth Simmons, Verlinda Thomas
Son: Samuel Williams
Exs: Son Zachariah Williams and son-in-law Abraham Simmons
Wit: William Smith, John Linthicum, Thomas Linthicum

WILLIAMS, LEONARD   L L f 109   5 Jul 1819
                                              L 3 p 36   3 Aug 1819

Daus: Elizabeth Shaw, Casander Waters
Ann Williams - 20 a. "Bentons Lot" on road from Frederick to Georgetown
Walter Williams - remainder of land
Ex: Son Walter Williams
Wit: Thomas Anderson, Horace Willson, Samuel Le--er (probate shows Samuel
     Boyer)

WILLIAMS, WALTER   L N f 293   4 Nov 1822
                                              L 3 p 192   19 Nov 1822

Wife: Dorothy Williams - 160 a. "Spring Garden Resurveyed"
Son: James Williams (under age 21) - lot and house in Clarksburgh
Ex: Wife Dorothy
Wit: Horace Willson, William Bell, Adamson Waters

WILLIAMS, WILLIAM   L B f 225   25 Feb 1779
                                              L 1 p 198   14 Mar 1788

Wife: Verlenda - dwelling plantation
Son: William Williams - "Ned's Quarter", "All I Can Git", "The Meadow", and
                        land in Granville Co., S.C. on the Savannah River

151

Son: Amos Williams - dwelling plantation at decease of his mother
Dau: Eleanor Williams
Ex: Wife Verlenda
Wit: Joseph Wilson, Basil West, Coborn West

WILLIAMSON, ALEXANDER	L B f 323	22 Dec 1785
	L 1 p 228	28 Apr 1787

Nieces: Elizabeth Chesley, Mary Chesley, Ann Chesley and Rebecca who is married, all children of sister Elizabeth Chesley, whose husband is dec'd. - house and plantation
Dau: Mary L. Williamson
Nephews: Alexander Chesley, Thomas Chesley
Exs: Henry Townsend, Benjamin Stoddard, Thomas Johns
Wit: Samuel Davidson, R.W. Lingan, James Dunlope

WILLMORE, ZACHARIAH	L H f 10	15 Feb 1812
	L 2 p 309	9 Mar 1812

Wife: Sarah Willmore
4 children: Edward, Edwin, Mary Ann, Eliza
Ex: Wife Sarah
Wit: Burgess Culver, Erasmus Marlow

WILLSON, CHARITY	L I f 211	24 Sep 1808
	L 2 p 458	21 Nov 1815

Dau: Martha Willson - 100 a. land purchased from testator's son John Willson
Sons: William Willson, Samuel Willson
Daus: Susannah Magruder, wife of Enoch Magruder; Margarett Jones, wife of Benjamin W. Jones; Charity Magruder, wife of George B. Magruder
William Howard
Grandson: William Willson Magruder
Ex: Son Samuel Willson
Wit: Richard Parrott, Ninian Magruder, Nicholas Travers

WILLSON, JONATHAN	L E f 337	7 Mar 1797
	L 2 p 92	18 Oct 1806

Son: John Willson - "Willson's Inheritance" where testator lives
Grandsons: John Willson, James Willson - 570 a. in Bedford Co., Va. purchased by testator from Esther Kennedy, widow of John Kennedy. James has sold his share to John
Youngest grandson: Charles Willson (under age 21)
Youngest granddau: William-mina Willson (under age 16), dau. of John Willson
8 grandchildren: Perry, John, Thomas, James, William, Charles, Martha Magruder, William-mina
Ex: Son John Willson
Wit: Joseph Benton, Jr., Jonathan Cash, Samuel Simmons

WILLSON, MARGRET   L I f 209   24 Aug 1813
                                           L 2 p 453   17 Nov 1815

Niece: Mary Tillard Douglass Willson
Niece: Elizabeth Ricketts
Sisters: Elizabeth Mulloy, Agnas Prater, Uphon Clagett, Martha Ricketts,
         Jane Riggs
Brother: James Willson
Alexander Warfield
Ex: Brother Robert Willson
Wit: Joseph Poole, Benjamin Poole, Dennis Lackland

WILLSON, WILLIAM   L A f 16   10 Jun 1777
                                           L 1 p 14   21 Aug 1777

Wife: Elizabeth Willson - all land
Son: Hezekiah
Possible posthumous child
Children: (not named)
Ex: Wife Elizabeth
Wit: Thomas Warner, Hezekiah Veatch, Josiah Wilson

WILSON, GEORGE   L F f 508   22 Apr 1809
                                           L 2 p 215   18 Oct 1809

Sisters: Ann Willmore, Agnes Wilson - land in Prince Georges Co.
Eleanor Ryan
Sarah Wilson
Brother: Zedekiah Wilson
Sister Mary Ryan
Ex: George Riley
Wit: Barton Harriss, Edward Willett, John Blewer

WILSON, HENRY   L B f 43   Not dated
                                           L 1 p 98   12 Jun 1781

Wife: Vilender
Children: (not named)
Exs: Wife and son Zadock
Wit: Peter Becraft, John Lee, Sr., John Kisner

WILSON, JOSEPH   L B f 433   5 Nov 1790
                                                           8 Feb 1791

Dau: Sarah Wilson - land where testator now lives pt. of "Two Brothers" and
                    pt. of "Valentine's Garden"; also, Mrs. Rebecca Owens'
                    right of dower in pt. of "Discontent" and pt. of
                    "Advantage" which was conveyed to testator by said
                    Rebecca Owens

Dau: Ann Worthington - 300 a. pts. of "Joseph and James" and "Conclusion" Lots at Montgomery County Court House to be sold
Plantation in Virginia
Son-in-law: William Worthington
Dau: Mary Davis
Wit: James Anderson, William Williams, Benjamin Nicholls

WILSON, ROBERT, Sr.	L C f 144	13 Aug 1794
	L 1 p 290	24 Sep 1794

Daus: Margaret, Sarah, Jane, Martha, Elizabeth
Son: Robert
Exs: John Veirs, Sr., Caleb Darby
Wit: Townshend Dade, Richard Gott

WILSON, WADSWORTH	L E f 5	4 May 1799
	L 1 p 522	23 Dec 1802

Wife: Eleanor Wilson
Sons: Leven Wilson, James Wilson
Daus: Frances Shepherd, Mary Burns, Eleanor Shepherd
Grandsons: Wadsworth Wilson Shepherd; Wilson Burns; Wadsworth Wilson, son of James Wilson
Granddau: Eleanor Burns
Ex: Son Leven Wilson
Wit: Hugh S. Dunn, John Harwood, John Beard

WINSOR, THOMAS	L G f 143	21 Dec 1809
	L 2 p 230	10 May 1810

Wife: Catharine Winsor
Daus: Rebeccah Lewis, Mary Lewis, Ane Brown, Catharine Winsor, Amia Winsor, Sarah Winsor
Sons: Zadock Winsor, Robert Bedden Winsor, Arnold Thomas Winsor, Alexander Winsor, Henry Winsor
Ex: Arnold Thomas Winsor
Wit: William Willson of John, Charles Miles, Adamson Waters

WOOTTON, RICHARD	L K f 234	10 Jun 1816
	L 2 p 530	25 Nov 1817

Son: John Wootton - "Collington Plantation" in Prince Georges Co.
Son: Singleton Wootton - 610 a. in Frederick Co. purchased from John Worthington
Son: Richard Wootton - land where he now lives
Son: Turner Wootton - estate at decease of wife
Daus: Margaret Davis dec'd., Elizabeth Beall, Martha Wootton (under age 21) - land in Anne Arundel and Calvert Cos.
Niece: Frances Rebecca Davis

Wife: Martha Wootton - remainder of estate plus 8 a. purchased from Lewis
       Beall, dec'd.
Nephew: Samuel Beall
Wit: Augustus Taney, Otho Willson, Benjamin Curran

WOOTTON, THOMAS S.   L B f 410   11 Jan 1789
                                                        30 Nov 1789

Nephew: Turner Wootton - estate given testator by his brother Singleton
         Wootton in Prince Georges Co.
Niece: sister of Turner Wootton (not named)
James Anderson
Ex: Nephew Turner Wootton
Wit: Thomas Drane, Elizabeth Gittings, Zadock Magruder

WRIGHT, THOMAS   L D f 304   26 Mar 1800
                                      L 1 p 452   4 Apr 1800

Ninian Mockbee
Ex: Ninian Mockbee
Wit: William Waters, Basil Waters, Bennett Smith

YOST, JASPER of Georgetown   L A f 14   23 Jun 1777
                                      L 1 p 12   4 Aug 1777

Wife: Helena Chaterina
Sons: Philip (minor), Jasper, John, Henry
Daus: Anna Elizabeth, Margaret, Anna, Susannah
Exs: Son John Yost, sons-in-law Peter Miller and Frederick Wetzel
Wit: John Sail, John Gibhart, Theodosus Crouse

YOUNG, CHARLES in his 26th year of age L I f 33   31 Mar 1808
                                        L 2 p 391   12 Aug 1814

No children at this time
Wife: Eleanor Young - all lots in City of Washington
Father-in-law: James Wallace, Sr.
Brother-in-law: James Wallace, Jr.

YOUNG, JOHN, Sr.   L M f 135   29 Jul 1820
                                      L 3 p 98   22 Aug 1820

Daus: Rebecca Douglass, Eleanor Young, Sarah Cowley
Son: John Young, Jr. - farm where testator lives for 6 yrs.
Grandchildren: John Young Fish (minor); child of son Benjamin Young, dec'd.
Dau. Eleanor Young and granddau. Harriot B. Pack - house yard and garden
                                                   where testator lives
Ex: Son John Young, Jr.
Wit: Abraham Jones, Charles Willson, Aeneas Belt

INDEX TO TRACTS OF LAND

NOTE: In this index only one spelling has been used for each tract name. The text of the book shows the spelling as it appears in the original will.

Able's Levils	37
Accord	64,86
Adamson's Choice	47
Addition	52,65,67
Addition and Troublesome, Res. on	63
Addition to Brooke Discovery	20
Addition to Brooke Grove	53,71 96,114
Addition to Deer Park	44
Addition to Georgetown	7,17
Addition to Hensley	101
Addition to Magruder's Purchase	92
Addition to Magruder's Purchase, Res. on	92,93
Addition to Mill Seat	22
Addition to Moore's Rest	1
Addition to Mother's Delight	40
Addition to Promise Fulfilled	54
Addition to Ray's Adventure	109
Addition to Scotland	149
Addition to Turkey Thicket	91
Addition to Waters Prospect	145
Addition to William and James	103
Addition to Williams' Range	151
Additions to the Fork	65
Additions to Magruder's Purchase Res. of the	92
Advantage	153
Albany	147
Aldridge's Discovery	1
All I Can Git	151
Allison's Park	1
Allisson's Adventure	86
Amsterdam	38
An Hours Work	49
Andrew's Folly	3
Anns Garden	36
As Good As We Can Get	103
Back Head	137
Back Pond	143
Banks Venture	118
Barren Ridge	52
Barron Hill	102
Basil's Lot	61
Bassheba	65
Batchelor's Forrest	6,10,11,106
Batchelor's Forrest Enlarged	30

Batchelor's Forrest, Res. of	10
Batchelor's Purchase, Res. on	8
Beall, Thomas of George, Addition to Georgetown	7
Beall's Addition	128
Beall's and Magruder's Honesty	93
Beall's Contest	29
Beall's Goodwill	86
Beall's Manor	142
Bear Garden	45,110,124
Bear Garden Enlarged	110
Beary's Meadow	15
Beatty's Addition to Georgetown	73,91
Beattys and Hawkins Addition to Georgetown	120
Beaverdam Mill	114
Bedfordshire Carrier	48,75,90
Beggars Purchase	53
Beginning, Res. on the	49
Benjamin's Lott	52,53
Bentons Lot	151
Black Acre	52
Black George	8
Black Oak Thicket, Res. on	149
Boon's Good Luck	17
Bordley's Choice	120
Boyleston's Discovery	30
Brandy, Res. on	123
Brook Meadow	5
Brooke Black Meadow	20
Brooke Discovery, Add. to	20
Brooke Grove, Add. to	53,71,96,114
Brooke Park, Res. on	71
Brooke Piney Grove	113,114
Brooke's Addition	20,114
Brother's Content	114
Brother's Industry	12,34,72
Browning's Folly	22,142
Buck Lodge	149
Burgesses Look Out	53
Busey's Adventure	128
Buxton's Delight	123
Buxton's Delight, Res. on	100
Camels Choice	121
Carenot	52
Carrolinor	106
Chamberlains Desire	30

156

Chance	29,141,145
Charles and Benjamin	4,15,68
	69,91,145
Charles and John's Choice	36,125
Charles and Thomas, The	117
Charles and William	29,33,34
Charley Forest	113
Chelmsford	40
Chestnut Ridge	96
Chiswell's Lodge	31
Clagett's Folly	32
Clagetts Purchase	32,75,81,111
Clean Drinking Manor	75
Clean Gleanings	64
Clewerwall	101,103
Club's Delight	56
Collington Plantation	154
Collyar's Resurvey Corrected	35
Conclusion	4,79,145,154
Conjurer Out Done	127
Conjuror's Disappointment	7
Content	110
Content, Res. on	128
Cook's Choice	36
Cook's Range	36
Cool Spring Manner	63
Cove, The	90
Cow Pasture	50,142
Crabb's Purchase	36
Culver's Chance, Second Add. to	50
Dan (Dann)	13,32,33,35,56,120,149
Dawson's Mill Land	28
Debate	44
Deer Park	21,110,124
Deer Park, Add. to	44
Deer Park Enlarged	45
Diamond	52
Dickerson's Delight	114
Discontent	153
Discovery	67,106
Dispute	13
Doull's Park	14
Drumelderey	15
Dry Spring	38
Dublin	36,120
Dublin, Res. on	36,120
Dunbarton	7
Dunghill	72
Earnhill	131
Edmonston Enclosure	45
Edmonston's Range	45,56
Edmonston's Refuse	145

Elders Delight	35
Elizabeth	58
Elizabeth's Delight	108
Ellis's Chance	86
Enster	8
Enster Rectified and Divided, Res. on	8
Eversfields Addition	125
Fair Dealing	101
Fair Hill	71,113,114
Fair Prospect	40
Fairwell	8
Farm, The	99,138
Farm, Res. on the	99,138
Father's Good Will	137
Fellowship	36,125
Fenwick	33,34
Fertile Meadows	24
Fertile Plains	147
Final Conclusion	116
Finish of Trouble Enough, The	90
First Bit Enlarged	145
Fishmarket	140
Fleming's Addition	48
Fleming's Addition to Hensley	48
Flints Grove	49
Fork, Add. to the	65
Forke, The	20,65
Forrest	49,50,59,143
Fortune	40
Fox Hall	52
Fox Race Ground	79
Frederick's Grove	52
Friends Advice	49
Friendship	63,68,92,99
Friendship Enlarged	99
Gaither's Forrest	52
Gaither's Meadow	146
Gaither's Purchase	51
Gaither's Range	51
Gap Filled Up, The	142
Gartrell's Good Will	144
Georgetown, Add. to	7,17
Georgi	86
Gittings Ha-Ha	83,96
Gleaning	86
Good Friday	52
Good Luck	51
Gravelly Hill	142
Greenbrier	1
Greenland	8,33,44
Green Marsh	118

Green Spring	52
Griffith's Park	58
Grove	52
Grove, Res. on the	80
Grubby Thicket	91
Gum Spring	71
Half our Work	138
Hamburgh	143
Hammond's Addition	60
Hammond's Strife, Res. on	52
Hanover	147
Hanover, Res. on	31
Hard Struggle	71
Harding's Choice	11
Hartly Hall	54
Harwood's Delight	61
Hawkins and Beatty's Addition	93
Hawkin's and Beatty's Addition to Georgetown	50
Hensley	48,101
Hensley, Add. to	101
Hensley, Fleming's Add. to	48
Herbert's Chance	72
Hermitage	43,53
Hermitage, Res. of	53
Hickery Hills	142
Hills and Dales	34
Hobson's (Hopson's) Choice	51,62 63,72
Hold Fast of What You Have Got	52
Hole	25
Holland's Addition	68,69
Honesty The Best Policy	145
Hope Improved	109,134
Hopewell	99
Howard's Chance	35
Hunting Hills	130
Hutchcraft's Range	38,134
Inman's Plains	58
Inspection	5
I Was Not Thinking on It	30
I Will Not, Yet I Will	17
James and Mary, Res. on pt. of	80
James Brooke's Reserve	145
James' Gift	8,10
James' Gift, Res. of	6,10
James's Park	103
Jeremiah Park	62
Jeremiah's Park, Res. on	63
John and Jane's Choice	46
John's Delight	18

Joseph	78
Joseph and James	154
Joseph's Goodwill	110
Joseph's Park	65
Jumhoyle	127
Kilmamock	29
King Cole	98
Labyrinth	6,32,81
Lakin's Desire	52
Lakin's Lot, Res. on	36
Lakin's Lott	36
Last Coat, The	65
Laws Purchase	32
Lay Hill	9
Leakings Lot	25
Leeke's Lott	83
Leeke's Lott, Res. of	83
Little Park	110
Little Worth	81,110
Little Worth, Res. on	53
Locust Thicket	44,136
Lucky Range	36,144
Lyby	100
Magruder's Chance	32
Magruder's Court	145
Magruder's Farm	91
Magruder's Hazard	13
Magruder's Industry	72
Magruder's Purchase	92
Magruder's Purchase, Add. to	92
Magruder's Purchase, Res. on the Add. to	92,93
Magruder's Purchase, Res. of the Additions to	92
Maiden's Bower	145
Maiden's Fancy	144,145
Meadow, The	51,151
Meadow Hall, Res. on	8
Meadows, The	52
Mercy's Inheritance	128
Meredith's Hunting Quarters	86
Mersars Land	2
Mexico	35
Mill Land	58
Mill Race	51
Mill Seat, Add. to	22
Mill Trail, Res. on	36
Mill-Use	93
Miller's Beginning, Res. on	30
Mistake, The	91
Mitchell's Garden	51

Mitchell's Range	51,142
Mitchell's Range, Res. on	54
Moab	52
Molls Rattle	100
Molls Rattle, Res. on	100
Moore's Rest, Add. to	1
Morton's Island	54
Mother's Delight	40
Mother's Delight, Add. to	40
Mount Airy	142
Mount Nebo	49,50
Mount Prospect	126
Mount Radnor	21
Mt. Pleasant	54
Mt. Zion	60,61
Ned's Quarter	151
Needwood	36
Netherlands	47
New Design Place	58
Newtown	102
None Left	118
Not Worth Naming	53
Outlet	128
Orpus, Res. of	82
Overplus	54
Owens Rest	6,11
P--ks Lot	1
Panthers Ridge	145
Paradise Enlarged	13
Partnership, Res. on	150
Peasant Farms	57
Penn Brooke	21
Penn's Inheritance	109
Philadelphia	8
Philenia and Sarah	113
Pickaix	66
Pig Park	15
Pines	131
Piney Creek	20
Piney Grove	71
Piney Luck	93
Pint Lookout	109
Pippin	47
Piss Ant Hills	110
Pleasant Fields	137
Pleasant Hills	54
Pleasant Plains of Damascus	32,113
Pollymony	27
Poor Stony Hill	99
Precious Springs	35
Presley	52

Prevention	8,37
Principal, The	141
Pritchetts Purchase	32
Progress	124
Promise Fulfilled	54
Promise Fulfilled, Add. to	54
Providence	52
Quince Orchard	32,68
Raddle Snake Denn	36
Ray's Adventure	38,71,132,134
Ray's Adventure, Add. to	109
Resurvey on the Addition and Troublesome	63
Resurvey on the Addition to Magruder's Purchase	92,93
Resurvey on the Additions to Magruder's Purchase	92
Resurvey on Batchelor Forrest	10
Resurvey on Batchelor's Purchase	8
Resurvey on the Beginning	49
Resurvey on Black Oak Thicket	149
Resurvey on Brandy	123
Resurvey on Brooke Park	71
Resurvey on Buxton's Delight	100
Resurvey on Content	128
Resurvey on Dublin	36,120
Resurvey on Enster Rectified and Divided	8
Resurvey on the Farm	99,138
Resurvey on the Grove	80
Resurvey on Hammond's Strife	52
Resurvey on Hanover	31
Resurvey of Hermitage	53
Resurvey on pt. of James and Mary	80
Resurvey of James' Gift	6,10
Resurvey on Jeremiah's Park	63
Resurvey on Lakin's Lott	36
Resurvey on Leeke's Lott	83
Resurvey on Little Worth	53
Resurvey on Meadow Hall	8
Resurvey on Mill Trail	36
Resurvey on Miller's Beginning	30
Resurvey on Mitchell's Range	54
Resurvey on Molls Rattle	100
Resurvey of Orpus	82
Resurvey on Partnership	150
Resurvey on Richard's Fancy	145
Resurvey on Shady Grove	37
Resurvey on Small Purchase	36
Resurvey on Well's Invention	91
Resurvey on Wildcat Spring	141
Resurvey on Wolf's Cow, 2nd	18

Resurvey on Younger Brother	136,137
Richard and Nathan	68
Richard's Fancy, Res. on	145
Richland	3
Rich Level	51,52
Ricketts' Folly	118
Ridges, The	91
Rockey Point	47
Rockey Spring	17
Rome	108
Roses Delight	136
Rum Punch	36
Sapling Range	146
Sapling Ridge	3
Saturday Morning	65
Scotland	149
Scotland, Add. to	149
Second Add. to Culver's Chance	50
Second Add. to Snowden	5
Seneca Landing	40
Shady Grove, Res. on	37
Shawfields	106
Shepherd's Hard Fortune	15,107
Sherewood Forrest	58
Shop field	16
Simpson's Avenue	49
Simpson's Chance	52
Sine of the Meadows	35
Sisters Goodwill	44
Slipe, The	124
Small Purchase, Res. on	36
Smallwood's Entrenchment	127
Snoden Purchase	52
Snowden, Second Add. to	5
Snowden's Addition	5
Snowden's Add. to his Manner	5
Snowden's Manor Enlarged	15,22,69 114,142
Snowden's Mill	12
Spring Garden	20
Spring Garden Resurveyed	151
Spring Hill	63
St. Georges	16
Strawberry Vale	122
Strong Beer	128
Stubb Hill	35
St. Winnexburgh	108
Sugar Tree Bottom	4
Taylinton	106
Taylor's Pasture	106
That's All	58
This or None	128
Thomas and John	123

Thomas Beall's Addition to Georgetown	7,89
Thomas' Discovery	2
Thomas' Discovery Fortified	54
Thomas's Choice	35
Three Brothers	13
Threlkeld's Add. to Georgetown	50
Timber Creek	144
Timber Neck	51,52
Tom's Lot	44
Two Brothers	153
Trail's Addition	137
Trap, The	91
Trouble Enough	14,84,126,132,134
Trundle's Inheritance	138
Turkey Thicket, Add. to	91
Tusculum	58,72
Valentine's Garden	153
Ward's Inheritance	141
Warfield's Vine Yard	142
Water's Conclusion	144
Waters' Lott	144
Waters Luck	144
Waters Prospect, Add. to	145
Water's Purchase	144
Well's Invention, Res. on	91
West part of Discontent	110
What You Will	145
What's Left	51,52,53
Wheeler's Hope	86
Whole Included, The	13
Wickhams Park	110
Widdow's Lot	39,40
Widow's Purchase	29,141
Wildcat Spring, Res. on	141
William and James	102
William and James, Add. to	103
William and John	82,123
William and Mary	145
William and Mary and Daniel's Inheritance	139
William Meadows otherwise Netherlands	47
Williams' Range and Add. to	151
Willson's Inheritance	152
Wolf's Cow	49,147,149
Wolf's Cow, 2nd Res. on	18
Yazzo	52
Yorkshire	80
Young Man's Folly, The	103
Younger Brother	136
Younger Brother, Res. on	136,137

INDEX TO PROPER NAMES

A name may appear more than once on a page
[ ] indicate page on which that person appears as a witness to a will

ADAMS-ADDAMS, A.	[147]	Hendry (Hendery)	143	Edward	3,[113]
Alexander	105,129		[23,139,148]	Eleanor P.	140
	[29,127]	Hendry Jr.	143	Elizabeth	140
Ann	1	Henry	2	James (Jeams)	3,155
Benedict L.	1	Hezekiah	2		[17,37,47,48,154]
Benjamin	118	James	143	James, Dr.	[55]
Catharine	118	John	2,[71]	James W.	[140]
Eleanor	35	Jonathan	1	John	3
Esther	147	Joshua	2	Kitty Ann	140
Hennaritta	1	Loyd	2	Mary	140
James	1	Nancy	142	Philemon	114
John	1,[104]	Nelly	2	Priscilla	3
Kezia	147	Polly	2	Richard	3,[3]
Sarah	10	Presus	2	Richard Jr.	[3]
Stephen	1	Richard	[132,150]	Robert	3,[55]
W.	[147]	Ruth	2	Sarah	[114]
Williams	147	Sarah	30	Stephen	114
ADAMSON-ADDAMSON		Silvester	2	Susan	76
Basil	[116]	Thomas	2	Thomas	[74,145,151]
John	104,[36,81,125]	William	2	ANDREWS, Ann	3,66
ADLUM, William	[124]	Zachariah	2	Charles	3
ADLY, Dorothy	75	ALLNUTT-ALNUT, Aden	18	Charles Kilbourn	3
ALDRIDGE, Ann	1	Amelia	18	Comfort	3
Dolly	1	Ann	31	Edward	3
Elizabeth	1,5	Benoni	2,3	Elizabeth	3
Isaac	1	Daniel	2	Jonathan	3
Jacob	[144]	Eleanor	2,40,57	Phillip	3
James	1	Elizabeth	38,40,57	Rachel	3
John	1,54	James	2,3,40	Richard	3,[29]
	[25,30,64,113,144]		[31,43,139]	Ruth	3
Joshua	1	Jane	2	William	3
Rebecca	1	Jesse	2,31,[18]	ARNOLD, David	4,108
Thomas	38	John	2,[18]	Eleanor	108
ALLEN, Alexander	[12]	Joseph	2	Epharim	4
Archibald	1	Lawrence	2,40	John	4
Elizabeth	1		[31,43,139]	Lucy	4
Sarah	123	Rebecker	2	Nancy	108
Thomas	1,[1]	Robert D.	[54]	Nelly	108
ALLEIN, Benjamin	[46]	Susanna	2	Peter	4,108
ALLISON-ALLESSON		Talbert	2	ASHON, Virlinda	124
Alpheus	143	Thomas D.	[88]	ASTLIN, Joseph	[54]
Ann	1,2,143	William	2	ATKINS, Joseph	[127]
Benjamin	1,[28,71]	ALPHIN, Ann	[19]	ATKINSON, John	[35]
Charles	1,[128]	Edward	[19]	ATLER, Jane	[19]
Daniel	2	ANCRIM, Elizabeth	47	ATWOOD, Cela	4
Eleanor	2	ANDERSON, Amelia	134	Charles	4
Elisha	1	Ann	3,140	Ellioner	4
Elizabeth	2,65	Catherine	3	George Perry	4

161

James	4	Dorothy	97	Archibald	[8,150]
John L.	4	Elizabeth	97	Archibald Allen	8
Mary	4	John	5,97	Archibald Brooke	44
Willy	4	John Sr.	5	Archibald Edmonston	11
AUBREY-AWBREY, William	4	Lucey	5	Axy	10
AUGHTERBONY, Patrick		Margaret	84	Basil	7,9,10
	[141]	Mary	97	Basil M.	[14]
AUSTIN, Amos	4	Nancy	5	Basil Musgrove	8,14
Ann	67	Reazen	5	Benjamin	8,10
Barrach	4	Samuel	5,[72]	Brooke	22,[30,73,97]
Deborah	67	BARING, Edward	23	Caleb	7
Hezekiah	4	BARKLEY, Charles	[55]	Cela	8,[14]
John	4	Sarah	[55]	Celina	6,9
John Sr.	4	BARNES-BARNS		Cephus	8
Margett	101	Elizabeth	5	Charles	10
Thomas	125	Hannah	137	Charlotte	93
Zachariah	4	Jacob	5	Clement	[106]
AYRES, John	32	John	143,[69]	Daniel	8,9,[18]
AYTON, Ann	52	Joseph	5	Daniel Jr.	7
Beal	4,[115]	Nancy	5	Daniel Sr.	[7,24]
Eleanor	4	Richard Weavour		Dorothy	7
Henry	4	(Weaver)	5	Eden	6,11,[127]
Jane	4	Thomas	5	Edward Sr.	6
Richard	4	Weavour (Weaver)	5,[52]	Eleanor	9
Samuel	4	BARNETT, James	[100]	Elemleck	7,9
		BARRETT, Eleanor	29	Eli	6
BAGGERLY, Henry	[126]	BARRUCH, George	126	Elijah	6,10,11
BAILEY-BAYLY-BAYLEY		Nancy	126	Elisha	9,11
Rebecca	133	BASEL, Susaner	137	Elizabeth	6,7,8,9,10
Rebeckah R.	39	BATES, Benjamin	5		98,154,[24,48]
William	[75]	Henrietta Maria	5	Elizabeth Brook	8
William Jr.	133	Fleming	[6]	Elizabeth W.	15
BAKER, Abednego	[18]	Lucy	5	Emmery Montgomery	7
John	[90,133]	Martha	5	Enoch	10,[71]
Larkin	[32]	Micajah	5	Erasmus	7
Samuel	[22]	Tace	5	Esther	120
BALCH, Anna	7	William	5	Eveline	10
Elizabeth	7	BATSON, Mary	113	George	7,133
George	7	BAWLDING, Margaret	129	Hanna	9
Harriet	7	BAXTER, Elizabeth	6	Helen	98
Lewis W.P.	7	Gabriel	6	Henrietta	6
Stephen B. (Rev.)	7	Mary	6	Hester	25
Stephen B.	[27]	BEADEN, John	33,[36]	Hezekiah	7,9
BALL, Daniel	[72]	BEALL-BEAL		Horatio	9
Henry	[85]	Alexander	6,7,8,110	J.F.	[9,17]
James	75		[84]	James	7,9,110
John	[2,28]	Alexander Edmonston	8		[48,88,150]
Mary	29	Alexander Robert	8	James of James	8
Rachel	66	Alpheus (Alpheous)	7,9		[11,24,84]
Richard	[41]		106	James of James the 3rd	
Sarah	75	Andrew	10		[14]
William	29	Ann	7,8,106	James of Ninian	8
BALTZER, John Jr.	78	Anna	7,9	James of Robert	8
BARBER, Ann	5	Archibald	6,7,37	James A.	10

James Brook(e)	7,8	Sarah	7,10	BECKWITH, Ann		34
James E.	9	Sebert	8	Charles		[132]
James Edmonston	6,7	Selah	7	Elizabeth		14
Jane 6,8,9,11,37,110		Selea	8	George		34
Jemima	8,11	Thomas	7,98,133	John		12
Jemme	8		[22,78,144]	Kezia		12
Jeremiah	7,8,9,[46]	Thomas of George	111	Lucy		13
John 7,8,[70,84,106]			[93,97,131]	Samuel		14
John H.	[61]	Thomas B. (Capt.)	7	William		13
John L.	[7,10,24]	Thomas B. [86,125,135]		BECRAFT, Benjamin		12,65
Joseph	9	Thomas Brook	7	Benjamin Jr.		[94]
Joseph Sr.	9	Thomas Edmonston	[24]	Jonathan		12
Joseph Belt	11	Tyson	37,[45,70,78]	Jonathan N.		[34]
Josiah	9	Upton	[25,29,38,98	Luranah		65
Josias	102		109,111,141]	Mary		12,99
Kinsey (Kinzey)	10	Walter	[126]	Peter	12,[32,35,43	
	[62,72]	William	75		81,106,153]	
Lawson	96	Zachariah	8,11	Peter, Dr.		[12]
Levi	[106]	Zadock	10	BEDDO, Absolem		12
Levin (Leven)	25	Zebedee	7,8	Deborah		12
	[31,70,94]	Zephaniah	8	Dorcas		12
Levin C.	7,[84]	BEALMEAR-BELMEAR		Eleanor		12
Lewis	155,[38,98]	Elizabeth	92,[92]	Harriott		12
Lloyd	8,10,11	Rachel	92	James		12,[125]
Margaret	8,9	Samuel	[78]	Martha		12
Margery	8,11	BEAN-BEANES-BEANS		Mary		1,12
Mary 9,11,110,146,150		Christopher	11	Nancy		12
Middleton (Midleton)		Josiah	11,[29,135]	Sarah		12
	10,102	Josiah Sr.	33	BEEDING, Josiah		[4]
Nancy	1,6,8	BEAR, Catherine	11	Thomas		[49]
Nathaniel	9	Elizabeth	11	BELL, Frances		57
Nehemiah	9	George	11	Joseph		[100]
Ninian	8,9	Jacob	11	William		[151]
Norman	98	John	11	BELT-BELTT		
Patrick S.	7	Margaret	11	Aeneas		13,136
Polly	7	Mary	11		[25,61,107,155]	
Priscilla	98	Michael	11	Alfred		13,136
Rachel	6,9	BEARD, John [60,139,154]		Ann		13
Richard	67,96	John Sr.	[13]	Ann (Anna) Campbell		13
	[63,66,70,74]	BEATTY, Charles	11			136
Richard of Samuel	10	Charles, Dr.	130	Betsy		144
Robert	8,10,102	Charles A.	[34]	Carlton		13,77
	104,[130]	Charles Affordly	11	Carlton Sr.		13
Robert Sr.	[128]	Charles W.	[27,89]	Charlotte		137
Robert B.	[29]	James	11	Dolly		13
Robert L.	[47]	John Meddagh	11	Elizabeth	13,53,77,136	
Ruth	8,9	Martha	11	Esther		13
Sabrina	6,9,10	Mary Franckfeld	11	Evan		16,[16]
Samuel	6,8,9,10,11	Randle Hulse Cradock	11	Greenbury		13
	106,154,[150]	Thomas	11	Henne Ann Campbell		136
Samuel Jr.	[22]	Thomas Johnson	11	Henny Campbell		13
Samuel Sr.	11	Velinder (Volinda)	12	Higginson		13,14
Samuel Charles	[6]		101	John 13,14,79,[19,144]		
Samuel D.	11	BEAVEN, Charles	[128]	John Smith		13

Joseph	14,[41]	Deborah D.	15	BLEWER, John	[153]
Joseph S.	[90]	Edward	116	BLOWERS, Ann	38
Leonard	13	Eleanor	15	Creasy	74
Lloyd	13,136	Eleanor Bowie	15	BLOYCE, Jonathan	[7]
Margaret	13	Elisha Clagett	15	Zadok	[130]
Mary	14,77	Elisha D.	15,16	BOGELY, Ann	16
Mary Ann	74	Erasmus	[53]	Sarah	16
Otho	13	Jeremiah	15	BOGLER, Ann	98
Rebecca	13	Jeremiah (Rev.)	15	BOHRER, Abraham	16
Rufus	13	Jeremiah of Richard	[9]	Barbary	16
Salla	67	John	15	Benjamin	16
Sarah	13	John Wilks	15	Benjamin S.	[92]
Sarah Ann	77	Lucy	91,93	Elizabeth	16
Thomas	[46]	Mary	116	George	16
Tilghman	13,136	Mary Clagett	15	Jacob	16
Westley	13	Michael R.	16	John	16
William	13	Mildred	15	Mary	16,17
BELWOOD, Henry	[4]	Nicholas	15,[6]	Peter	16
BENJAMIN, Abraham	[115]	Ocatia	15	BOLAND, George	87
BENNETT, Casandra	15	Richard	15,16,[6]	Margrett	87
Daniel	[44,66]	Sarah	90	BONIFANT, Benjamin	17
Eleanor	15	Sarah G.	16	James	17,[9,82]
Joshua	[97]	William	15	John	17,[82]
William	[129]	BIER, Philip	[12]	Samuel	17
BENSON, Ann	14	BIGGS, Ezebel	88	William	17
Anne Henrietta	14	Hennerita	16	BONSIDE, James	75
Fleetwood	14	Jane	16	BOONE, Anne	17
Margaret Smith	14	John	16,88	Arnold	17
Ninean	107	Samuel	16	Isaiah (Isiah)	17,[73]
Sarah	14,107	BIRD, Sarah	43	Jo.	[91]
Thomas	[41]	BIRDSALL, John	[16]	Mary	17
William	14,107	Wilson	[16]	Mordecai	17
	137,[51]	BIRDWHISTELL, Eleanor	16	Samuel	17
BENTLY, Caleb	130	James	16	BOOTH, Robert	29
BENTON, Ann	15	Susanna	16	William	83
Benjamin	14,15	Thomas	16	BOSWELL, Leonard	17,[55]
Erasmus	14	William	16	Nicholas	[38]
Henrietta	15	BIRNSIDE-BURNSIDE		Otho	18
Hezekiah	14	Ann	16	Rena Anna	17,18
Joseph	14,15,91	Aquilla	16	William	18,[80]
Joseph Jr.	[67,108,152]	Henry	16	BOUCHER, John Thomas	97
Levin (Leaven)	14	James	16	BOURNE, George	96
Mordacai	14	John Nelson	16	BOWIC, Peter	94,135
Nathan	14	Joseph	16,[89]	BOWIE, Allen	18,[15,53]
Nathaniel Offutt	14	Margaret	16	Allen Jr.	[56,125]
Rachel	14	BLACKLOCK		Charles	92
Samuel S.	15	Richard	[91,121]	John	18,[6,46,87
Sarah	121,[76,85]	Thomas	[121]		106,108,118,146]
Sarah Ann	15	BLACKMORE, Rebecah	40	Mary	34
Theodore	15	Sarah	40	Ruth	18
Thomas	14,15	William	40	Thomas	18
William	14	BLAKE, Catherine	41	Washington	18
BERRY, Benjamin	15	Sally	41	William	92
Cassandria	15	BLANCHARD, William	[95]	BOWLES, Elizabeth	6

164

Richard C.	6	Hannah	120	BROWN-BROWNE	
BOWLING-BOLING		Isaac	120	Andrew	[143]
George	17	Robert	116,[73]	Ane	154
Joseph	17	Sarah	151	Elizabeth	83
Margaret	17	BRIGHT, William J.	[23]	James	68,83,[68,83]
William	17	BRISCOE, Robert	19	James of James	[74]
BOWMAN, Frederick	18	Sarah	19	James of Thomas	[74]
George	18	BROOKE, Ann	21	Jeremiah	21
Jacob	18	Basil	19,20,21,44	John A.	[69]
Matilda	18,71		[68,91,127,130]	Joseph	21
Perry	71	Clement	[148]	Joshua	42
Rezen	[39]	Deborah	20,21	Mary	21
Richard	18	Dorothy	21	Nancy Waters	142
Richard P.	18	Eleanor	20	Nathan	[98]
Shadrach	18	Elizabeth	19,20,21,133	Sarah	68
BOYD, Abraham	[7]	Gerard (Ger.)	20,21,32	Sarah Scott	[122]
Andrew	88		127,[26,130]	William	22
Ann	88	Hannah	21	BROWNING, Benjamin	22
Mary	88	Henry	20	Daniel	[9]
Sarah	19	Hester	17	Drusilla	84
William	19	James	17,20,21,44	Edward	22
BOYER-BOWYER			[4,68]	Edward Sr.	22
Adam	18,[11]	James Jr.	20	Elias	22
Mary	18	John Thomas	133	Elizabeth	22
Peter	18	Joseph	[50]	Jeremiah	22,[9]
Richard A.	111	Margaret	133	Jesse	22
Samuel	[151]	Mary	21	John Baker	22
BRADDOCK, John	[49	Nicholas Basil	20	Jonathan	22,[22,45,85]
	98,105]	Peggy	21	Josiah	70
BRADEN, Robert	147	Richard	20,44,133,[107]	M.	[67]
BRADLY, Robert	[135]	Roger	20,21,130	Mescheck (Masheck)	22,67
BRADSTREET, Lyonel	19		[130,145,148]	Mesheck	[13,44,67]
William	19	Samuel	20,21,115,[15]	Nancy	67
BRAGG, Mary	19	Sarah	21	Nathan	22,[128]
William	19	Susannah	20	Priscilla	22,128
BRANIFF, Patrick	[86]	Thomas	20,21	Rachel	22
BRASHEAR-BRASHEARS		BROOKES, Arabella	21	Rebecca	22
Delilah	22	Henry	21	Samuel	22,67,[128]
Edward	43	James Bowie	21,[85]	Verlinda	22
Nasey	[44]	Letitia	21	William	22
Nancy	43	Martha	21	Zadock	[85]
BREATHERT, Rebecca	61	Walter	21	BRUCE, Ariana	75
BRENT, Ann	[26]	BROOME-BROME		Elizabeth	77
Catherine W.	[27]	Alexander	21	Harriot	112
Daniel	27,[86]	Benjamin M.	21	Henrietta	75
Jane	27	Isabell Ann	21	Jane	75,77
Robert	26	John M.	21	John	[36]
Robert Young	27	Mary	21	BRUNEN, Byrno	[30]
William	27,[26]	Mary H.D.	21	BRYAN, Charity	103
BREWER, William	49,[48]	Sarah M.	21	John	103
BRIAN, Susannah	125	Thomas	21,[54]	BRYDEN, James	[114]
William	125	BROOMLY, Mary	112	BRYN see Burns	
BRIGGS, Elizabeth Ann		Mrs.	111	BUCHAN, William	[99]
	151			BULLITT, Sophia	[122]

Thomas J.	122	BUSSON, Enoch	[81]	Alexander	[106]
BURCH, Jesse	80	BUTLER, Ann	23	George	25,35
Thomas	42	Elizabeth	23	Henrietta	25
BURDETT, Nathan	35,[3]	Henry	24	James	25,35,[39]
BURGESS, Ann	23	James	24,[22]	John	25,26
Basil	23	Margaret	23	John R.	4,26
Betsy	146	Tobias	[30]	Lydia	25
Edward	23,104,[5,96 104,119,134,137]	Walter	24	Margrate	[49]
		BUTT, Aaron (Aron)	24	Mary	25,26
Edward Sr.	[109]	Ann	24	Sarah	25,35
Elizabeth	23	Basil	24	CANBY, Amos	26
Ephraim	23	Elizabeth	24	Charles	26
Jane	23	George	[117]	Eliza S.	[26]
Jenny	146	Hazel	24	Joseph	26
John	23,58,[133]	Jane	24	Martha	26
Nancy	23,146	John	24	Mary	26
Peggy	146	Keziah	24	Thomas	26
Sarah	23	Lidia	24	Whitson	26
Thomas	23	Mary	24	CANDLER, Daniel	14,26 [106]
BURKE, John	129	Proverb	24		
BURKET, Deborough	126	Richard	24	John	26,106,[21,55,121]
BURNS-BURN-BURNE-BYRN		Richard D.	[11]	Rosanna	14
BYRNE-BRYN		Rignal	24	Rosetta	26
Augustine	25	Ruth	24	Sarah	63
Eleanor	154	Samuel	24	William	26
John	25	Swearingen	24	CARN, Walter	[74]
Martha	25	BUXTON-BUCKSTON		CARR, Mary	43
Mary	23,106,125,154	Ann	24	Richard	[84]
Mathaias (Matthias)	23	Brittania	24	William	43
	[40]	Eleanor (Ellenor,		CARRINGTON, Samuel	[29]
Matthias Jr.	[34]	Eloner)	23,24,137	CARROLL, Daniel	26,27
Matthias Sr.	[34]	Fanny	95	Elizabeth	27
Virlinda	23	James	24	Elleanor	27
Patrick	25,[43]	John	24,[57]	George	26
William	[96,143]	John Jr.	[34]	George A.	27
William Sr.	17	John of Thomas	24	John	26,27
Wilson	125,154	Mary Ann	137	Nancy	27
BURNSIDE see Birnside		Mercey	128	William	26,27
BURRESS-BURRISS		Rachel	24	CARTEN, Dothary Brook	8
Charles	132	Sarah	24,137	CARTENHOUR, John	102
Ruth	24,132	William	23,24	Sally	102
Virlinda	24	BYRN see Burns		CARTWRIGHT, Barbara	27
BURTON, Basil	[30,82]			Henry Greenfield	27
William	84,[144]	CAGLESON, Samuel	[88]	John Sliegh	27
BUSEY, Eleanor	81	CAHELL, Astere	25	Julia	27
George Washington	117	Dennis	25	Thomas	27
John	120,[11]	Joseph	25	William	27
Joshua	117,[93]	Mary	25	CARY, William	[17]
Samuel	117	William	25	CASANAVE, Ann	86
BUSSARD, Daniel	142	William Jr.	25	Peter	[89]
John, Dr.	110	CAMPBELL-CAMEL		CASE-CAISE	
John R.	[12,81]	Aeneas (Aneas)	13,25 [23,27,49,55,65 108,138,141]	Brock	[31]
Milton Mortimer	142			Edward Browning	22
Perry Andrew Lycurgus	142			Elexander	19

Elizabeth	18	Samuel	29,[10,108]	CHILTON, Elizabeth H.	43
James	18,19,22	Thomas	29,[138]	Joshua	43,[57]
Josias Browning	22	William	29,141,[28]	Thomas	[27]
Margaret	19	William Sr.	29	William S.	[57,117]
Mary Ann	19	CHAMBERLAINE		CHINA, Elizabeth	31
Robert	19	Catherine	41	Shadrick	31
Sarah	22	CHAMBERS, Ann (Anne)	29,30	CHISHOLM, Archibald	[50]
Thomas	22	Darcus	75	CHISWELL, Ann	31
CASEY, Alice	28	Eleanor	30	Frances Elizabeth	31
Anna Stacy	28	John	30,[19,144,149]	John Augustus	[31,94]
Elizabeth	28	John of Wm.	[89]	Joseph	[94]
John	27	Kesiah	29	Joseph N.	31
Keziah	22	Nancy	29	Joseph Newton	31
Mary	28	Sarah	30	Newton	[67,119]
Pamela	27	William	29,30	Peggy Presberry	31
Philip	28	William T.	[149]	Rebeckah P.	31
Rebecca	28	CHANDLEE, Deborah	120	Sarah	31,49
Rebecca S.	28	George	120	Stephen Newton	31
Thomas	27	CHANDLER, Deborah	21	Thomas Fletchall	49
William	[27]	George	21	William	49,50
CASH, Ann	28	CHENE, Margaret C.	[73]	CHRISTIMAN, Elizabeth	131
Dawson (Dorson)	28	CHENEY-CHANEY		CLAGETT, Ann	31,32,33
Henrietta	28	Elizabeth	144		92,93
Isaiah	28	Fannutta	30	Ann P.	149
John	28	Henry	30	Anna	31
Jonathan	28,[152]	Hezekiah	30	Anne Magruder	32
Rezin	28,[34]	Richard	30,[7]	Ara	62
Richard	28	Samuel	30	Charles	[110,119]
William	28	Shadrick	31	David	31,32,[31]
CASHELL, George	[10]	Susanna	30	Elizabeth	62
CASTOGRAVE, George	95	William	[49,141]	Henry	31,32,92,[102]
CATLETT, Polly	54	CHAPPELL-CHAPPEL		Hezekiah	32
Susanna	10	John	[117,127]	Horatio	32
CATON, Verlinder	119	Thomas	[75,76]	Jane	23,[30]
CATRON, Joseph	[125]	William B.	[127]	John	32,33,[79,93]
CAWOOD, Ann	132	CHESHIRE, Birch	30	John Sr.	32
Elenor	132	Jane	30	John H.	62,[101]
Erasmus	29	John	30	Joseph	32,62,[69,101]
Isaac	[17]	CHESLEY, Alexander	30,152	Joseph White	148
Mary	28	Ann	30,152	Josiah	31,32
Priscilla	29	Elizabeth	152	King Magruder	32
Stephen	28,29	Mary	152	Margrett	23
CECIL-CECILL		Rebecca	152	Mary	32,33,[110]
Ann	29	Thomas	152,[76]	Mary Anna	32
Archibald	29,[28]	CHEW, Cassandra	112	Nathan	33,[64]
Benjamin	29,[3]	CHILDS, Cephas	30,31	Nathan M.	[23]
George	29	Edmond P.	30,31	Nathan Magruder	32
James	29,[10]	Eleanor	30,31	Ninian	23,33,[142]
Jemima	29	Elizabeth	30,31	Rachel	101
John	29,[10,28,108]	Enos	30,31	Rebeckah	33
Mary	29	Henry	30,31,[91]	Rebeckah Magruder	32
Phillip	29	Joseph	30,31	Samuel	31,32,33,93
Richard	[138]	Mary	30,31	Samuel Magruder	32
Sabrit (Talbert)	29	William	30,31,[98]	Sarah	32,150

167

Sarah Ann	[110]	Charity	34	COMPTON, Joseph	32
Susanna	62	Elizabeth	12,34	CONN, Henrietta	147
Thomas	31,32,33	Francis	34,[136]	Leanna	147
	[77,104,148]	Gustavus	34	CONNELLY, John	[87]
Thomas John Jr.	[81]	Gustavis	[43]	Matthew	[23]
Thomas M.	[93,148]	Jacob	12,34	Phillip	[37]
Uphen (Uphon)	97,153	Joseph	12,34	Thomas	[42]
Verlinder	89	Martha	34	CONNER-CONNOR	
Walter	32,[76,81,90]	Oswald	[116]	Richard	[19]
William	32,33,[18,21]	Rebecca Sanders	34	William	[87]
William Magruder	32	Samuel	[61]	CONSTABLE, Ann	35
Zachariah	31,32	Sena	98	Eleanor	35
CLARK-CLARKE		Wilford	34	John	35
Ann (Ane)	33,34	William	34	Rachel	35
Baley E.	33,34	CLEMONS, Basil	57	Robert	35
Baley Liverot	33	Chloe	57	Ruth	35
Eliza	33	George	57	Samuel	35
Elizabeth	40,58	CLINGAN, Mary	101	Stephen	35
Henson (Hanson)	33,34	CLOPPER, Nicholas	[123]	Susanna	35
	[11]	CLOUD, Abner	[50]	Thomas	35
Henrietta	126	Artemesia	127	COOK-COOKE	
Henry	33,34	Emsey	127	Ann	104
Henry Sr.	33	Naoma	127	Basil	36
James	40	Susannah Pemmet	127	Elizabeth	35,36
Jane	34,109	Trammall Hickman	127	James	36,[27]
John	34,[69,113]	COATS, Ann	2	John	35,36,69
John Beeden	33	Charles	2	Nathan	36,92,[36,137]
Johnson	33,34	COCKLAN, Margaret	116	Mary	35
Joseph	50	COCKRAM, Joshua	[68]	Rachel	36,68,69
Judson	33,34	COHAGHAN, William	133	Rezen	35
Lawson	33,34	COLE, Matilda	[122]	Ruth	36
Levin	33,34	COLEMAN, J.W.	[80]	Sarah	36
Margaret	14	Lydia	80	Zadoc(k)	35,36,92
Mary	126	Thomas W.	[80]	Zadoc M.	[137]
Mason Earls	33	William	80,[121]	COOKENDORFFER, Hannah	[136]
Moriah	33	COLLEY, Ann	149	Micheal	[136]
Nancy	139	COLLIER-COLLYAR-COLIER		COOLEY, Henry	[29]
Neill	14	Ann	35,56	James	[124]
Nelson	34	Eleanor	35	COOPER, Arra	142
Robert	50,126	James	2,35	CORNISH, W.A.G.	[94]
Thomas	109	Jane	56	COSTIGAN, Dennis	36
William	139,[25,33]	John	35	Mary	36
CLARKSON, Elexus	34	Lilbourn (Lisbon) W.	35	Michael	36
Ignatius	34	Sarah	35	COUPLAND, Hugh	37
Notley	34	William	2,35	COURTS, Eleanor	75
Vilettee	34	William Jr.	35	Elizabeth	27
William	34	William Sr.	35	COWLEY, Anderson	124
CLEMENTS, Ann	34	COLLINS, Daniel	[74]	Elizabeth	132
Aseaner	98	Eleoner	[64]	Sarah	155
B.H. Jr.	[24]	Elizabeth	123	Thomas A.	[124]
Basil	34	James	97	COX, Abraham	[131]
Bennett	[138]	Rueben	41	Mary	47,[131]
Bennet Hanson	34	Susanna	127	CRABB, Jeremiah	21
Catherine	34	William	35	John	[115]

CRADDICK, Charles	73	CRUMMEL, Nathan	22	William	54,55,121
Mary	73	CULLIAM, Francis	[96]		[80,129]
CRAMPHIN, Thomas	[1,18	CULP, Ann	35	William Jr.	127,[26,29
	59,73,77]	Elizabeth	38		63,80,101,127]
CRAWFORD-CRAFFORD		George	38,[104]	DAVID, John	[80]
CRAUFORD		George Sr.	38	DAVIDSON, Samuel	[93,152]
Alexander	37	John	38,[25]	DAVIS-DAVISS	
Betsey Sutton	37	Katherine	38	Amos	146
Eleanor	106	CULVER, Burgess	[42,78	Ann	39
Elizabeth	11,37		143,152]	Baxley	23
John Sutton	37	Elizabeth	[134]	Charles	71,[149]
Lethe	37	Henry	78	Dorcas	126
Margaret	11	Nancy	70	Eleanor	39
Nancy Owen	106	Polly	[70]	Eli	126
Nathaniel	37,122	William	70,[42,45,109]	Elizabeth	18,23,[146]
Patty Allen	37	CUMMINGER, hrs.	49,50	Ephraim	146
Rachel	11,37	CUNNINGHAM, Martha	87,88	Esther	126
Robert	37	Walter	88	Frances Rebecca	154
Robert B.	106	CURRAN, Benjamin	[155]	Gideon	38
Thomas	39	CUSHMAN		Griffith	[122]
CRAYCRAFT, Eleanor	115	George Washington	38	Harriot	126
CRETIN, John	81	John Franklin	38	Isaiah (Isiah)	39,40
Mercy Ann	81	John H.	38	Leonard	39
CREW, Lemuel	[6]	CUSTIS, Miss	111	Lodowick	39,[109]
Margaret	[114]	CYBERT, Rachel	137	Loradia	71
Micajah	[114]			Luke	39,[54]
CROSBY, Joseph	59	DAKEN, Henry	135	Margaret	154
CROSS, Ann F.	64	DADE, Robert T.	[148]	Massa	23
Benjamin	58,64	Townshend	[71,154]	Mary	154
Priscilla	74	DAILEY, John	[28]	Middleton	[134]
Thomas	[129]	DANBY, Michael	19	Rezin	39
CROUSE, Theodosus	[155]	DARBY, Aden	38,39	Richard	126,[25]
CROW, Basil	37	Ann (Anne)	38	Solomon	25,58,126
Edward	37,38	Anna	38	Susan	39
Edward Sr.	37	Asa	38	Susanah	39
James	37	Basil	38,[3,31,40]	Thomas	18,58,146,[52,53
Joshua	37	Caleb	38,154,[67,117]		54,96,100,107,114
Lucy	37	Drusillar	38		115,119,120,146]
Martha	37	Charles Alexander	39	Thomas John	52
Nancey	37	George	2,38	Thomas N.	[61]
Priscilla	37	John	38,39,[124]	Thomas Noland	25
Samuel	37	John Washing(ton)	39	William	39
CROWN, Dorothy	37	Nicholas R.	39	William Sr.	39
Elisha	37	Rada	38	Zachariah	39
Garrett	[36]	Rezin	38	DAVISON, Henry	[106]
Jerrard	37	Ruth	39,58	DAWE, Robert	[122,125]
Joseph	37	Samuel	38,[18,39]	DAWS, Rachel	108
Mary	37	Sarah	53	DAWSON, Abraham	[68]
Samuel	37	Verlinda	2	Ann (Anne)	2,147
Sophia	37	Zadock	38	Benoni	40
Susan	37	DARNALL, Henry	85	Elenor	40
Thomas	37	Robert	41	Elizabeth	2,40
Truman	[39]	DARNE-DARNES		James	2
CRUMBLICK, Jacob	[37]	Elizabeth	54	James M.	[147]

Jane	40	DILLEHAY, Arthur	[99]	William	42
Mary	40,126	DILLON, Lydda	73	Zachariah	42,[1,125,129]
Nicholas	40	DIXON, Charlotte	12	DOYLE, Alexander	42
Nicholas Lowe	[38,149]	Richard	12	Anne	42
Rebecah	40	DOHERTY-DOUGHERTY		Elizabeth	42,[127]
Robert D.	31,40	Rebecca	50	Gracy	42
	[29,58,66]	Patrick	35	James	42,[127]
Robert Doyne	40	DONALDSON, Rachel	142	John	42
Sarah	31,40	DORSEY, Amelia	58	Joseph	42
Susannah	2	Anna	58	Margaret	42
Thomas	2,40	Caleb	[89]	Mary	42
Virlinder	40	Eliza	54	DRANE, Mary	59
William	2,40	Evelina	54	Thomas	42,56,63,[155]
	[43,125,149]	Henry Chew	52	Thomas O.	59
DAY, James	60,85,[11	Rachael	92	DRAPER, William	[138]
	18,22,23,33]	James M.	[20]	DRURY, Charles	[46]
Sarah	142	Joshua W.	[13]	Ignatius	56
DEAKINS-DEAKENS		Lloyd	[83]	Mary	56
Francis	40,80	Lucetta	[144]	DUBOIS-DuBOIS	
Francis, Col.	79	Maria A.	[20]	J.	[24,79]
Jane	40	Robert E.	[20]	John	[89]
John	[106]	William Hammond	20	DUCKER, Nathaniel	123
Leonard Marbury	40	DOUD, John	[26,55,121]	Sarah	123
Nancy	106	DOUGLASS-DOUGHLASS		DULEY, Elizabeth	37
Tabythey	106	Ann	41	Jonathan	[4,41,68,148]
William Jr.	40,[73]	Charles	41	Kitty Eleanor	37
DEAVOR-DEVER		Elizabeth	41,113	Margaret	121
Elenor	83	Hugh	41	Mary	37
Henry	[144]	Jane	41,113	William	[18]
DECANDRY, Ch.	[56]	John	41,113,123	DUNLOP-DUNLOPE	
DELLS, John	96		[48,56,67]	Elizabeth	111,112,[75]
DENNING, James	[60]	John Wallace	[72]	George	112
DENNIS, Abraham	[143]	Josias	41	Helen	112
Easter	40	Levy (Levey)	41,65	Henry	112
William	40	Margaret	58	James	112,[152]
DENT, John	10,[101,121	Mary	15,41	John	[112]
	128,129]	Mary Ann	113	Mary	112
Verlinda (Valinder)		Priscilla	110	DUNN-DUNNE	
	10,102	Rebecca	41,113,155	Eleanor	1
DEUR, John	[1]	Robert	[72,93]	H.	[6,37]
DICK, Margaret	111,112	Samuel	41,65,113	Hugh	[59]
Robert	112	Sarah	113	Hugh S.	[13,94
DICKERSON, Elizabeth	41	Susanah	41		115,126,154]
Hannah	41,68,69	DOULL, James	[90,91,102]	Sarah	1
Sarratt (Surratt)	41	DOWDEN, John	[142]	William Sr.	[30]
	68,69	Mary	39	DURITTY, Mary	42
Zadock	[25]	Sarah	41	DUVALL, Ann	43
DIGGES-DIGGS		Thomas	39,[39]	Aquilla	42,43
Catherine	27,41	Zachariah	41,110	Benjamin	43,[12,45]
Edward	[40,119]	DOWNS, Ann M.	42	Claudia	43
Eleanor	105	Henry	42	Daniel	[74]
Elizabeth	105	Mary	42	Eleanor	43
Mary	105	Richard	[125]	Eli H.	[143]
William	41,[117,136]	Richard M.	42	Elizabeth	43

Frederick	42	Mary	44,45	Nancy		69
Levin	42	Nancy	9	Rezin		45,46
Lewis	42,43	Olivia	45	Richard	45,46,[15]
Lewis W.	43	Polly	142	Sarah	45,46,70
Mareen	43	Priscilla	44	ETCHISON, Elisha	[23]
Mary	115	Robert	44,45,125	Ephraim	[43]
Samuel	[7]	Roger	44	EVANS, Charles	[16,102]
Sarah	43	Sarah	44	Eliza	151
Washington	[45]	Thomas	44,45,[110]	Elizabeth	7,151
William	43	Thomas Sr.	44	William	46
Zadock	42	William	44	EVEY, John	[141]
DWYER, James	[146]	EDWARDS, Benjamin	10,[89]	EWING, Nathaniel	27
DYER-DYAR		Charles, Dr.	147		
Ann	43	Deborah	54	FARR, Agsnath	46
Arn Sr.	[109]	Elvira	80	Cyrus	46
Catherine	43	John	[99]	Edward	46
Eleanor	43	Margaret	10	Elizabeth	46
Henry	43	Samuel	[138]	Hannah	46
Thomas	[75]	William	[87]	Isaac	46
DYSON, children	139	ELDER, Ann	88	James	46
Jeremiah	43	Johannah	45	Jane	46
John	139	ELGAN, J.	[37]	FARRALL-FAIRALL-FERRELL	
John B.	43,[3,40]	ELGIN, Anne	17	Ann	46
Lydia	43	ELLICOTT, George	20,38	Eleanor	132
Maddox	[2,132]	ELLIOTT, Mark	[141]	Elizabeth	82
Samuel	43,[2]	Mary	4	Henry	46
		Jacob	118	James	46,132
EASTON, Drusilla	118	Richard	[10]	John	46,[5,8]
Levin	[11]	ELLIS, Ann	59	Kezia	46
EDELIN-EDELEN		Elizabeth	45	Mary	46
Leonard	44	John	45	Mary Rosemond	46
Philip	44,[3,141]	Joseph	45	Rebekah	46
EDMONSTON-EDMONSON		Nathan	65	Verlinda	46
ADMONSTON		Pelly	17	FEE, George	47
-.-.	[56]	Philip	45	Thomas	47
Alexander	45,[110]	Ruth	45	William	47
Ann (Anne)	44,[8]	Sarah	74	FELL, James	[19]
Ann Henrietta	44	ENGLISH, Charles	92	FENWICK, George	[50]
Archibald	44	David	92	John	[134]
Brook	45	Eliza Ann Beall	92	FERGUSON, Addison	47
Decious	45	Jane	92	Ann Skinner	47
Dolly	45	John	92	Caroline	47
Dorrithy	44	King	47,[32,35,75	Catharine	47
Eden	44,45,142,143		76,81,97,126]	Elizabeth	47
	[12,140]	Lydia	92,110	John	46,47
Edward	44	ERSHIRE, David M.	112	Nancy	47
Elizabeth	44	ESSEX, Elizabeth	46	Nathaniel	46
Franklin	45	Peggy	46	Rezin	47
Hannah Ann	143	ESTEP, Alexander	46	Robert	[39]
James	6	Ann Lyles	45	William Evans	46
Jane	6	Betsey (Betsy)	45,69,70	FIELDS, Ann Allison	2
Jean	44,75	Eleanor	45,46,70	Martha	82
John	44	Eleanor Maria	45	Mary	75
Lucretia	142	Elizabeth	45,46	Matthew	75

FISH, Ann		47	Betty		49	James		51,[6,59]
Francis		47	Cynthia (Cinthy)		49	John		51
Eleanor		47	Daniel		50	Jonathan		51
Elizabeth		47	Dorcas		139	Joseph		51
George		47	George		49,50	Sarah		51
Harriot		47	George W.		50	FULKS-FOLKS		
Henrietta		47	James		49	Battus		[19]
James		47	John		49,50	William		[19,104,115]
John Young		155	Sarah Newton		49			
Joseph		[47]	Thomas		31,46,49,64	GAITHER, Agnes		52
Levin		47			[67,95,115,139]	Amelia		52
Mary		47	FLING, Rebecca		134	Ann Riggs		120
Priscilla		47	Thomas		[93]	Basil		51,52
Richard		47	FORD, Cassandra		137	Beal(e)		52,53
Robert		47	Elizabeth		14	Beal of Gerard		52
Robert Sr.		47	James		7	Benjamin		51,52,53
William		47	Nancy		7			[36,47,68,97]
FISHER, Ann		48	Prissilla		14	Brice		51
Aquilla		47	Sabra		9	Burgess		51
Artaxerxes		47	FORREST, Joseph		[54]	Cassandra		52
Eleanor		47	Richard		[27]	Daniel		51,52,120
Elizabeth		32,47	Samuel		77	Deborah		52,53
George		47	Uriah		111,122	Edward		51,146
Hilleary		[102]	FORSEYTH, Ann		84	Eli		51
John		47	FOSSET, James		144	Elisha		51
Martin		47,48,128	FOWLER, Ann		50	Elizabeth		52
	[1,67,123,128]		Elisha Jr.		50	Elloner (Eloner)		51,52
Mary		48	Elizabeth		75	Ephraim		51,52,100,[18
Matilda		47	Henry		[41]		51,54,89,107,146]	
Nelson		48	FRANEWAY, Joseph		[10]	Ephraim of Wm.		[18,21
Priscilla		76	FRAZER-FRAZIER				53,71,86,133]	
Sary Ann		56	Cinthia		109	Eviline		21
Selah		47	Cleopartra		109	Frederick 52,53,54,[114]		
Thomas		47,48	James		50	George R.		51
William		47,48	John Stone Jr.		108,109	Gerrard		52
FISTER, Henry Jr.		[16	Joshua		50	Greenbury (Greenberry)		
		141]	Rachel		109		51,53,80,[78,110]	
FITZHUGH, Ann		64	Richard		50	H.C.		[51,57]
McCarty		64	FREE, John Read		129	Harriot		53
FLEMING-FLEMMING			FREEMAN-FREMAN			Henrietta		51,120
Ann		48	Aaron		50	Henry		51,52,[7⁻,77]
B.W.		[81]	Ann		50	Henry, Col.		52
Burgess		48	Samuel		50	Henry Chew		52
Catherine		48	FRENCH, Ariana		[112]	Henry of Daniel		52
Cephas		48,[102]	George		50,[107]	Henry of Frederick		52
Elizabeth		48	FRY, Jonathan		[23]	James		53
James	48,149,[17,129]		FRYER, John		51	James Wilson		110
John		48,97,[4,10	Margary		137	Jane		53
		32,65,105]	Richard		51	John		110,[115]
Mary		48	Walter		51,[123]	Johnsey (Jonsey)		51,53
Robert		48	FYFFE-FIFFE			Lyla		52
Robert W.		48,49	Abijah		51	Margaret		21
FLEMMON, Elizabeth		23	Ann		104	Martha		21,52,53
FLETCHALL, Ann		49,50	Elizabeth		51	Mary		52,53,110

172

Matilda	53	Edward W.	55,[31,47,98]	GLAZE, Basil		88
Nicholas	51	Elisha	55	Jonathan		[88]
Samuel Riggs	51,120	Elizabeth	55	Mary		33,88
Sarah	52	James	55	Mary Offord		32
William	51,52,100	John	55	Nathinal		88
William Beal	51	Kitty	55	Samuel		88,[24]
William Henry	52	Mary	26,55	William		149,[14
GALWITH, John H.	[29]	Mary Ann	55			30,35,45]
GANTT, Francis	[64]	Matilda	55	GLOVER, Hugh		45
T.T.	[64]	Rebeccah	55	GLOYD, Washington		[104]
GARRETT-GARETT-GARROTT		Richard	[101,127]	GODMAN, Edward		56
Aron	53	Samuel	55	Elijah		56
Barton	53	Samuel Franklin	55	Ely		116
Edward	53,[125]	Sarah	55	Julia		56
Eleanor (Elenor)	65	Thomas	55	Rachel		56
	[65]	Vhelander	55	Samuel		56
John	53	William	55	Samuel Israel		[115]
John M.	[107]	Z.	[98]	Sarah		56
Lemelick	53	Zachariah	55,128,[127]	GOLDEN, John		[116]
Middleton	53	Zachariah Sr.	[110]	GOLDSBURRY, Ignatius		56
Susannah	53	GEBHART, John	[155]	John		56
GARTRELL-GATRELL-GATRIL		GENTLE, Fielder	56	Jonathan		56,[141]
Aaron	53	Samuel	56	GOOCH, John		19
Benjamin	53,[83,96]	Sarah	56	GOTT, Eleanor		56,57
Caleb	53	Stephen	56	John		57
Francis	[83]	William	56	Richard	57,[148,154]
Ignatius	53,54	GIBBONS, Elenor	87	Sarah (Sary)		57
Mary	13,53	GILPIN, Ann	133	Sebell		56,57
Richard	[69]	B.	[143]	GRAFF, Andrew		[100]
Ruth	54	Elizabeth	133	GRAHAM, Judith Swann	57
Samuel	53,[54]	Hannah	133	GRANGER, Jonathan	60,[149]
Sarah	54	Lidia	133	GRANT, Violet		30
Stephen	53	Samuel	133	GRAY-GREY		
Thomas	54	Sarah	133	Barney		77
William	53,[39]	Thomas	133	Benjamin		[137]
GARVIS, Alley	54	GITTINGS, Amelia	56	William		[125]
Hillery	54	Ann	56	GREEN, Allen		57,58
Jarrett	54	Ason	56	Ann Butt		24
Polly	54	Benjamin	56,[29,135]	Benedict		57,[98]
Washington	54	Eleanor	15	Clement		[122]
Zadock	54	Elizabeth	56,[155]	Elizabeth		4
GASKINS, John	[128]	Elizabeth Garrett	53	Francis		57,[98]
GASSAWAY, Amelia	15	James	56	Hugh		57
Ann	4	Jeremiah	56	Jane		57
Brice J.	[128]	Joseph	11	Jemima		58
Charles	53,54,55,89	Kinsey	56,[12,72	Kitty		58
Nicholas	89		102,140]	Luranna		92
Ruth	9,10,54	Kinsey of Benjamin	[14]	Margaret		58
Thomas	54	Michael D.	[85]	Rachel		57
GATHREL, Lucy	150	Sarah	56	Richard		57,96
GATTON, Ann	55	Tabitha	11			[24,38,83]
Aquilla	55,110	Thomas	33,87,[11,33,80]	Susannah		58
Azeriah	55	Virlinda	56	Thomas		58,[17]
Benjamin	55,[55]	GLADMAN, Ann Henritta	14	Thomas W.		58

William	57,58	Samuel	58,[37]	Maryan		131
GREENFIELD		Sarah	54,146	HARDIN, Ann		90
Basil	16,[121,140]	Thomas	146	HARDING, Anna		59
Elizabeth	35	GRIMES, Jane	[19]	Basil		59
Harriott	35	GROOME, Richard	[14]	Benjamin		59
Sarah	35	GROSSMAN, Elizabeth	[51]	Charles		39,59
Thomas G.	[75]	GUE, George	114	Christiann		18
Truman	[118]	GUN, Alex.	88	Clement		59
Walter	[140]	Margary	88	Edward		59,[14,43
Walter S.	[101]	GUNBY, Col.	116			56,59,87]
GREENTREE, Benjamin	[4]			Eleanor		39,59
GREENWELL, Barnabas	107	HADLEY, James	[130]	Elias	59,[8,47,53]
Bennet	[141]	HALL, Alexander	[62]	Elizabeth		59
Philbird	[56]	Ann	58,[104]	Henry	87,[81,131]
Rachel	107	Johanna	150	Joeaster		59
GRIFFIN, Ann	42	Joseph	[15,22	John		59,[41]
GRIFFITH			64,69,107]	John of Edw.		[107]
Amelia Dorsey	120	Nicholas	58	John S.		18
Ann	54	Rebecca	29	Josiah		59
Basil	54,96,[68]	Richard Bennett	62	Keziah Butt		24
Benjamin	119,[58]	HALLSAL-HALLSALL		Lewis		59
Catharine	122	Lucy	42	Mary		60
Charles A.	54	Mary	42	Mary Elizabeth		74
Charles G.	[58]	Stacy	42	Millisent		59
Charles Greenbury	[39]	Zachariah	42	Mr.		80
Davage	54	HAM, George	[25]	Nathan		59
Elizabeth	58,[13]	HAMBLETON, John	128	Philip		59
Greenberry	54	Samuel	[64]	Polly		59
	[69,90,143]	HAMILTON, John Gainer	47	Rezin		59
Greenberry Jr.	[50]	Sarah Fields	29	Rebeccah		98
H.	[13,52,54]	HANKER, Nicholas	[115]	Richard Abraham		74
H. Jr.	[52]	HANKS, Sarah	14	Ruth Butt		24
H.G.	[37]	William	14	Sarah		59
Henry	58,120	HANLY, Dorothy	139	Thomas N.H.		74
	[18,52,57]	HANNES, Darkey	82	Thomas Noble Harwood		59
Henry Jr.	[43]	HANSON, Benedict	57	Vachel		59
Henry of L.	[134]	Juliet	57	Walter		59
Hezekiah	[39]	Letitia	57	William		59
Howard	[119]	HARBIN, Dorcas	58,59	Zach.		[86]
Ignatius	54	Eleanor	59	HARIMAN, Sarah		146
John	54,58,[119]	Elias	58,59	HARPER, Ann		121
John H.	[58]	Gerrard	59	Edward		[18]
Joshua	58,[13]	James	58,59	Elizabeth		61
Juliett	58	Jeremiah	58	John		[106]
Lyde	58	John	58	Mary		2
Mary	119	John Hatton Bevly	58	Thomas		2
Nacy	44	Joshua	59	HARRIS-HARRISS		
Pheby	58	Mary	59	Ann		146
Philemon (Phillemon)		William	58,59	Barton	60,61,[153]
	54,58,[131]	HARDESTY, Mary	59	Deborah		146
Polly	120	Samuel	[52]	Dorcas		146
Rachel	54	HARDEY-HARDY		Elenor		61
Rebecca	53	Fielder, Mrs.	[2]	Elizabeth	57,60,61,73
Ruth(y)	15,96	George	[74]	Jesse	60,61,[100,146]

John		60	Elizabeth	47	Cassandra		121
Joseph	60,61,94		George Washington	47	Daniel		120
Joseph Jr.	[63]		Margaret	47	HERBERT, Elisha		135
Maddison Franklin	60		HAYS-HAYES		James		135
Mary	60,61,146		Abraham	[59]	Jesse		[117]
Mary Ann		60	Abraham S.	63,[74	Margaret		135
Nancy		57		103,105]	Mary		135
Nathan	61,[99,100]		Anne Rawlings	62	HERRING, George		[11]
Priscilla		60	Charles	62,[62]	John		[33]
Samuel		57	Eleanor	62,63,126	John Sr.		[77]
Sarah	60,61		Elizabeth	62,63,[45]	HERSEY, Benjamin		[88]
Thomas		57	George	62,94,[82]	HEUGH, Andrew		64,[8
Zadock	[137]		George B.	62,63,[100]			16,75]
HARRISON, Ann		60	Jeremiah	62	Ann		64
Elizabeth		60	Leonard	63,128,[59,66]	Charles		64
Greenbury		60	Leonard Jr.	[80]	Christina		64
Henry		60	Levin	62	Elizabeth		64
Joshua		60	Lily Rawlings	62	Harriet		64
Josias		60	Notley	63,100	Jane		64
Linny		60	Patty	62,63	John	64,[46]	
Marry	[19]		Priscilla	62,63	Margaret		64
Nathan		60	Richard	62	Martha		64
Peggy		60	Samuel S.	63,[42]	Mary		64
Rebecca		60	Thomas	62	Sarah		64,98
Sarah Hawkins		60	William	62,63	HEWETSON, Susannah		135
HARWOOD, G.W.		[117	William of William	[82]	HEYDEN, George		[147]
	139,143]		William H.	62,63	HICKEY, John		[35]
Henry	61,[139]		William S.	63,[63]	HICKMAN, Betty		64
Gassaway W.	61		HEBBURN,-----	80	Elisha		[27]
John	61,[17,25		Samuel	63	Elizabeth	49,64,65,125	
	139,154]		HEDGES, Nicholas	[78]	Gerrat		124
John H.	61		HEETER, Charlotte	115	Greenberry	65,124	
Levin	61		George	115	Hanson		64
Mary	61		John	[41]	Jean		49
Maryann	61		HEIGHTON, Josiah	29	John	64,65,124	
HATTON, Thomas	6		Josias	[28]	Joshua		64
HAWKER, Deanna	62		Milly	29	Joshua Jr.		143
Elizabeth	62		Stephen	29	Litha		65
Lidia Butt	24		Thomas	29	Margaret		123
Susanna	62		William	29	Mary	2,64,65,143	
William	62		HEMPSTONE-HEMPSTON		Mary Waters		64
William Sr.	62		HEMSTONE		Nancy	65,[125]	
HAWKINS, Amy	60		C.T.	[74]	Peggy		123
Dorothy	62		Christian	[13]	Richard	64,125	
Eleanor	62		Eleanor	63	Sarah	64,125	
Elizabeth	91		William	67,[74,136]	Sitha		65
James	62,[5,67		HENDERSON, Jennett	92	Thomas	49,64,65	
	122,129,140]		John	64,[21]	William	49,64,65	
John	62,[10,103,121]		Lidia	109		135,[141]	
Juliet	62		Richard	63,92	HIGDON, Anne		108
Nathaniel	62		Sarah	63,64,92	Ignatius		43
Peter	62		HENOP, Frederick	[12]	John	[16,77]	
Sarah	60		HENRY, Aaron	[9]	Mily		43
HAYMOND, Eli Fee	47		Ann	147	Peter		108

Thomas	[105]	James	66	James	68,[58,96,120]
Virlinder	108	Michai	66	John	68
HIGGINS, Benjamin	65	Pilip	66	Liones	68
Eliza	[65]	Rebecca (Rebeckah)	66	Martha	9
Elizabeth	65		[35]	Mary	68,83,143
Emily Jane	133	Thomas	66,[3,35]	Mary Ann	7
George W.	133	Thomas Sr.	66	Nathan	36,68,69
James	12,65,[12,56]	HOBBS-HOBS			[21,144,148]
James B.	65,84,86	Elizabath	150	Nathan Jr.	7,10,68
James Becraft	65	Jesse	66		[21,90,106,109]
Jamima	65,66	John	[9,17,116]	Nathan Sr.	68
John	65	Marcy	67	Nehemiah	[22,69]
Joshua	133	Martha	67	Philip	[54]
Joshua C.	133	Polly	67	Rosetta	143
Leonora	12	Priscilla	67	Samuel	68
Lucretia Ann	65	Rezin	66	Sarah	7,68,69,145
Margarete	133	Samuel	66,67,[128]	Sary	69
Martin	65	Samuel Sr.	66	Solomon	41,55,68,[4
Maryelenor	149	William	66		25,109,118,142]
Matilda	65	HOCKER, Dorcas	5	Stephen	68
Montgomery	65	Nancy	5	Susanna	68,69
Richard T.	133	Nicholas	[94]	Thomas	69
Thomas L.F.	[11]	Philip	5	William	68,69,143
William	66	Samuel	[66]	William of Nathan	69
HILL, Thomas	[143]	Weavour	5	Zadock	68
HILLEARY-HILLARY		William	[77]	HOLLY, Mary	42
Ann	110	HOEY, Peter	[71]	HOLMES, Basil	69
Elizabeth	66	HOFFMAN, Peter	[12]	Eleanor	45
Henry	66	HOGGINS, Benjamin	67	Ely	69
Henry Jr.	143	Ellender	67	Isabella	69
John	66,[136]	John	67	John	69,70,78
Joseph	110	Kitty	67	Josiah	69
Margaret	110	Mary	34	Mary	[69]
Rignal	66	Mary Elenoer	67	Nancy	69
Sarah	66	Milliann	67	Richard	45,69,70
Thomas	66	Peter	67,[142]	William	69,[82,124,129]
Tilghman	66	Richard	67	HOLT see Hoult	
HILTON, Ann	66	Richard Jr.	[79,141]	HONBURG, Eliza	[112]
Archibald	66	Tamer	67	HOOK, James	23
Cloe	134	Teacle	67	HOPKINS, Eleven	70
Darcus	66	William	67	Leavin	70
Delila	66	HOLLAND, Abraham	[69,136]	Gerrard of Richard	[20]
Easther	66	Alice	14	Mary	17
Elizabeth	66	Amelia	52,53	Philip	17
James	61,134	Anthony	[97]	Richard of Gerrard	[20]
John	134	Archibald	69,107	Stephen	70
John Sr.	[134]	Arnold	68,69,[91,148]	HOPWOOD, John Jr.	[124]
Jonothan	134	Asa	[24]	HORNER, Jeane	87
Otho	66	Benjamin	14,69,147	Louisa	87
Priscilla	61	Benjamin Sr.	68	Mary	87
Samuel	63	Cassy (?)	69	Samuel	87
Trueman	[86]	Eleanor	107	HORTULAMUS, Antje	[122]
William	66,[62]	Elias	7	HOSKINS, Margaret	131
HINTON, Elizabeth	59	Eliza	7	HOSKINSON, Andrew J.	70

Ann	70	Thomas	71,[89]	Jesse	[67]
Elisha	70	Thomas Sr.	71	IJAMS-IAMS	
Elizabeth	70	William	71,152	Mordeca	[128]
Elizabeth T.	70	HOWEL, Patty	117	Richard	97
George	70	HOWISON, Eleanor	46	ISRAEL, Mary	58
George Sr.	[126]	HOWS-HOWSE-HOUSE			
George B.	70	Ann	71	JACKSON, J.M.	[112]
Hilleary	70	Edward	71,[18]	Nicholas	44
John	70	James	[71]	Philip	[44]
John N.	70	John	71,[149]	Samuel A.	[33]
Josiah	70	Mary	71	JACOBS, George	[44]
Margaret	62	Nathaniel	71	John	[86]
Nathan	70	Reuben	71	Thomas	[44]
Norris	70	Richard	71	JAME, Richard	[29]
HOULT, Ann	70,71	HOWSER-HOUSER		JAMES, Daniel	135
Barbery	70,71	Christian	72	Richard	33
Darkes	71	Lewis	[51]	Thomas	135
Elizabeth	70,71	Martin	72,[101]	JAMISON-JAMMISON	
Lawrence O.	28,[84]	Mary	72	Eleanor	104
Lawrence Owen	71,[47]	Nathan	72	Francis	104,105
Ralph	70	Philip	72	Laurence	104
Rebecka (Rabeckah)		Tessy	67	JANES, Henry	[32]
	70,71	William Pritchell	72	Willy	[81,84,118]
William	71	HOY-HOYE		JANNEY, George	17
HOWARD		John	[112]	Susannah	17
Alcindia Graham	57	Paul	40,[20]	JARBOE-JARBO	
Amy	99	HOYLE, John	[57]	Henry	[95]
Ann	71	HUDDLESTON, Jonathan	[16]	Joseph	[4,58]
Baker	71	William	16,[118]	Raphael	[56]
Benjamin	71	HUFF, Samuel	[131]	Valinda	126
Charles	[57]	HUGHES, Benjamin	17,72	JARRAT-JARRETT	
Eleanor	63,71	Edward	72,[90]	Benjamin	99
Elisha	88,89,[87]	Elizabeth	17,72	Daniel	[129]
G.	[13,68,99]	John H.	[43,61]	Eleanor	99
George	71,[62]	HUMBERT, Elizabeth	116	John	99
Greenberry (Greenbury)		HUMPHRYS, Cassandra	81	Thomas Ray	99
	71,99,[22	HUNGERFORD, Charles	[67]	William	99,[63]
	72,117,143]	William B.	104	JARVIS-JERVIS	
Hannah	71	HUNNICUTT, Jane	114	Gerard	109
Henry	71	HUNT, James	72,[101]	Zadock	109
Henry of John	57	Ruth	72	Widow	32
Jacob	71	William P.	[101]	JAY, Lydda	73
John	71	William Pitt	72	JEFFERSON, Basil	73
John A.	[94]	HUNTER, Daniel	72	Benjamin	73
Joshua	[121]	Henry	72	Hambleton	73
Leonard	[87]	Susannah	72	Henry	73
Mary	133	HURDLE, Anna	42	John	73
Priscilla	71	Elizabeth	42	Leonard	73
Rebecca	71	Leonard	42	Violetta	73
Sally	71	Sarah	42	William	73
Samuel	71	Thomas	42	JENES, John	[40]
Sarah	116	HUTCHINSON, Francis	[119]	JOHNS, Ann	5
Sarah Fauntlery	57	HUTTON, Charles B.	[41]	Aquila	73,[73]
Susanna	71	HYATT, Asa	[128]		

177

Elizabeth	40	Charles Courts	75,77	William	75,76,125
Leonard H.	111,150	Charles O.	102	JORDAN, James	[147]
Leonard Hollyday	73	Edward	75,[50]	JOSEPH, Ann	77
Margarett Crabb	73	Eleanor (Elenor)	76,77	Ann Northcraft	77
Richard	73,[73,111]		137,[76]	Basil	77
Richard Henry	73	Elizabeth	61,76,101,115	Charlotte	77
Richard W.	40	Elizabeth Ann	74	Clement	77
Richard Weavour	5	Elizabeth E.	67	Dorcas	77
Sarah	73	Evan	75,76,77	Eleanor	77,114
Thomas	73,152,[75]	Evan Jr.	[76,85]	Elizabeth	77
JOHNSON, Basil	74	Galen (Gaylon)	76,77,149	John	77
Benjamin	73	Hanbury	76,115,[94]	Joseph	77
Elizabeth	133	Henry	75,76,77	Susannah	77
Greenbury	74		[76,85,132]	William	77
James	73,[17]	Henry of Edward	32	JOYE-JOY	
Jefferson	74	Horatio	74,77	Eleanor	108
John	73,74,[71]	Isaac P.	76	Enos	78
Jonathan	73	James E.	[137]	Helan	78
Joseph	74	John	75,76,77	John	78
Josias	73	John of Nathan	85,[76]	Susanna	78
Lydia	74	Joseph	[28,88]	William	78
Margaret	71	Joseph Jr.	[28]	JUDY, George J.	[87]
Mary	74	Joseph G.W.	[137]		
Mary Ann (Maryann)		Joseph J.W.	[107]	KARRICK, Walter	[145]
	73,74	Joseph James Wilkinson		KEAGEN, Ann	107
Rachel	73		77	KEETH, Priscellar	124
Reason Augustus	74	Josiah	82,[45]	KELLY-KELLEY	
Resin	73	Josiah Jr.	[56]	Benjamin	78
Reuben	74	Laurance	[76]	Benjamin B.	[122]
Richard	74,[68]	Leanah	42	John	[82,122]
Samuel	73,74	Liddia	75	Joseph	78
Susannah	11	Lodge	[76]	Hannah	78
Thomas	74	Louisa	75	Thomas	78,[82]
Thomas Sr.	74	Margaret(t)	125,152	KEMP, Jacob (Jake)	78
William	74	Maria	77	John	78
William J.	149	Mary	75,76	Peter	12,78
JOHNSTON		Nancy	76,77	Sarah	78
Berthewlomy	[70]	Nathan	75,76	KENNEDY, Esther	152
Sterling	[100]	Nathan V.	76	John	152,[36]
JONES, Abraham	74,77,124	Priscilla	76,77,[85]	KENNY, David	35
	[124,155]	Priscilla P.	76	Sarah	35
Ann	67,75,76,77,149	Rebecca (Rebekah)	47	KERBY, John B.	[91]
Ann V.	76		76,102	KEY, Francis S.	85
Anna	82	Richard	77,[134]	Philip B.	41,112
Aquilla	76,[76]	Sarah	75,76,77	KING, George	[112]
Arianna (Ariana,		Sarah Elizabeth	74	Henry	[42]
Arraanna)	75,76	Stephen Lloyd	67	Richard	[126]
Basil	77	Sucky Courts	75	William	[89]
Benjamin W.	77,152	Susan	76	KINSEY, Elizabeth	88
Brook(s)	76,77,80	Susanna(h) C.	75	Joseph	88
	[4,73,149]	Susanna Courts	77	KIRK, Susannah	29
Caterine	149	Teresa	79,80	KIRWAN, Catherine	41
Charles	75,76	Thomas L.	76	Mary	41
Charles C.	75	Walter	77	KISNER, John	[153]

178

Priscilla	11	Lily	80	Sharlotte	104
KLEIN, Peter	78	Rebecca	80	LAZENBY, Alexander	82
KNEWSTEP-KNEWSTAB		Thomas	80	Cephas	82,[7,90,108]
Robert	78,79	William	80	Elias	82
Thomason	78	LANGFORD, Amelia	129	Henry	82
KNIGHT, Joseph	[118]	LANHAM, Aaron	75,76	James	82,[80,108]
Mary	94		81,[32]	John	82
William	[118]	Ann	24	Joshua	82
KNOTT-KNOT		Aquila	81,[47]	Margaret	82
Caleb	79,80	Archibald	81	Martha	82
Edward	63,79,80	Catherine	47,81	Robert	82
Francis	79,80,[77]	Elizabeth	81	Thomas	82
Henry	79	Elleanor	81	LEACH-LEECH-LEATCH	
Jane	79,80,[145]	George Horatio	81	Ann	45,[70]
John T.	79,[80]	Hezekiah	81	Daniel	[7]
Joseph	63,79	Jemimah	81	Eliza	[98]
Leonard	80,102	Leah	81	Elizabeth	119
Lewis	63,79	Lethe	81	Jesse	98,[31,98,105]
Lucy B.	102,103	Marcia Ann	81	John	18,82
Mary	79	Margaret	81	Josiah	[29,35]
Mary Ann	79	Maryann	81	Leah	149
Philip (Phillip)	44,79	Mercy Ann	81	Martha	82
	[67]	Ruth	81	Mary	82
Rosella	80	Samuel	81	Nancy	82
Samuel	80	Sarah	81	Rachel	18
Stanislaus	79,80	Stephen	81	Thomas	82,[96]
Thomas	44,67,79	Susannah	81	Thomas Sr.	[149]
	[21,67,94,144]	Thomas	81	Sarah	149
William	79	Walter	81,[47]	William	32
William Jr.	[71]	William	[37]	William Jr.	82
Zachariah	79	Zadock (Zadok)	81	William Sr.	82
	[60,77,145]		[47,65]	LEADSOM, Judith	136
KURTZ, Christian	[95]	LANSDALE, Catharine	81	Margaret	136
		Isaac	80	LEE, Daniel	82,[135]
LACKLAND-LACKLEN		Isaac L.	[70]	Eloner	137
Dennis	17,80,[58,66	John	85	James	82,[43]
	94,124,138,153]	LASHLEY, Cesiah	82	John	82
Eli	80	George	81,[63]	John Sr.	82,[153]
George L.	80,[143]	John	82	Susannah	[45]
James	32,80,[32,53]	Lucy	82	LEEKE, Ann	83,[83]
James C.	80	Robert	82	Cassandra (Casandrah)	83
John	[47]	Thomas	81	Catherine	83
LAMPHIES, R.G.	[44]	William	82	Dinah	82
LANE, Har.	[109]	LAWMAN, Jacob Sr.	[74]	Elizabeth	83,114
Hardage	10,80	Lucy	130	Henry	83,[52,74]
Harvey	80	Mary	130	Henry 3rd	[50]
James B.	80	LAWRENCE, Otho	[131]	John W.	[58,83]
Rachel	10	LAWSON, James	126	John Waters	83
LANCASTER, Ally	80	Thomas	[100]	Joseph	83
Ann	80	LAYMAN, William	[46]	Joseph of H.	[83]
Charity	80	LAYTON-LATON		Joesph Jr.	83
Charles	80	Ashford	[22,141]	Margaret	83
Edward	80	Ashur	141	Mary	82,83
Fanny	80	Sarah	141	Obed	83

Richard	83	LINTHICUM-LINTHICOME		Levin (Leven)		86
Samuel	83,[83]	LYNTHICUM		Luther		86
Sarah	83	Ezekiah (Ezek.)	85	Mary Ann		65
LEEMAN, Arthur	63		[50,123,125]	Samuel Noland		86
LEGG, Charles	[79]	Frederick	85	Susanna		86
LETTON-LITTON-LYTTON		Jane	85	Thomas Hussy		86
Brice	84,[49]	Jean	151	Verlinder (Verlinda)		86
Burton Summers	84	John	85,[118,151]	William		86
Caleb	84	Sarah	115	William Francis		86
Harriot	84	Thomas	85,[151]	William Gipson		86
John	84,150	Thomas Fletchall	50	LUCUS-LUCAS		
Mary	[70]	Zachariah	51,85	Amos		86
Michael	47,84,150	LIVERS, Anthony	[148]	Elisha		86
	[2,28,132]	LIVINGSTON, Anna Maria	27	Henry		[89]
Michael Hartly	84	LOCKER, Patrick	49	John	86,[25]
Ninian Willett	84	LODGE, Brock	85	Matilda		86
Ralph	84	Frances	115	Sarah		86
Reuben Pike	84	Henry	85	William		86
Vanwick Michael	84	Johannah	85	LUFFLIN, Joseph	[109]
LEWIS, Alice	84	John	85	LYDDAN, Bridget		87
Ann B.	84	Julian	85	John		87
Daniel	84	Laurence	85	Judas		87
David	84	Lucinda Russ	85	Laurence		[85]
Drusiller	84	William	[75,77]	Margaret		87
Elenour	[55]	William B.	115	Michael		87
Elizabeth	84	William O.	85	Patrick Sr.		87
Jeremiah	84	LONG, John	[50]	Peter		87
John	[55]	LOVE, Jean	75	Timothy		87
John W.	84	LOVELESS-LOVELASS		LYLES, Margaret		61
Jonathan	84	LOVELACE		Richard		[25]
Joseph	84	Benjamin	[65]	Richard Sr.		[74]
Levin	85	Catrine (Katherine)	8,47	LYNN, David	87,120
Levy	84	El-onis	[65]	Elizabeth		87
Lewis D.	84	Elizabeth	107	Rose		20
Margaret	84	Lucy	[65]	LYON, Benjamin	[121]
Mary	45,84,154	Margery	8	Elenor 127		
Maxainno(?)	84	Zadok	107			
Nathan	84	LOWE, Anna	95	McATEE-MACCATEE-MACKATEE		
Rebeckah (Rebeccah)		David	48	MACKETTEE-MACKATIE		
	85,154	Letitia	85	Ann		89
Thomas	84	Margaret	48	Charity		87
LE-ER, Samuel	[151]	Milla	95	Cloe		88
LIEZEAR-LISHURE		LUCKETT, Ann	86	Elizabeth Clements	89
Rachel	148	Charity	86	Ellender		88
Reuben	9	David	86	Francis	88,117,[96]
LINGAN, James M.	85,[95]	David Lawson	86	Francis X.		87
James Maccubbin	63,64	Eleanor	86	Francis Xavier		87
Janet	64	Elizabeth	86,103	George	87,88,89
Nicholas	73	Francis William	86	John		87
R.W.	[152]	Jane	65	Lucy	88,89,130
LINSTED-LINSTID		John	86	Margaret	87,117
Anna Maria	84	Juliett	86	Mary		[89]
Thomas	[49]	Kitty Callander	86	Nelly		87

Sarah	87,108	Robert	[58]	Mary Ann	92,[92]
William	87,88,[117]	MAGRATH, William	[37,131]	Mira	92
McAULIFFE, Florence	[87]	MAGRUDER, A.	[93]	Molly	13
McCABE, Dr.	147	Alexander	90,91,93	Nancy Turner	138
Mary	147	Ann (Annie)	91	Nathan	91,[69]
McCARTHY, Timothy	87	Aquila	91	Nathaniel	91
McCAULEY		Archibald	90,[93]	Nathaniel E.	[80]
George Washington	[88]	Basil	89,90,91,94	Ninian (Ninean)	90,91,92
McCORMICK, Christina	38		[19,66]		93,[44,81,90,91,152]
Edward	38	Carlton	13	Ninian (Ninean) Beall	
George	38	Catharine (Catharine)			92,93,[102]
James	38		48,89,90,91	Otho	136
McDONALD, Lucy	1	Charity	152	Patrick	93,[72]
McDUGLE, Benjamin	[118]	Charles	93,152	Perry	152
McELFRESH-MACCLEFISH		Daniel	90	Philip	91
MACKLEFREASH		Deborah	149	Priscilla	91
Charles	[128]	Edward	90,[93]	Rachel	92
Richard	[83]	Eleanor	21,90,92	Rebecca (Rebekah)	91,92
Sarah	85		93,[92]	Rector	[69]
Sarah Ann	50	Eli	90	Robert P.	37,92,110
McFARLAND		Elias	93		111,[47]
Charlotte Matilda	87	Elizabeth	85,90,91,92	Robert Pottinger	92
Margaret	87,88		93,109,110,[90]	Robert White	89,90
Mary	87	Elizabeth Turner	138	Ruthey	93
Samuel	87,[58]	Enoch	152	Samuel	92,93,[103]
McGILL, Mary D.	23	George	90	Samuel Sr.	93
McGLOCKLIN, Henry	[40]	George B.	148,152	Samuel B.	93,[14]
McINTOSH, Elizabeth	65	George Beall	91,93	Samuel Brewer (Br.)	92
McKAY, Ann	88	George Fraser	89		93,[91,93]
James	88	Greenbury	89,90	Samuel Jackson	93
William	88,[118]	Hariot	91	Samuel Wade	93
McLAUGHLIN, James	[1]	Henry Brookes	21	Sarah	77,91,138
McMASTER, John	88	Hezekiah	90,[44,93]	Sarah Ann	151
John Jr.	88	Isaac	91	Sarah B.	77
Joseph Garrison	88	James	90,93,152,[86]	Susanna(h)	90,152
Juliet	88	Jane	90	Theodorus	90
Mary	88	Jeffrey (Jeffry)	91	Thomas	92,94,152
McNAMARA, Peter	[100]		[15,81,148]	Thomas Contee	93
		John	90,152	Verlinda (Violander)	
MacCALLUM, Jane	88	John B.	77,[81,93]		90,91
MACCUBBIN-MACKUBIN		John Beall	91,[69]	Walter	91,93,[14]
John C.	[129]	John Bowie	92	Warren	93,[1]
Zachariah	[15,78]	John Burgess	6,89,90	William	92,93,152
MACKALL, Leonard	[90,150]	Jonathan W.	92,[145]	William Jr.	91
MACKLAIN, John	89	Joseph	13,90,92,93,[48]	William Beall	[119]
Priscilla	89	Josias	93	William Burrett	94
MACLISH, Absolem	12	Josias Hardin	90	William Offutt	91
Margaret	12	Julian	89		[101,103]
Robert	12	Lech'd (?)	[119]	William Willson	152
William	12	Levin	93	Williminy	77
MADDEN, Ann	135	Lloyd	13,93,[136]	Zachariah	93
John	135	Lucy (Lucey)	91,93	Zadock	92,[8,22
MADDING, Mordecai	[16]	Margaret	91,92,93		111,118,155]
MAGINNIS-MAGINNISS		Martha	152	Zadock Jr.	[109,142]
Rhodalph	95	Mary	6,85,91	Zech.	[90]

Name	Page
MARCH, Catharine	116
Mary Ann	116
MARKHAM, Elizabeth	130
MARLOW, Erasmus	[152]
MARQUESS, Ann	94
Deborah	94
Elizabeth	94
James	94
MARTAIN, Honore	120
MARTIN, Lenox	[29,100]
Sarah	100
MASON, Alexander	[115]
Ann	94
Archibald	[5,22,124]
Frances	94
John T.	[40,130]
Leannah	94
Magruder	94
Selby	94
Richard	94
Verlinda	94
MATHEWS-MATTHEWS	
Betsy	44
James	44
Mary	44
Priscilla	44
Wm., Rev.	27
MAY, Frederick	[27]
MAYNARD, Sarah	11
Susanna	11
MEDDAGH, John	11
MEDLEY, Ann	4
Basil	34,94
E.B.	[24]
Elijah	3,113
Elisha	[31]
John	[108]
John Baptist	94
Mildred	34,94
Mary	112
Thomas	34,94
William	[3]
MEEM, James	[78]
MELTON-MILTON	
Alexander	94
Anne	94
Eleanor	94
Elizabeth	94
Henrietta	94
Joseph	94
Mary Ann	94
Rachel	94
Raphael	94
MERRICK, Jacob	18
Michael	18
Rachel	18
Verlinde	18
MELVIN, James	[78]
MICHEL, Lucy	[11]
MIDDLETON, Mary	50
MILES, Charles	[5,146 154]
Edward	95
Henry	95
Joseph	95
Nancy	113
Tracy	95
MILLER, Peter	155
MILLS, Elias	[60]
Jesse	[60]
MILTON see Melton	
MINOR, Charles	[26]
MITCHEL-MITCHELL	
Ann(e)	22,94
Eleanor	94
John	[1]
Lucretia	22
Norris	75
Rachel	94
Sarah	94
Spencer	[33]
Walter	22
MOBLE, Mary	97
MOBLEY, Charity	74
Delilah	5
John	5
MOCKBEE-MOCKEBEE-MACKBEE	
Alfred (Alphud)	95
Allen	89
Basil	37,[98]
Cordelia	95
Deborah	89
Emmaline	37
Hezekiah	95
James	37
Louisa	37
Martha	95
Mary	95
Ninian (Ninean)	95,155 [51,123]
Ninian Jr.	95
Rejoice	95
Zephaniah (Zepheniah)	95,[75]
MOFFETT, Ann	48
Jane	48
Mary	48
MOLYNEAUX, Robert	[27]
MONTGOMERY, Henrietta	86
MOODY, Mary	15
MOORE-MORE	
Benjamin	95
Elizabeth	95,96
George	96
Hariet	96
Horatio	96
James	82,95,[30]
James of Arch.	[130]
James Henry	[30]
John	114
Keziah	95
Levin	95
Lucy	83
Mary	96
Mordecai	[94]
Nancy	114
Nathan	[83]
Priscilla	95
Sarah	75,82,150
Thomas	5
William	96
Zachariah	96
Zedekiah	96
MORAN, Andrew	141
Zachariah	141
MORELAND, Margaret	[66]
MORGAN, Mordecai	[17]
William	[17]
MORSELL, H.	[30]
James S.	[39]
William	[131]
William Jr.	[131]
MORTON, Thomas	[132]
MOUNT, Samuel	19
MOXLEY, John	[70]
MUDD, Joshua	95
MULLICAN-MULLIKIN	
MULICAN-MULLIKIN	
Ann	96
Archibald	139,[47]
Basil (Bassel)	96,97 [16]
Dorcas (Darcus)	96
Elizabeth	96,113
John	41,96,97
Leurana	73
Lucy	41
Rachel	96
Sarah	96
Tabitha	74
Teresa	96
Willey	96

William	96,97,[68]	William	135	Darcus		100
Zadock	[47]	NICHOLLS-NICKOLLS-NICKELL		Elenor		132
MULLOY, Elizabeth	97,153	Archibald	[28]	Eliza		100
MUNCASTER		Benjamin	98,[154]	Elizabeth Margaret		100
Zachariah	[151]	Benjamin of Thos.	[107]	George		99,[132]
MURDOCK, Addison	97	Cassandra	98	John		99
John	97	Cephas	98	Luther		100
William	97	Edward	98	Mary		63,99,100
MURPHY-MURPHEY		Isaiah	98	Mary Anne		99,100
Aquila	[94]	John	87	Otho		100
Cassandra	97	Naoma	98	Rebecca		132
Charles	97	Pegga	98	Solomon		99
Deborah	97	Prissilla	98	Thomas		99
John	97	Priscilla Sr.	98	William		63,99,100
Joseph A.	[66,79,80]	Samuel	98,[44]	William of George		[61]
Josue	97	Sarah	120	William of William		100
Mary	97	Simon	[78]	NORTHCRAFT, Casandra		100
Michael	20,[145]	Thomas	98,110,[16]	Catrine		100
Sophia	71	Thomas C.	[85]	Edward		100,[96]
William	97,[15	Westly	98	Elizabeth		100
	108,128]	NICHOLSON, Alies	[64]	Erasmus		100
William Jr.	[94]	Asa	63	Hezekiah		100
MURRAY, Jane	[86]	John	[73]	James		100,[96]
Matthew	131	Joseph	[89]	Mary		100
MUSGROVE, Amos	97	NICHOLUS-NICHOLAS		Parmelia		100
John	97	Ann	99	Richard		100
Nathan	97,[52,53,54	Asa	99	NOWTON, Ignatius		[130]
	107,115,119,146]	Barbary	12	NUCOLS, Thomas		[113]
Nathan Sr.	[114]	Elisha	99	NUGENT, Betsy		100
Rachel	42	Elleonor	99	Evan		100
MYERS, Elizabeth	17	James	99	John		100
Valentine	[150]	John	98,99	Polly		100
MYLER, Mat	[113]	Marget	99	Sally		100
		Mealey	99	NUSBAUM, William A.		[81]
NAYLOR, George	[27]	Nancy	99			
NEAL-NEALE-NEEL		Naoma	98	O'BRIAN, Charles		24
Barton	43	Phillip	99	ODEL, Baruch (Baruck)		100
Charles	[88]	Simon	12			[33]
Joseph	[90,99]	William	99	Margaret		100
Mary	43	NIXON, Amey	99	ODEN, Benjamin		98
Rebecca	103	Elizabeth	99	Rachel		[104]
NEEDHAM, John	98,[42,99]	Hugh	99,[30]	OFFUTT-OFFOTT		
Richard	98	James	99	Aaron		101,121
Sarah	98	Jonathan	99	Alexander		31,101,103
Sarah Ann	98	Jonathan Jr.	[30]			[102]
William	98	Joshua	99	Andrew		101,[89]
William Abington	98	Richard	99,[33,138]	Ann		31
NEIGHBOURS, Nathan	[79]	NOBS, John	[39]	Baruch		101,102,103
NELSON, Joshua	[108]	NOLAND, Catherine	25	Basel		101
NEWCOMB, Mary	46	Thomas	25	Betsy		102
NEWELL, Susannah	133	NORRIS-NORRISS		Brooke Burgess		101
NEWHOUSE, William	[79]	Ann Mariah	100	Cassandra		101,102
NEWLIN, David	[46,57]	Benjamin	99,100	Catharine		80
NEWMAN, Kasiah	135	Charlotte	100	Catherine C.		102,103

Catharine Christie	104	Thomas	103	Eleanor	106
Charles	101,[32]	Thomas Jr.	103	Elizabeth Ann	14
Clarissa	102	Thomas Sr.	102	Esther	125
Colmore	102,[101]	Thomas B.	[123,127]	Harriot	106
Debby	102	Thomas Burgess	102	James	106,[1,80,109,133]
Eleanor	10,101	Thomas H.L.	[103]	Jeremiah	[134]
Elisha	103	Thomas Hussey Luckett		John	[53]
Elizabeth	92,101		102	Lucy	106,[133]
	103,122	Thomas Levi	103	Moses	106
Elizabeth Chew	104	Thomas Odle	101	Nathan	14
Fielder	103	Thomas Wootton	103	Oliva Cattrol	14
George	102	Verlinda	102	Patrick	[56,70]
George H.	103,129	William	92,101,102,103	Polly	8
	[101]	William of James	[103]	Priscilla	106,[8]
George W.	102,[127]	William Jr.	103,[91]	Rebecca	106
George Washington	102	William III	103	Richard J.	[24,38
Hannah	101,102	William M.	[115]		92,121]
Hezekiah	101,104	William Mockbee	101	Robert	[110]
Humphrey Burgess	101	Zachariah	10,102,103	Robert Sr.	[8]
James	12,101,102,103		104,[32,75,104]	Samuel Taylor	106
James of Wm.	[121]	Zadock (Zadok)	12,101	Ursulla	106
James Sr.	97	Zephaniah (Zepheniah)		Verlinder	106
James Doull (Duell)			104,[1]	OSBOURN, Francis	111
	101	Zepheniah B.	103	OULD, Paulina	51
Jane	101,103	Zephaniah Burgess		Robert	51
Lawrence	[28]		102,104	OWEN-OWENS	
Lucy	10,102	OGDON, Benjamin	104	Ann	107
Lucy Burgess	104	Henry	104	Benjamin Jr.	[144]
Margaret (Margett)	102	O'LEARY, Arthur	[87]	Cloe	37
	103,104	OLIVER, Charles	104	Daniel	106
Martha	101	Nelly	104	Edward	9,106,107,120
Mary	101,102	William	104,[82]	Elias	[121]
Mary Ann	103	O'NEALE-O'NEAL-O'NEILL		Elinor	107
Molly	102	Ann	104	Elizabeth	43,107
Mordecai B.	[127]	Barbara	105	John Candler	106
Mordecai Burgess		Barton	105	Joshua	106
	102,104	Bernard	105	Lawrence	[119]
Nathan	102	Elizabeth	85,105	Mary	106,107
Nathaniel	101,103	Henry	104,[25]	Nancy	9
Nathaniel of Samuel		Jannet	105	Octavia	107
	[70]	John	105	Rachel	106,[10]
Ozgood	103	Joseph	105	Rebecca	153
Ozias	101,[48,91,129]	Lawrence	28,[111]	Richard	[130]
Ozias, Dr.	12	Margaret	104	Robert	70,107
Rachell	101	Mary	105	Rosanna	106
Rebecca	12,101	Mary Ann	104	Singleton	106
Rezin	101,103,[33]	Sarah	105	Tavy	9
Rezin Beall	10,104	William	105,115	Washington	9,107
Samuel(1)	101,103,104	William Jr.	[116]	OWING-OWINGS	
Samuel C.	102	O'REILEY, Henry	[34]	Rachel	9,54
Samuel Chew	104	ORME, Archibald	110,125		
Sarah	101,102,103		[29,53,106,116]	PACK-PECK	
Sarah B.	16	Archibald Brook	14	Christena	107
Serena Milema	103	Charlotte	106	Harriet	107

Harriot B.	155	PEARSON, Anna Maria	27		Rachel		109,110
Mary	97	Mary	27		Roger	109,111,[92]
Nathan	107	PECK see Pack			Stephen		111
Richard	2,107	PEDDICOART-PEDDICOARD			Thomas		109
Thomas	78,107	Jasper	14,[113,133]		Thomas J.		111
Thomas Sr.	107	Rebecca (Beckey)	13,14		Zadock		111
William	32,107,[78]	Sarah	14		PETER, Alexander S.	111
Zadock	107	PEERCE see Pearce					112
PAGNO, Mary	14	PELLEY-PELLY			Ann		112
Nicholas	14,107	Ann	16		David		111,112
PALMORE, Mary	[131]	Benjamin	16		Elizabeth		112
PALMMER, Sarah	45	Harrison	109		George	111,112,[112]
PARHAM, Frederick, Dr.		Mary	109		George, Capt.	111
	136	PENN, Charles	[109]		Hamilton		111
John, Dr.	136	Edward	20		James		111
PARKER, David[34,41,117]		Elizabeth	109		Jane		112
PARKERSON, Elizabeth	56	John	[120]		Janet		112
PARKLINGTON, John	[56]	Joshua	114		John	111,112,[46]
PARRADICE, James	20	Lucrasia	71		Mary		112
PARROTT, Richard	[152]	Roby (Robey)	71,109		Robert		91,97,111
PARSONS, Lucretia	42	Stephen	54,96				112,[62]
PASLEY, Jonas	[118]	Zackeas	109		Sarah		111
PEAK, Elender	[147]	PERRY, Ann	111		Thomas	111,112,[111]
Thomas	[147]	Ann Waters	110		William		111,112
PEARCE-PEERCE		Aqualina	142		PETERS, Amsey	3
Ann	107	Basil	109		Charles Gilbert	112
Benjamin Notley	107	Basil M.	[81]		Elizabeth		112
Clement	130	Basil Magruder	110		John		112
Eleanor	108,[87]	Betsy	109		John S.		112
Elizabeth	87,108	Charles	109,110		Liney		112
Henrietta	33,34,108	Collen	111		Phebe		112
Henry C.	108,[34]	Elias Waters	110,144		Rachel		112
Henry Culver	107	Elisha	111		Ruth		112
Ignatius	108	Elizabeth	59		PETTY, Calvert	[116]
James	108	Erasmus	59,[59]		PHELPS, Edward	[113]
John	107,108	Erasmus Jr.	[11]		PHILLIPS, Bedder	[23]
John B.	[135]	Francis	109		Thomas H.	[117]
John Baptist	108	Gassaway (Gazway)[7,41]		PHILPOT, Casander	53
Katherine	107	George	4		Elizabeth		53
Leonard	108	Hanner	109		PIGMAN, Dorcas	113
Margrate	108	James	101,109		Ignatius		113
Rachel	108	James W.	[45,81]		John		113
Terecy	108	James Wilson	110,[22]		Joshua		113,114
Verlinder	108	Jemima	89,110		Matthew		113
Walter	108	Jemima (Jamima)			Nathaniel		[36]
William	108,109	Magruder	110,142		Philenia		113
William C.	108	Jeremiah	111		Sarah		113
William Gale	108	John	53,109,111		PILES, Ann		115
PEARRE, Alexander	108	Joseph	110		Francis		113,115
	[99]	Levi	111		Jane		113
Alexander Jr.	[94]	Lydia	109		John		76
Alexander Sr.	108	Marry	109		Leonard		113
James	108	Nancy	109		Mary		76
Joshua	108,[28,61	Peggy	109		Richard		113
	77,79,130]	Priscilla	109,110		PITTS, Archibald	39

PLATER, Thomas	54	
PLEASANTS, Basil	6	
Deborah	20,21	
Elizabeth	20	
Elizabeth Ann	6,113	
Hannah	6	
Henrietta	21,114	
Henrietta M.	113	
Isaac W.	[113]	
James	20	
James Brooke (Brooks)	113,114	
Joseph Jordan	6	
Margaret	21,113,114	
Margaret Willing	6	
Mary	21,114,[113]	
Sarah	21,113,114	
Tarlton Woodson	5	
Thomas	21,113	
Thomas Snowden	6	
William Henry	5,6,113,114	
PLOWDEN, Edmund	147	
PLUMMER, Bellinder Ann	67	
Betsy	144,[144]	
Delilah	120	
Dorcas	28	
George	120	
John	114,[63]	
Johnsey	[120]	
Joseph	114	
Joseph P.	[133]	
Mary	28	
Philemon	114,[53,96]	
Philemon Jr.	[53,74,83,96,100,115,119]	
Robert	[13]	
William	114,[54]	
PLUNKETT, Reverand	126	
Robert	[27]	
POLLARD, Priscilla	110	
Rebecca	109,110	
POOLE, Benjamin	[41,65,124,153]	
Henry	141,[121]	
John	76,114,115	
John Jr.	41,[65,77]	
John Sr.	59,[42,56,73,79]	
Joseph	[97,153]	
Joseph Jr.	[41]	
Matilda	141	
Milla	141	

Pollyann	141	
Priscilla	115	
Rebecca	115	
Richard	[21,97]	
Sarah	141	
PORTER, Charles	115	
David	115	
Denton S.	115	
Edward	115	
Eleanor	94	
Nathan	115	
Polly	115	
POSEY, Jane	16	
Jemima	16	
POWELL, Elen	147	
Fetney	147	
PRATER, Agness (Agnas)	97,153	
PRATHER, Aaron	24	
Ann	65	
Benjamin	115	
Deborah	4	
Eleanor (Eloner)	4,52	
Elizabeth	24	
Henne	121	
Henry of Walter	52	
Jane	10	
John	2,115	
Mary	115	
Ruth Allison	2	
Sarah	65	
Thomas	115	
Walter	138,[138]	
William	115	
Zephaniah	[115]	
PRICE, Benjamin, Capt.	116	
Sarah	2	
Richard	[120]	
William	2	
PRIEST, Joseph Eden	81	
PRITCHETT, Charles	115	
Elias	115	
Henson	[41]	
Liddy	115	
Margaret	117	
Mary	115	
Thomas	115	
William	115	
PROUT, Jonathan	127	
Sarah	127	
William	127	
PURDIS, Ann	[43]	

PURDUM-PURDOM		
Elizabeth	22	
Joshua	[33]	
Priscilla	22	
PURNELL, Ann	12	
QUAID, Thomas	[39]	
QUARY-QUERY		
Daniel	116,[10,26]	
Henry	116,[10]	
Margaret	116	
Nicholas	116	
QUEEN, Mary	142	
RABBIT, John	[24]	
RANDALL, Elizabeth	4	
Susana	4	
RATRIE, William	[17,126]	
RAWLINS-RAWLINGS-ROLLINS		
Ann	116	
Benjamin	116	
Elizabeth	116,[78]	
James	116	
James H.	116	
John	62,116	
Mary	62,116	
Mary Eloner	116	
Priscilla	116	
Richard	116	
Sarah	116	
Thomas	116,[78]	
RAY, Ann	117	
Asa	38	
Benjamin	[52,65]	
Eleanor	81	
Elizabeth Butt	24	
Eloisa	81	
George	[115]	
George Washington	38	
James	38,116	
John	117,[96]	
John Jr.	[52]	
Joseph	116	
Josiah	117	
Martha Ann	38	
Mary	116,117	
Nicholas	[109]	
Rebecca	117	
William Alford	38	
RAYMAN, William	[135]	
READ-REED-REID-REEDE		
Alexander	63	
Alletha	117	
Ann	117,132	

Anna		117	Susanna		69	John Hammond		119,146
Archibald Anderson		117	William	150,[2,24,37]		Julia		120
Catherine		132	RICHARDSON			Mary		133
Eastor		117	William Pierpont		[112]	Remus		120,[58]
Eleanor		117	RICKETTS, Ann		68,69	Reuben		119,120,133
Elizabeth	92,117		Anthony		19,118	Romulus		120
George Nelson		117	Anthony Sr.		118	Ruth		58,119
Henson (Hanson)		117	Benjamin		68,69,118	Samuel	120,146,[117,145]	
James		117			[19,21]	Sarah H.		146
John		117	Benjamin Sr.		118	Thomas		120,146
John Alferd		117	Druzilla		118	RIGNEY, Lucy		139
John M.		[142]	Elizabeth		119,153	RILEY, Amos		120
Joseph		117	Frances		137	Ann		116
Leven		117	Gerard		118	Benjamin		120
Mahala		117	Jacob		118	Camden		116,120,[21]
Margaret		117	Julyl meriah		137	Eleanor		120,121
Mary		117	Margaret		19	George		26,120,153
Maryann		34	Martha		97,118,153	Hugh		120
Matthew	117,[67]		Mary		118	Isaac		26,84,120,121
Robert	92,117		Merchant		118			[1,95,141]
Ruth		117	Nancy		19	James		120
Sarah		[37]	Rachel		137	James Taylor		76
Susannah		55	Rhoda		118	Martha		120,121
Thomas	117,[8,37,118]		Richard		119	Mary		120,121
William		117	Robert		118,[36]	Mary George		120
William Perry		117	Sally		118	Mary Ray		116
Zachariah		117	William		36	Sarah Martha Camden		120
REAT, James		[88]	Zadok		118	Sarey		26
REDMOND, James		[105]	RICKEY, Mary		11	Susanna Lanham		76
REEDER, Francis		117	RIDDLE, John		115	Tabitha		120
Henry		117	RIDGELY, William		58	RINE, Valentine		[9]
Hezekiah		117	RIDGWAY-RIDGEWAY			RINEY-RYNEY-RHINEY		
John		117	Isaac		119	Catharine		31
Simon	[60,62,108,126]		Jeremiah		119	Elizabeth		67
Simon Sr.		117	Rebecca		42	Margarett		96
REINTZEL, Anthony		78	Robert		119	ROBB, Adam		81,131
Daniel		78	Sarah		119			[81,84,131]
REMINGTON, Absalom		[116]	RIGBY, John		[50]	John N.		81
RHOADES-ROADS			RIGGS, Ahezriah		[70]	ROBERTS, Ann		121
Ann		126	Amelia Dorsey		120	Artemisa		127
Elisha		118	Amon	58,119,[79,146]		Billingsly		121
Jane		118	Caroline Elenor		146	Darcas		121
John		118	Charles		119	Eleanor		121
Nicholas	118,[15]		Edmund		119	Elizabeth		127
Thomas		[99]	Elisha		120	Henry		121
RICHARDS-RICHARD			George		120	James		121,127
Christina		118	George Washington		120	John		121
Eleanor		118	Greenberry		119	Joseph		121,[103]
Elizabeth		150	Henry		119	Mary		121
George		118	James		119	Richard		121
Jacob	118,[73]		Jane		97,153	Susanah Pemmet		127
Marion		118	John		119	William		121,[30,101]
Mary		118	John H.		68,[46,68	ROBERTSON, Benjamin		121
Sarah		[37]			104,120]	George		[150]

Mary	133	SCOTT, Amos	122	Henry	124
Priscilla Ford	121	Eliza	122	James	124
Samuel	121	Elizabeth	[51]	Mary	124
Sarah	121,126,133	Elizabeth Luckett	103	Ruth	124
Thomas	121,133	Gustavus	122	Samuel	124
William	121,[21,97]	Gustavus Hall	122	William	124
ROBINSON, Leonard	[149]	Isabella	[51]	SEERS, Hyram	[56]
ROBY, Benjamin	[145]	John C.	122	SELBY, Agnes	70
ROSE, Anna	7	Margaret	51,122,151	Ann	150
John, Capt.	7	Rachel	103	Brice	[14,25,26,60]
ROZIER, Henry	27	Robert	122	Charles	[137]
RUGLOSS, Mary	[69]	Sarah	122	Elenor	125
RUSSELL-RUSSEL		Thomas	122,[101]	Elenor Bowie	125
Ann	[43]	Thomas Jr.	122,123	James	[97]
Henry	[40]		[62,72,102]	John	124
Martha	[135]	Thomas Sr.	[102]	John Eversfield	124
Rebecca	6	William	122,123	Josha W.	[99]
RYAN, Eleanor	153	William B.	122	Leurana	125
Jemimah	73	SCRIVENOR, Elizabeth	123	Nathan	[97]
Mary	153	John	123,[97]	Rebekah	125
		Mary	123	Richard	125,[36]
SAFFELL-SAFFEL-SAFFLE		Polly	123	Ruth	70
Ann	122	Rezin	123	Sarah	14,125
Charles	122	Sarah (Sally)	123	Solomon Simpson	126
Drusilla	121	William	123,128	Thomas	14,125
Elizabeth	122	SEAGAR, John	123	Thomas Sr.	125
Hezekiah	122	Sophia	123	Verlindar	125
James	122	SEAR, Betsy	123	Walter Bowie	125
John	122	Elias	123,124	William Magruder	[97]
Joshua	122	Hester	123	Zachariah (Sachariah)	
Lamack	[44]	Hezekiah	124		125,[14]
Mary	122	Israel	123,124	SELF, John	125
Maryann	121	John	124	Polly	125
Samuel	122	John Thompson	123	William	125
Sarah	122	Joshua	123,124,[123]	SELMAN, Althea	14
William	122	Josiah	123	William	14
SANDERS, Azariah Weaver		Lawson	123	SEWALL, Eleanor	41
	39,40	Mary	123,124	Maria	41
Charles	[23]	Priscilla	124	Nicholas	41
Edward	34	Rebecca	124	Robert	41
Lucretia	39,40	Thomas	124	William	41
Rhodum Weaver	39	William	123,124	SHAAFF, Arthur	85
SANDS, William	26,[85]	SEARCY-SEARSEY-SCEARCY		SHANK, Deborah	143
SANSBERRY, Benjamin	1	Ann	49,50	SHAW, Adamson Tanihill	125
Thomas	1	Nancy	124	Ann	88
SARGEANT, John	61	Robert	124	Elizabeth	151
SAUBRAGE, Ann	121	William	124	Hessisah	125
SCHOLFIELD-SCHOOLFIELD		SEDGWICK-SEDWICK-SEGWICK		James	[137]
Andrew	[99]	Ann	14	James Alexander	81
Elizabeth	45	Benjamin	[129]	John	[140]
SCHOLL, Catharine	122	Elisha	124	Margaret	82
Frederick	122	Marian	14	Rebecca	125
Margarett	122	SEEDERS, Anne	124	Robert	125
Mountjoy	122	Bennett Sr.	124	Stephen	[68]

188

William	82,125	William	126	SNAIL, John	[155]
SHEARMAN, Mrs.	63	SIMPSON, Allen	126	SNELL, Elizabeth	128
SHEARS, Anne	48	Dorcas	126	George	128
SHECKLES-SHECKELL		James	126	SNIDER, Isaac	51
SHEKELLS		John	[60]	SOLLARS, Ann	128
Abraham	[109]	Mary	[44]	Robert	128
Ann	87	Musgrove	[44]	SOPER-SOAPER	
Elizabeth	[87]	Solomon	126	Ann	129
Richard	[51,111]	Thomas	[34]	Basil (Bazil)	128,[22]
Sarah	126	William	53	Basil Jr.	[141]
Theodore	87	SLATER, Anna	126	Basil Sr.	128,[141]'
SHEELE, Augustus Daniel		SMALLWOOD-SMALWOOD		Barton	129
	[77]	Director	127,[59]	Charles	[1]
SHEIR, Mary	117	Jain	127	Charles Sr.	129
SHELTON, Elizabeth	127	Joseph	[134]	Eleanor	3
Thomas	[148]	Sampson	127	Ignatius	128
SHEPHERD-SHEPHEARD		Sampson T.	127	James	[1]
Eleanor	154	William T.	127	John	128,[34]
Frances	125,154	SMITH, Alexander	131	Joseph	[95]
Thomas	125	Anna	68	Mary Ann	128
Wadworth	125	Benjamin	127	Nathan	129,[121]
Wadsworth Wilson	154	Bennett	[155]	Nelson B.	128
SHERLOCK, James	126	Charleton	[22]	Rebeckah	65
	[115]	David	127	Ruth	128
SHINGLER, Christiana	116	Deborah	68	Samuel	128,[16,22
SHOOK, David	115	Elizabeth	81		29,141,146]
SILVER, Eleanor Norris		Ignatius	127	Sarah	129
	100	Isaac	[144]	Susanna	128
Susannah Norris	100	James	106,127	Robert	[129]
William Norris	100	John A.	[49]	SPARROW, Ann	129
SIM, Ariana	64	John K.	150	Aquilla	129
Patrick	64	Joseph	105	Benjamin	[29]
William	64	Leonard	127	Charlotta	129
SIMMONS, Abigail	126	Margaret	44	Fardonando	129
Abraham	151,[80]	Mary	111	Jonathan	129,[129]
Elizabeth 126,151,[25]		Middleton	128,[102]	Priscilla	129
Elizabeth Magruder	151	Nancy	95,106	Sollomon	129
George	126	Octavia Owen	106	Thomas	129
Isaac	126	Rachel Ann	106	William	129
James	126	Rebecka	128	SPATES, Casandry	1
Margaret	126	Richard	111	Charles	1
Samuel	126,[152]	Robert	81	Hanny	123
Samuel of Samuel	[71]	Sarah	84,127	Hennelretta	123
Samuel W.	[151]	Sary	34	Priscilla	1
SIMMS-SIMS		Sicilly (Sicillia)	127	Richard	[48]
Ann	126	Volendar	131	Samuel	1
Elexious	126	W.	[7]	William	1
Francis	126	Walter	[94,103]	SPEAKS, Richard	[138]
Francis Xaverius	50	William	[10,66,85	SPENCER, Elizabeth	93
Ignatius	126		92,151]		129,141
Joseph	126	SMITHY, Thomas	[133]	Mary	57
Joseph Milburn	50	Thomas William	[89]	William	141
Thomas	126,[111]	SMOLTZER, Henry	[117]	SPRIGG, Eleanora	130
Walter	126	SMOOTE, Edward	134	Elizabeth	130

Frederick	[126,130]	Rebecca	131	Mary		132
James	130	STRIDER, John	64	Obed	9,[34,116]	
John	130	Margaret W.	143	Obediah		132
Lucy	130	Margaret White	64	Rachel		9
Margaret	130	SUGARS, Elizabeth Lewis		Samuel	9,132	
Mary	130		103	Susanna (Susanah)		65
Rezin	130	SULLIVAN, John	[133]	Thomas	132,[14]	
STABLER, Anna	6	SUMMERS, Benjamin	150	Van	39,132	
Deborah	6,113,114,130	Dent	131	William		132
Edward	114	Hosekeah	131			
Edward Jr.	[26]	James	131	TALBERT, Nathan		[6]
Elizabeth	6	Jane	70	TALBOTT, Benjamin		132
Elizabeth P.	20	John	131	James		132
Mary	6,113,114	John Dent	[73]	Lethe		91
Robertson	6	John L.	[73]	Paul		132
Thomas P.	20	John Litton	150	Sarah		132
Thomas Snowden	6	Mary	49	Thomas	132,[132]	
William 6,114,130,[83]		Owen	88	William		[136]
STAINS, Thomas	89	Paul	131,[121]	Wilson		132
STALLINGS-STALLING		Walter Dent	131	TALL, Arthur		48
Eleanor	130	Zadock	131,[45]	Ruth		48
Elizabeth	130	SUTER, Alexander	131	Stephen		48
Henry	[95]	James	131	TANEY, A.		[32]
Joseph Sr.	130	John	131,[52,82	Augustus		[155]
Sarah	50		116,130]	Roger B.		85
STAR, John	82	John Jr.	131,[62]	TANNEHILL-TAWNYHILL		
STARKEY, William	88	Margret	131	John		59
STEEL, Matthew	[7]	Mary	8	Leonard		59
STEPHENS-STEVENS		Nathan	131	Ninian		[97]
Cloe	60	Robert	131	Rebecca		[8]
Eleanor	72	Sarah	131	Samuel		59
James	72	Tabitha	84	Susanah		91
Lewis	104	William	[15]	TAPSCOTT, Ann		57
Mary Buchanan	72	SWAN-SWANN		TARVIN, Elizabeth		[135]
Nancy	142	Ann	132	John		[135]
STEUART, Helen	[150]	Cassandra	41	TASTELL, Elizabeth		50
John	[26]	Hezekiah	62	TAYLOR, Antony		136
STEWART, David	80	Thomas Turner	132	Allen Griffin		57
STIER, Jacob	[60,61,72]	Zedekiah	[115]	Benjamin Sr.		149
STIMSTON, Dorcas	[86]	SWANY, Elizabeth	25	Charles William		57
STOAKES, Sarah	62	Mary	25	Henry		133
STODDART, Benjamin	111	SWEARINGEN-SWEARINGER		Howard Tapscott		57
	152,[40]	SWEARINGHAM		John	133,[27]	
STONE, John	130	Daniel	132	John Marzhel		57
N.	[138]	Eleanor	9	Margaret		133
STONER, Jacob	130	Elemelick	132,[12,34]	Mary		131
Margaret	130	Elizabeth	9	Rawleigh Colston		57
STONESTREET, Polly	98	Hezekiah	132	Sarah		68
STORY, Henry	131	Jo.	[117]	Teresa		133
STRAUSE, Christiana	131	John	132	Walter		133
Eliza	131	Josiah	132	TEMPLEMAN, John		39
George	131	Julia	80	THOMAS, Ann		15
Henry	131	Lucy	39	Elizabeth		133
Hiram	131	Martha	9	Evan	134,[20,150]	

Francis	80	Susanna	116	Notly	137
Henryetta	133	TILLARD, Edward	45	Osburn (Ozbern)	137,[16]
Hezekiah	133		[46,121]	Rachel	136
Jacob Williams	151	Elizabeth	45	William	42,63,136,137
John	87,[17,20,133]	Martha Eleanor	45		[56,96,103]
John 3rd	133,[71]	Rezin	45	TRAMMELL, Samuel	[49]
Martaine	70	Sarah	45	Simpson	29
Pheby	139	TILLEY, Charles	[130]	TRAVERS, Nicholas	[152]
Richard	20,71,133	Robert	[64]	TRIPPETT see Tipit	
	[21,38]	Zachariah	[130]	TRUNDLE, Basil (Basiel)	
Richard Jr.	21,133	TIPIT-TRIPPETT			126,138
	[38]	Eleanor	135	Daniel	136,137,138
Samuel	133,134,[21]	John	135		[43,84]
Samuel Jr.	133,[4,71]	Joseph	135	David	137,[132]
Samuel 3rd	[8,20]	Mary Magdaline	135	Delilah	138
Sarah	133	Nelson	135	Esther	126,136
Verlinda	151	TODD, Alex	[4]	Hannah	137
William	133,[83]	Basill	[4]	James	137,[132,143]
THOMESON, Chaney	134	Sarah	58	John	137
Elizabeth	134	TOMLINSON, Henry	135	John L.	139,[84]
THOMPSON-TOMSON		William	[150]	Mary	139
Agness	134	TOOLE, Elizabeth	29	Massey	138
Ann	142	TOPPING, James	136	Otho	[139]
Clement	[86]	Judith	136	Otho Hezekiah	137
Cordelisa	134	Margaret Leadsom	136	Rachell	137,138
Evan	134	TOWNSEND, Henry	152	Ruth	137
Harriott	134		[30,76]	Thomas	137,138
J.	[112,131]	TRACY-TRACEY		Thomas Sr.	137
James	134	Eleanor	75	TUCKER, Elizabeth	22
John	134,[112]	Mary	134	Jonathan	[67]
Richard	94,[133]	Philip	134	Rachel	66
Sarah	[70]	William	[57,149]	Randal	[105]
William	[30]	TRAIL-TRAILE-TRAILL		Richard	66
Zachariah	[60]	Abigail	63	TUELL, Henry	[112]
Zachariah Jr.	134	Ann	136	TUMBELL, John	[19]
Zachariah Sr.	134	Archibald	137	TURNBULL, John	[13]
THOMSON, Kenneth	[107]	Ashford	137	TURNER, Arie Anna	138
THRASHER, Elizabeth	135	Basil	136,[137]	Samuel	138
John	135	Cassandra	136	Thomas	138
Margaret	134,135	Darkus	136		
Sarah	135	David	136	UPTON, Ann	138
William	134,135	David Jr.	51	Darcy	138
THRELKELD, Henry	135	David Sr.	136	Elizabeth	138
John	122,135	Edward	137	Filmon	138
Joseph	135	Edward Northcraft	137	George	138,[99]
Mary	135	Evan	138	Jimminor	138
Thomas	135	Frances	137	Leah	138
Sarah	135	James	100,136,137	Theador	138
THRIFT, Absalom	102	James Jr.	100,[57]	Tilghman	138
Elizabeth	101	James Sr.	137	USHER, Eleanor Allison	2
Jane	102	Margaret	136		
THUILLAIR, Charles	135	Mary Ann	137	VAN HORN, Gabriel P.	33
John	135	Massa	136	VARNELL, John	80
TICE, Jacob	[30]	Nathan	137	VAUGHAN, N.M.	[6]

VEATCH-VIECH		William	31,[3,40 139,142]	Sarah	140
Alexander Contee				Thomas	140
Hanson	139	VYRMEER, William	[105]	WARD, Amos	141
Ann Jenkins	139			Ann	129,141
Benjamin	62	WADE, Abigel	140	Anne Mary	141
Elijah	139	Ann	140	Asa	141
Elizabeth	138	Catharine	89	B.	[103]
Elizabeth Ann	139	Elizabeth	102	Benjamin	141,[51]
Hanson	139	Gala Ann	89	Edward	141
Hezekiah	139,[55,60 61,72,123,124 137,146,149,153]	James	90,140,[12,103]	Elizabeth	59
		Jesse (Jessee)	140 [102,125]	Esra	141
				Hezekiah	[121]
Jemima Fraim	138	John	89,102	John	141
John	138,[124]	Levi	89	Joseph	129,141
John T.	139	Martha	110	Mary	66
Kesiah	138	Perry	[92]	Mary Ann (Maryann)	129,141
Nathan	[138]	Samuel	89		
Ninian	138	William	140	Priscilla	128
Orlando	138	WAILES, John	[20,89]	Robert	141
Richard	[55]	WALKER, Elijah	[51]	Sarah	141
Sarah	71	Elisha	[5]	Sarah B.	141
Silas	138	James	[38]	Sarah Moran	141
Solomon	138,[124]	WALLACE, Alexander	140	Silas	141
Susannah	138	Ann	15	WARFIELD-WARFEL	
Thomas	139,[39,55]	Charles	140,[8,14,140]	Abraham	74
Thomas Sr.	139 [13,136]	Edwin	21	Alexander	74,142,153
		Eleanor	140	Arnold	142
VEAUXBLEAD		Elizabeth	140	Charles	[145]
John Baptist	135	Fanny	140	Charles A.	[39]
VEIRS-VIERS		James	140,[14,82 140,148]	Charles Alexander	[71,146]
Daniel	139,[132]				
Darcus	43	James of Wm.	140	Edward	[32]
Edward	139	James Jr.	155	George F.	[8,21]
Elijah	139,[2,129 139,147]	James Sr.	155	George Fraser	94
		John	140,[72,93,140]	John	69
Elisha	139	John of Wm.	[8]	John W.	[85]
Hezekiah	139	Martha	21	John Worthington	142
John	139,[28]	Mary	140	Mary	142
John Sr.	154	Robert	60,140,[3,8 38,49,60,98]	Susanna	68,69,89
John Mason	139			Zachariah	128
Levi	139,[129]	William	140,[14]	WARING-WARRING	
Mary	139	William M.	140	Henry	38,85
Nathan	43,139	WALLICK, Ann	140	Marsham	42,147
Polly	139	Christian	140	Susan	105
Ruth	139	Mary	140	WARKER, Margaret	74
Sarah	139	WALTER, Ann	140	WARMAN, Stephen	142
Solomon	139	Clement C.	[6]	Thomas	142
William	139,[132,139]	Walter B.	[95]	WARNER, Thomas	[153]
VERMILLION, Sarah	[42]	David	141	WARREN, Ally	142
VINSON		Elizabeth	140	George	142
Frances Elizabeth	31	George	140	Henry	32
John	142	Hepsibah	141	John	142
Thomas F.W.	[105]	Rebecca	140	Mary	142

Thomas	142	Richard Sr.	144	Nancy		88
WATERS-WATTERS		Richard R.	144	WEBB, Benjamin		86
Adamson	143,[151,154]	Rosetta	144	Fanny		86
Amelia	144	Samuel	144	Henrietta		86
Ann	144	Sarah	144	Mary		85
Ann S.	144	Somerset	144	Susannah		86
Anna	144,145	Somerset R.	143	WEBBER, John		[114]
Artridge	144	Susannah	144	WEEKS, Bissett		[130]
Azel	143,144	Thomas	144,145,[84]	WEEMS, J.		[112]
Baker	145,[143]	Tilghman	145	John		[40]
Basil (Basel)	145,146	Walter	146	John, Dr.		111
148,[72,100,143,155]		William	142,145	WELLMAN, Rachel		73
Benjamin (Benj.)	142		[92,100,155]	WELSH-WELCH		
	143,[22]	William Sr.	145	Betsy		146
Benjamin Jr.	143	Zachariah	100,145,146	Cassandra		16
Casander	143,151		[95,100,143]	Hamutal		146
Charity	142	WATHAN-WATHEN-WARTHEN		Mary		39
Courtney	145	Ann	145	Rachel		58
Cresay	144	Ann Statia	145	Samuel		58
Deborah	144	Barthon	79	Samuel Sr.		[43]
Dorothy	44	Barton	145	WESLEY, Samuel		[42,127]
Elizabeth	143,144	Benedict	145	WEST, Basil		[3,152]
Elleanor (Elloner)		Gabriel	145,[63]	Benjamin		66
	143,145	Henry	145,[63,79]	Coborn		[152]
Ezekiel	[5]	John	[89]	Elizabeth		115,123
Freeborn G.	143	John H.	[117]	Henry		66
Freeborn Garretson	142	Leonard	67,145	Jean		137
Godfrey	146		[61,67,130]	Joseph		66
Hannah	142,143	Monica	145	Joseph Sr.		[136]
Hazel	68	Willfred	145	Joseph D.		28
Horace	92,143	WATKINS, Gassaway	10	Nancy		103
Ignatius (Ignasious)		Greenbury	89	Norman (Normond)		123,146
68,143,145,148,[21]		Jeremiah	[32,33,85]		[72,80,140]	
Issac	[40]	Joseph	89	Osborn		[3]
James	2,143	Leonard	139,[86]	Rachel		110
Joale	58	Mary	10	Richard	105,146,147	
John	144,[147]	Nicholas	84		[72,102,103]	
Joseph	144,[69]	Rachel	84	Ruth		115
Joseph Jr.	143	Robert White	89	Samuel	146,[31,103]	
Joseph Sr.	143	Thomas	10,89,93	Sarah	66,103,146,147	
Josephus Burton	144	Thomas S.	[136]	Thomas		66
Katy	144	Wilson Lee	89	Verlinda		66
Margaret	144	WATSON, Eleazer	79	William		146
Mary	143,145,146	Henry Sr.	14	William of John		[3]
Nacy	144,[13]	John	14	WHARTON, Ann		147
Nancy	92	Zephaniah	[71]	C.H.W.	[32,105,119]	
Nathan	[5]	WATTER, Hiland, Mrs.	[2]	Charles H.W.		[20,32]
Nathaniel M.	92	WATTS, John	[123]	Charles Henry Waring		147
Plummer	144,145	Richard K.	[16,84]	Jesse		147
Plummer Jr.	[84]	Richard Key	[123]	WHEELER, Alfred		42
Prospect	145	WAUGH, A.M.	[131]	Ann		148
R.K.	[105]	WAYMAN, Cassandra	110	Clement	148,[25,43,64]	
Rebeckah	144	Charles	146	Deborah		59
Richard	144,[144]	WEAVER, John	88	Elizabeth		42,147

Henry Hooper	[104]	Ann	51,149	Isaac	[18,23]
Jane	101	Drusilla Lewis		Jacob	151
John Hanson	59,148	Trundle	137	James	151
Nancy	66	Elizabeth	33,132	John	150,[40]
Ruth	[46]	George	132	John M.	[50]
Samuel	148	Horatio	51,149,[73]	Leonard	151
Samuel Hanson	66	James E.	149,[74]	Lucy	106
Sarah	66	Jesse	67,148,[51,67]	Margaret	151
Thomas	[25]	John	132,[47]	Martha	150,[107]
Thomas T.	43,[64]	Josiah	149	Mary	46,144
WHELAN, Daniel	[139]	Letha	137	Masey	106
Otha	147	Levi	137	O.H.	[131]
Rebekah	147	Mary	132	Overton	[58,97]
WHETZEL-WETZEL		Rachel	149	Patty	106
Frederick	47,155	Rebeckah	149	Rebecca	93
	[35,64]	Rezin	149	Ruth	106
WHITAKER, Alexander		Ruth	149	Samuel (Sammuel)	93,151
	[59,126]	Thomas	149	Sarah	93,150,151
John Alexander	25	Thomas H.	[12]	Thomas O.	150
Robert	[1,135]	William	67,149,[59]	Thomas Owen	150
WHITE, Benjamin	31,50	William Sr.	149	Thomas Swearingen	12
	147,148,[67,95]	WILLET-WILLETT-WILLIT		Thomas T.	[77]
Benjamin of Nathan	[4]	Ann	48,149	Verlinda (Verlenda)	93
Eleanor	148	Burgess	49,85,149,[31]		151,152
Elizabeth	147	Catharine	90	Walter	151,[59,65]
Guy	148	Edward	90,149,[28,153]	Walter C.	[9,106]
Harriot	148	Edward Sr.	[116	Walter Cade (Caid)	150
John	[108,147]		135,149]		[87]
Joseph	25,147	Grace	150	William	150,151,[154]
Mary	8,11	John	149	William P.	[9,87]
Mrs.	80	Mary	149	William Prather	150
Nancey	145,148	Ninian (Ninean)	48,149	Zachariah	93,151
Nathan	31		[17,48,91]		[95,150]
Nathan S.	148,[57]	Oratio	149	WILLIAMSON, Alexander	152
Nathan Sm	148	Robert	149,[98]	Mary L.	152
Peggy	148	Robert White	149	WILLIS, Nicholas, Rev.	147
Peggy P.	31	William	149,[17]	WILLMORE, Ann	153
Rebecca	147	WILLIAMS, Amos	152	Edward	152
Rebeckah P.	31	Ann	12,151	Edwin	152
Samuel	148,[15,68	Barbara	150	Eliza	152
	91,144]	Benjamin	59,106,133	Mary Ann	152
Samuel Jr.	[69]		[68,69,82]	Sarah	152
Samuel Beall	148	Charles	150,[78,110]	Zachariah	152
Samuel R.	[68]	Clement	150,[15]	WILLSON, Alexander	[36]
Sarah	131,148	Colmore	49,[50,61	Amelia	70
Stephen	148		113,124]	Ann V.	76
Stephen of N	[57]	Dorcas	120	Charity	152
Stephen N.	147	Dorothy	151	Charles	152,[38,41
Thomas Clagett	148	Eleanor	106,152		77,142,155]
William	147,[135]	Elisha O.	150,[62,97]	Dorothy	134
Zachariah	8	Elisha W.	[112]	Elizabeth	118,153
WIGHTT, Truman	148	Elizabeth	59,93,151	Hezekiah	153
WILCOXON-WILCOXEN		Elizabeth Ann	151	Horace	[23,151]
WILLCOXEN-WILLCOXSON		Harriet	106,150	James	97,152,153
Amos	149	Hillery	[149]	Jane	134

194

John	110,134,152,[34]	Zadoc(k)	35,153	Eleanor	107,140,155
Jonathan (Jonothan)		Zedekiah	153	H.H.	[20]
	66,134,152	WIMSETT, Ann	129	John	107,[77,136]
Margret	153	WINDSOR-WINSOR		John Jr.	155
Martha	152	Alexander	154	John Sr.	155
Mary Tillard Douglass		Amia	154	Mary	140
	153	Arnold T.	[118]	Nicholas	86
Otho	[122,155]	Arnold Thomas	154	Notley	26,27,42,86,[27]
Robert	97,153	Bazel	[113]	Polly	86
Samuel	134,152	Catharine	154	Richard	[5]
Sarah	34,93	Elenor Ann	134	Sarah L.	76
Thomas	134	Elizabeth	134	Solon	140
Thomas P.	[7,38	George Washington	134	YOUNGHUSBAND, Mary	114
	60,142]	Henry	140,154,[143]		
William 34,84,152,153		Jane	84	ZEIGLER, Christopher
	[1,31,135]	Lozanser Baten	134		[128,141]
William of John	9	Robert Bedden	154		
[3,5,122,145,154]		Sarah	154		
William-mina	152	Thomas	154,[60]	--EMMONS, John D.	[57]
WILMINGTON, Ann	10	Zachariah Thompson	134		
John	10	Zadock (Zaddock)	154	-----, David (mulatto)	128
WILSON, Agnes	153		[38]	Ealse (mulatto)	128
Alexander	19	WINEMILLER, Casander	141	Jeremiah	20
Ameli	137	John	[16]	Johannes	[18]
Ann	33,34,91	WOOD, Edward	73	Joseph (mulatto)	128
Barsheba	139	WOOTTON-WOOTON		Massy	115
Caroline	33	Charles	[103]		
Eleanor	154	John	154,[49,55,65]		
Elizabeth	154	Martha	154,155		
George	153	Richard 47,110,121,154			
Henry	75,153	[36,55,60,101,138]			
Hezekiah 125,[137,138]		Singleton	154,155		
James	19,154,[28]	Thomas S.	155		
Jane	154	Turner	154,155		
John	19,[144,145]	WORTHINGTON, Ann	154		
John S.	[125]	C.	[17,40,73]		
Joseph 70,153,[71,152]		John	154		
Josiah	[153]	Ruth	109,110		
Keziah	35	William	154		
Leven	154	WRIGHT, Thomas	155		
Lucy	91				
Margaret	82,154	YATES, Sarah	[21]		
Martha	154	YOST, Anna	154		
Miliah	82	Anna Elizabeth	155		
Nancy	125	Helena Chaterina	155		
Nathaniel	[126]	Henry	155		
Robert	154,[147]	Jasper	155		
Robert Sr.	154	John	155		
Sarah	153,154	Lodowick	[137]		
Thomas	19	Margaret	155		
Vilender	153	Philip 47,155,[35,121]			
Wadsworth	154	Susannah	155		
William of John	104	YOUNG, Benjamin	155		
Zachariah	[82]	Charles	155		